Arthur Pigou (1877–1959)

Pioneers in Economics

Series Editor: Mark Blaug

Professor Emeritus, University of London
Consultant Professor, University of Buckingham
Visiting Professor, University of Exeter

This important series presents critical appraisals of influential economists from the 17th century to the present day. It focuses in particular on those economists who were influential in their own time and whose work has had an impact – often inadequately recognized – on the evolution and development of economic thought. The series will be indispensable for a clear understanding of the origin and development of economic ideas and the role played by the leading protagonists of the past.

A full list of published titles in this series is printed at the end of this volume.

Arthur Pigou (1877–1959)

Edited by

Mark Blaug

Professor Emeritus,
University of London

An Elgar Reference Collection

Published by
Edward Elgar Publishing Limited
Gower House
Croft Road
Aldershot
Hants GU11 3HR
England

Edward Elgar Publishing Company
Old Post Road
Brookfield
Vermont 05036
USA

A CIP catalogue record for this book is available from the British Library

A CIP catalogue record for this book is available from the US Library of Congress

ISBN 1 85278 499 7

Printed in Great Britain by Galliard (Printers) Ltd, Great Yarmouth

Contents

Acknowledgements

The editor and publishers wish to thank the following who have kindly given permission for the use of copyright material.

American Economic Association for articles: Robert Cooter and Peter Rappoport (1984), 'Were the Ordinalists Wrong About Welfare Economics?', *Journal of Economic Literature*, **XXII** (2), 507–30; Pieter Hennipman (1988), 'A New Look at the Ordinalist Revolution: Comments on Cootes and Rappoport', *Journal of Economic Literature*, **XXVI** (1), 80–85; Peter Rappoport (1988), 'Reply to Professor Hennipman', *Journal of Economic Literature*, **XXVI** (1), 86–90.

Basil Blackwell Ltd. for articles: R.F. Harrod (1934), 'Professor Pigou's Theory of Unemployment', *Economic Journal*, **XLIV**, 19–32; David A. Collard (1983), 'Pigou on Expectations and the Cycle', *Economic Journal*, **93**, 411–14; Krishna Bharadwaj (1972), 'Marshall on Pigou's *Wealth and Welfare*', *Economica*, **XXXIX**, 32–46.

Canadian Journal of Economics for article: Harry G. Johnson (1960), 'Arthur Cecil Pigou, 1877–1959', *Canadian Journal of Economics and Political Science*, **XXVI**, 150–55.

Duke University Press for article: Margaret G. O'Donnell (1979), 'Pigou: An Extension of Sidgwickian Thought', *History of Political Economy*, **11** (4), 588–605.

MIT Press Journals for article: S.E. Harris (1935), 'Professor Pigou's Theory of Unemployment', *Quarterly Journal of Economics*, **XLIX**, 286–324.

Review of Economic Studies Ltd. for article: A.B. Atkinson and N.H. Stern (1974), 'Pigou, Taxation and Public Goods', *Review of Economic Studies*, **XLI**, 119–28.

Southern Economic Journal for article: Jacques Melitz (1967), 'Pigou and the "Pigou Effect": Rendez-vous with the Author', *Southern Economic Journal*, **34** (2), 268–79.

University of Chicago Press for articles: R.H. Coase (1972), 'The Appointment of Pigou as Marshall's Successor', *Journal of Law and Economics*, **XV** (1), 473–85; A.W. Coats (1972), 'The Appointment of Pigou as Marshall's Successor: Comment', *Journal of Law and Economics*, **XV**, 487–95; T.W. Jones (1978), 'The Appointment of Pigou as Marshall's Successor: The Other Side of the Coin', *Journal of Law and Economics*, **XXI** (1), 235–43.

Every effort has been made to trace all the copyright holders but if any have been inadvertently overlooked the publishers will be pleased to make the necessary arrangement at the first opportunity.

In addition the publishers wish to thank the library of the London School of Economics and Political Science and The Alfred Marshall Library, Cambridge University for their assistance in obtaining these articles.

Introduction

Arthur Pigou, professor of political economy at Cambridge University from 1908 to 1943, is best known for his authoritative statement of the theory of the old economic welfare. His *Theory of Unemployment* (1933) furnished Keynes in *The General Theory* (1936) with the best example of the classical economics Keynes so decisively rejected. Having unfairly served as Keynes's whipping-boy, Pigou nevertheless managed in old age graciously to acknowledge that Keynes had been largely correct.

In his fundamental work *The Economics of Welfare* (1920), Pigou elaborated Marshall's invention of the concept of externalities into a general economic theory of government intervention. Externalities occur when the actions of one economic agent unintentionally harm or benefit others, as a result of which the *private* costs or benefits of an activity diverge from their true *social* costs or benefits. Such cases of market failure, he argued, require government intervention in the form of taxes or subsidies to close the gap between private and social cost-benefit ratios. This liberal theory of state action in the economic sphere has been with us so long, and has entered so deeply into the fabric of political life in the twentieth century, that its obvious weaknesses may not be immediately apparent. It is only in recent years that economists have come to realise that market failure as such is an insufficient reason for government intervention, since taxes and subsidies themselves generate a divergence between the private and the social calculus: there is 'government failure' as well as 'market failure'.

The Economics of Welfare was old welfare economics, in the sense that Pigou was perfectly happy to employ definite interpersonal comparisons of utility as if they had 'scientific' standing. Thus he concluded that any increase in national income which did not involve a shift from the income of the poor to the income of the rich was to be defined as an improvement in economic welfare; naturally, he left himself free in any particular case to decide for himself who were the poor and who were the rich.

Pigou was born at Ryde in the Isle of Wight in 1877, the son of a retired army officer. He won a scholarship at an early age to the famous public school, Harrow, from which he won another scholarship to King's College, Cambridge, graduating in 1901 with a thesis on *Robert Browning as a Religious Teacher*, his first published book. He began lecturing on economics at Cambridge in the same year, a task which he carried on without interruption until the Second World War. In these early days he was a brilliant lecturer, and his repeated insistence to students that 'It's all in Marshall' was largely responsible in the interwar years for the Marshallian orthodoxy of Cambridge economics. His early books – *Tariffs* (1903), *Industrial Peace* (1905) and *Import Duties* (1906) – do little to explain his accession in 1908 to Marshall's Chair in Economics at the early age of 30. But *Wealth and Welfare* (1912) and *Unemployment* (1914) give a first hint of his true powers, the later *Economics of Welfare* (1920) being a reworking of *Wealth and Welfare*. *Essays in Applied Economics* (1923), *Industrial Fluctuations* (1927) and *A Study in Public Finance* (1928) were other major contributions.

From 1927 onwards, ill-health undermined the liveliness of his lecturing and the vigour of his writing. He gave up mountain-climbing, the full-time hobby of his youth, and gradually became the academic recluse of later years, famous for his absentmindedness and slovenly appearance. His stream of output, however, never lapsed. The notorious *Theory of Unemployment* (1933) was succeeded by *The Economics of Stationary States* (1935), *Employment and Equilibrium* (1941), and a whole series of short popular expositions: *Socialism versus Capitalism* (1937), *Income: An Introduction to Economics* (1946), *Lapses from Full Employment* (1947), *The Veil of Money* (1949), *Keynes's General Theory: A Retrospective View* (1950), and *Essays in Economics* (1952).

Pigou has probably been more underrated than any other major economist, and he has only recently been adequately defended against Keynes's abuse in *The General Theory*. It is indeed impossible to discover Keynes's description of Pigou's ideas in Pigou's own *Theory of Unemployment* – in particular, that the only cure for the Great Depression was to force real wages down; Pigou, like Keynes, did not believe it feasible to reduce real wages substantially, and looked to public works to relieve unemployment. On the other hand, it is difficult to discover any coherent, operational theory of unemployment in what is actually one of Pigou's most abstract and complicated books. Many of Pigou's other works contain remarkable hints of things to come in economics, particularly in monetary theory; for example, in *Unemployment* (1913) he provided an exposition of the concept of the 'balanced budget multiplier' that Keynes might have envied 23 years later, and in an essay on 'The Value of Money' (1917), he all but spelled out the 'real balance effect' that Patinkin was to make his own in his famous *Money, Interest, and Prices* (1956). But Pigou's crowning achievement remains that of the monumental *Economics of Welfare*.

Secondary literature

A. Robinson (1968), 'Pigou, Arthur Cecil', in D.L. Sills, ed., *International Encyclopedia of the Social Sciences*, (vol 12), Macmillan Free Press.

D. Collard (1981), 'A.C. Pigou, 1877–1959', in D.P. O'Brien and J.R. Presley, eds, *Pioneers of Modern Economics in Britain*, Macmillan.

Note

Several paragraphs in this Introduction were borrowed from my *Great Economists Before Keynes* (Wheatsheaf Books, 1986).

[1]

PROFESSOR PIGOU'S THEORY OF UNEMPLOYMENT

The Theory of Unemployment. By PROFESSOR A. C. PIGOU. (London : Macmillan & Co. 1933. Pp. xxvi + 319. 15*s.*)

THE reviewer of Professor Pigou's *Theory of Unemployment* must needs feel abashed by the task which confronts him. For this work is a supreme intellectual achievement, a masterpiece of close and coherent reasoning. Professor Pigou has summoned his full powers of analysis and applied them with unflagging vigour. The book contains about three hundred pages and almost every one is tightly packed with ratiocination. Moreover, it is a coherent whole with all its parts interrelated, and the significance of the parts can only be fully apprehended when their relation to the whole is apprehended.

The difficulty which, it must be acknowledged, this book presents to the reader is not due to any obscurity in its writing. On the contrary, Professor Pigou shows here, as always, a superb command of clear expression. Terms are not used without definition and the definitions are pellucid and precise. Indeed his conscientious care to be unambiguous should be taken as a model at this time when intrinsically obscure economic writing abounds.

His method of presentation is extremely austere. The polished surface of his pages is free of ornamentation. Every word is relevant and carries the argument on. It has been his custom in earlier works to illustrate particular points by quotations from specialist writers. This form of relaxation for the reader has been reduced to a minimum in the work under review. Moreover, he wastes no time in barren controversy; it is his purpose to construct and not to destroy. He resists the temptation to use his great powers to lay other economists low. When particular views have to be refuted for the sake of his argument, his victims are almost always anonymous in these pages. If a name is invoked, it is usually to quote with approval. Nor, despite his own high standards, is there any expression of methodological arrogance or contempt for the clumsier weapons of others. He contents himself with one reference in the Preface to those "writers on economic subjects, unacquainted with this tool [the differential calculus], who resent its use by others." A touch of irony may also be detected in the expression "popular writers," who are made to suppose that "when the elasticity of demand for labour's contribution of processing is greater than unity over the relevant range, improvements in productivity necessarily lead to increases in the quantity of labour demanded at the standing real-wage rate" (p. 114). A crude enough error in all conscience!

Yet in spite of the great beauty, the exquisite workmanship, the painstaking lucidity of these pages, it cannot be denied that they make tough and laborious reading. One is tempted to search for the true cause of the difficulty. It is the case that close reasoning of this kind necessarily requires a severe effort of attention. It is the case also that Professor Pigou is sometimes a little cryptic, so that the reader has either to take his conclusions on trust or, in the absence of a superior mathematical intuition, to verify them by a more elaborate method with pencil and paper. I do not refer only to the solution of equations but to sections of the literary argument which have mathematical implications. But these facts do not explain the whole, or even the most serious part of, the difficulty.

This is due to somewhat different causes. In order to build up his system, Professor Pigou has to sort out the facts of real life so as to frame certain clear-cut concepts for use in his analysis. Now the student of economics, for whom this book is primarily intended (*vide* Preface, p. v), usually has a certain framework of concepts which he has acquired by dint of studying the principal literature of the subject. At every point when Professor Pigou sorts out the phenomena so as to define a new concept, and these points occur frequently, the reader is bound, if he is to profit by this book, to ask himself how far the concepts so framed correspond with those which pre-exist in his own mind, whether they are more or less relevant to the real world, and what relations the conclusions reached with their aid ought to have to his own preconceived ideas. If the conclusions differ from his own views, is this difference apparent only and due to a difference of definitions? Or is it a real difference? If so, a good deal of translation is needed to discover if and why his own ideas were erroneous. A fundamental work of this kind will not have served its full purpose unless the reader can permanently embody some of its propositions in his own working stock of principles. He will probably be unwilling to abandon his old concepts completely and start his economic life *de novo*. In this case he will be compelled to do much translation and re-translation, if he is to derive the full benefit of Professor Pigou's work, and this process entails enormous labour. I do not suggest that Professor Pigou could by any device have spared the reader this trouble, if he was to say what he had to say. For unfortunately the technique of economic analysis is at present only standardised in very small measure, and any set of concepts that would prove easy for one reader would probably be extremely irksome to some other.

But there is a difficulty in Professor Pigou's work closely connected with this fact which might perhaps have been avoided. The salient steps in his arguments are not strongly underlined. It is really only at these steps that it ought to be incumbent on the reader to translate Professor Pigou's concepts into his own for purposes of verification and true understanding. But, in fact, since he is never quite sure when a salient step is occurring, he feels it necessary to do a great deal of translating and retranslating at points where this is not really necessary, that is, at stages in the reasoning which are, in fact, subordinate, but which he does not clearly perceive to be subordinate until he has finished the whole book and reads it for a second time. He is thus led into much labour which he might have avoided. The surface of the text is uniform and monotonous. There is, it is true, a great charm in this manner. If Columbus sets the discovery of America on an equal footing with his other daily adventures without emphasis or passion, the reader's thrill is enhanced and not diminished. This monotony of surface would call for nothing but praise, if only the subject-matter were not so difficult. Unfortunately, on this particular voyage, the reader does not know beforehand what America is or whether its discovery is of any importance. If this is never explained for him, he is in serious danger of completing his study of the journal without ever appreciating the great thing that he has been told.

The principal weapons which Professor Pigou uses for his attack on the problem of unemployment are the theory of marginal productivity and a theory which bears close kinship with the old Wages Fund theory, and which we may christen the Wage-Goods Fund theory. This revival is a welcome one. "Popular writers" have been in the habit of stating that the old classical theories of this type have been long since disproved and superseded by the marginal productivity theory. Such statements are both erroneous and harmful. These old theories are firmly founded on tautology, and may well prove, as is evidenced by Professor Pigou's book, to be most useful analytical tools. Nor is there any incompatibility between them and the modern theory of marginal productivity. Professor Pigou is able to use both the old and the new in the utmost harmony, without apology or defence: he fits them neatly together with great artistry. His use of the Wage-Goods Fund theory does not imply a rejection of the Wages Fund theory in its strict classical form, for these two may also be fitted together. But for the purpose in hand Professor Pigou does not require the Wages Fund theory.

Professor Pigou has two main themes, the volume of employment in particular industries and the volume of employment as a whole (as well as their mutual reactions). Of his treatment of the former topic, which he conducts with great subtlety and beauty both in the earlier and final parts of the book, and of the many interesting propositions which he deduces, space forbids me to speak. I shall confine myself to some remarks on his treatment of employment as a whole.

Even here I shall limit myself severely, and consider mainly his advocacy of the case that wage reductions are likely to be associated with an expansion of employment. This proposition is of great general interest and it is of importance to scrutinise most closely how securely it is founded.

Professor Pigou begins by analysing the matter in "real" terms and then proceeds to a monetary analysis. There is, however, embedded in his real treatment one monetary chapter.[1] I shall consider this first, for it forms an indispensable link in the chain of argument favourable to the view that in the real world a wage reduction would lead to increased employment, and then proceed to consider his "real" treatment generally.

"Meditation along these lines," he writes, "has suggested to some persons the view that in actual life reductions in the money rates of wages would simply be reflected in a proportional fall in prices; so that no effect whatever either on the real rate of wages or on the volume of labour demanded would be produced."

He examines this view and rejects it. His grounds are as follows. He supposes wages to constitute the whole of prime costs. These fall, therefore, in the same proportion as wages. The purchasing power of wage-earners falls in the same proportion. But, "at the outset nothing has happened to non-wage-earners' money income." Consequently purchasing power as a whole and, while output is constant, the general level of prices will fall less than wage-earners' purchasing power and prime costs. Consequently there will be, on average, an excess of price over prime cost and a stimulus to expansion. The crucial proposition is that

[1] Part II, Chapter X.

"at the outset nothing has happened to non-wage-earners' money income." In that the question is really begged. Has nothing happened?

It must be remembered that payments to supplementary factors are residual. It cannot be known what happens to these even "at the outset," until it is known what happens at the outset to the general level of prices. Yet what happens to the general level of prices depends on what happens to the volume of non-wage-earners' money expenditure. This in turn depends on what happens to their incomes. No solution, therefore, can be reached on these lines.

By way of hypothesis we may suppose that at the outset profit-earners maintain their old real level of purchases. If they do this, the stream of purchasing power and the level of prices will be reduced by as much as the level of prime costs and wages.

This is a matter of very simple arithmetic, but the opposite view is so widely prevalent that it may be well to set it out explicitly. Let x, the unknown term, represent the fall in the amount of money expended as a fraction of the old amount. This will also represent the initial fall of prices before the reaction on output is taken into account. x is equal to the sum of two fractions, namely, the fraction showing the reduction of wage-earners' money expenditure divided by the previous expenditure of the whole community, and the fraction showing the reduction of non-wage-earners' expenditure divided by the previous expenditure of the whole community. Let q be the fraction of total expenditure formerly contributed by wage-earners and $(1 - q)$ the fraction formerly contributed by non-wage-earners. Let p be the reduction of wages expressed as a fraction of the old wages. The first of the two fractions, the sum of which is equal to x, viz. the reduction of wage-earners' expenditure divided by the previous expenditure of the whole community, is therefore

$$pq.$$

If non-wage-earners maintain their old level of real purchases, the proportional reduction of non-wage-earners' money expenditure is equal to the fall of prices, x. Thus the second fraction is—

$$x(1 - q).$$

It is required to find x. We have the equation—

$$pq + x(1 - q) = x$$
$$\therefore x = p$$

i.e. the reduction of purchasing power and consequently the fall in prices is equal to the fall in wages. Two corollaries flow from this.

1. Since the fall of prices is proportional to the fall in wages, the fall in non-wage-earners' incomes is proportional to each. Consequently non-wage-earners will find their money income reduced by exactly the amount required to make their income balance their expenditure at the old standard of living, and they will lack the means to expand purchases. If they do not expand purchases initially, they will have no inducement to do so later.

2. Since the fall in prices is as great as the fall in prime costs, there will be no inducement to expand output. No new employment will be given.

The distinction which Professor Pigou draws between wage-goods and non-wage-goods, though vital to his general analysis, does not affect this particular argument. The distinction would indeed be of importance on one assumption, namely, that the non-wage-earners purchased no wage-goods at all. In that case wage-goods prices would fall in proportion to wages, non-wage-goods prices would be sustained, and non-wage-earners' incomes as a whole would be sustained, since what they lost on the lower prices received in respect of wage-goods would be precisely equal to what they saved on prime costs. But if they spend any money on wage-goods at all, their money incomes will be reduced owing to the reduction of the prices of the wage-goods they purchase and, by competition, the process of weakening in the non-wage-goods prices will be set up and, provided that non-wage-earners do not increase the real volume of their purchases, all prices will be reduced by the same amount as wages. The "process of weakening" referred to is a mathematical and not a temporal one. The total fall of non-wage-goods prices may be regarded as the sum of an infinite series, the summation of which is effected instantaneously in time.

It remains to consider how far the hypothesis that non-wage-earners maintain their old real level of purchases without increase or diminution is a proper one. It certainly seems to be justified by the consequences deduced; for, if they do this, they will find themselves with no spare money income left on their hands. It can be shown, however, that if they adopt a different policy and maintain their old money level of expenditure, they will also be justified by results; their old money incomes will be maintained; prices will fall less than prime costs and there will also be a stimulus to expand output. It might be argued that, since, whether they maintain real purchases or money expenditure, they will be solvent, and since, by maintaining money expenditure (which means increasing their real level of purchases), they will be better off, they will tend to do the latter. Such an argument is invalid, however, *because it proves too much.* For at any time, with or without a reduction in money wages, they can put themselves in a better position in the short period by increasing real purchases. The extra money that they spend comes back to them; they gain at the expense of wage-earners, real wages being reduced.

There is, in fact, as Mr. Keynes has so well shown by his principle of the widow's cruse, something indeterminate about the volume of profit-earners' joint expenditure. What normally holds them in equilibrium is that they can only expand real purchases and remain solvent if they act jointly. But unless there is a general stimulus to expand they will not usually act jointly, and so the whole system will remain in equilibrium.

The fact that profit-earners can, when a money-wage reduction occurs, jointly expand purchases and remain solvent, cannot be used as an argument that they will jointly expand in consequence of a money-wage reduction, for they could do that without a wage-reduction. If they have not already done so, there is nothing in the nature of a money-wage reduction to make them do so subsequently. But if they do not do so, prices will fall by as much as prime costs, they will have no unspent income left over, and they will have no subsequent stimulus to expand purchases; and there will also be no stimulus to expand output.

It is true that a wage-reduction accompanied by ballyhoo may incline employers to expand purchases. But so might ballyhoo without a wage-reduction. It is the ballyhoo that is the operating factor.

It appears from the foregoing that we have here a weak link in Professor Pigou's chain of argument, and that we cannot with any confidence expect a money-wage reduction to cause a real-wage reduction in a closed system.

We must now address ourselves to the important question whether a real-wage reduction is likely to cause an increase of employment. Put broadly, and omitting details, Professor Pigou's position may be set out as follows. If wages are contracted to be paid in wage-good units, the demand for labour in the wage-goods industries as a whole depends on the labour productivity function, in such wise that the marginal net product of a unit of labour must be equal to the real wage per unit stipulated for. The volume of employment in other industries is a function of the volume in the wage-goods industries (see p. 90 and Pt. I, Chap. V); more particularly, it is equal to the product of the wage-goods industries and of the export industries whose products are exchanged for wage-goods, less the amount of wage-goods paid back into those industries as wages, and less the amount of wage-goods consumed by non-wage-earners, all divided by the amount of wage-goods per unit of labour stipulated for. The Wage-Goods Fund may be further augmented by savings on unemployment pay, etc., and by reductions in outstanding stocks of wage-goods.

It is advisable, therefore, to consider very closely the nature of the demand for labour in the wage-goods industries. Professor Pigou assumes that the elasticity of the labour productivity function has negative value, *i.e.* that prime labour costs in the wage-goods industries are rising. (Cf. p. 45, line 2, "We know that η is negative.") And it is the case that in every industry operating in conditions of perfect competition they must be rising.

In his Preface (p. vi) he states that "many complications of detail associated with the imperfection of markets are left aside." He has, it is true, explicitly dealt with the problems of monopoly in certain passages (especially Pt. II, Chap. IV, and Pt. III, Chap. VII). But he does not consider them in connection with his treatment of the demand for labour in the aggregate; and it is precisely in this connection that the prevalence of imperfect competition may affect the argument, not merely in matters of detail but in its essential nature.

The presence of imperfect competition has two important consequences. 1. Marginal labour costs may be falling in the equilibrium of the short period. It must be noted that throughout the book Professor Pigou is concerned with the short period. 2. The real wage of labour stipulated for is equated not to the marginal net product of labour, as defined on p. 41, but to the marginal revenue derived from the employment of labour.

1. It would be wrong to brush complications connected with imperfect competition aside as of subordinate importance in the general theory of unemployment. In this country, for example, by far the greater part of industry is working in conditions of imperfect competition, in the sense that particular firms are confronted by demand curves of less than infinite elasticity. In these circumstances the elasticity of the labour productivity function may have positive value. It is true that if a firm is producing the amount of output for which its fixed equipment was designed, the probability that marginal costs will

be falling is not a great one. But for short-period equilibria in which output has fallen to some value below that for which the plant was designed, the probability becomes much greater. (In perfect competition, *per contra*, marginal costs *must* be rising even in the short-period equilibrium of a depression.) It is quite a feasible proposition, therefore, that on balance marginal costs in British industries at the present time are falling or, anyhow, constant and would not rise over a wide range of expanding output.

Let us suppose that this is so. It follows that the wage consistent with an equilibrium with a higher volume of wage-good output would probably be higher than or equal to and not lower than that appropriate to the lower volume. If this is so, the defence of wage-reduction would have to proceed on different lines. It would then be recommended not as the introduction of a wage appropriate to an equilibrium with a higher level of output, but only as a temporary stimulus to expansion, to be replaced by a higher wage when the stimulus had become effective. In judging such a recommendation it is necessary to advert to the second principal feature of imperfect competition.

2. If the wage-good wage stipulated for is equal to the marginal net wage-good product, a reduction in the wage-good wage must tend to stimulate output. And this is the case in conditions of perfect competition. It might be objected that a reduction of the wage-good wage might reduce the demand for and value of wage-goods, as well as reducing their cost of production and so obviate the stimulus to expansion. Such an objection would be erroneous. Considering wage-goods industries as a unity, nothing can reduce the value of wage-goods *in terms of wage-goods*. Now, if initially the wage-good wage is equal to the wage-good product at the margin, a reduction of the wage-good wage must make it less than the wage-good product at the margin for the old level of output. Output will be stimulated until the rising labour cost at the margin raises the wage-good cost per unit of output to the level at which it stood before the rate of wage-good wage was reduced. Consequently, in Pt. II, Chap. IX, Professor Pigou argues that the slower the rate at which labour costs rise, the greater stimulus to output a given wage-reduction would exercise. At first sight it might seem that if labour costs are not rising at all but falling, Professor Pigou's argument would stand *a fortiori*.

But the position is radically altered if the wage-good wage stipulated for is not equal to the marginal net wage-good product, but is something less. In that case it is necessary to consider explicitly the effect on the demand for wage-goods consequent upon the reduction of wages.

Now the demand schedule for wage-goods in terms of wage-goods cannot be affected by a reduction of wages. It does not follow that the marginal revenue in terms of wage-goods derived from the sale of wage-goods cannot be so affected. The elasticity of the demand for wage-goods in terms of wage-goods is infinite; it must not be inferred from this that the marginal revenue in terms of wage-goods derived from their sale is equal to their value and constant at all levels of output; this would only be true if there were, in fact, only a single sort of wage-good. In the chapter already referred to (Pt. II, Chap. IX), Professor Pigou imagines, in order to make the exposition simple, that there is only a single sort of wage-good. This supposition does not affect the validity of his argument provided that conditions of perfect competition are assumed. But to use this supposition in order to consider the reaction of a real wage-reduction in conditions of imperfect competition would involve a fallacy.

Each particular wage-good has its own demand curve. If a wage-reduction occurs, the value of some wage-goods in terms of wage-good units at the old level of output may rise while that of others falls. The rises must exactly balance the falls if a computation is made weighting each good as it is in fact weighted in the make-up of a wage-good unit. But, in addition, the elasticities of the demands for particular wage-goods may alter, and it is by no means necessarily the case that the decreases of elasticity are balanced by opposite increases. But the marginal revenues derived from the sale of various wage-goods depend on these elasticities. If the elasticities grow less the marginal revenues will decline. If the decline of marginal revenues is greater than the real wage-reduction, there will be a contraction of output in the wage-good industries.

There seem to be some general grounds for supposing that a decrease of elasticity would occur. The reduction of wages involves a transfer of command over wage-goods to non-wage-earners. The demand of these is likely to be less elastic than the demand of wage-earners. Not only would there be a slump in the value of wage-goods compared with other goods—this would not matter as wages are assumed to be fixed in wage-goods—but the demands for particular wage-goods would become much less elastic at the old level of output. This consequence would not, of course, follow if the whole of the extra wage-goods over which the employers secured command were utilised for putting extra labour to work; whether they would do this or not would no doubt depend on whether forces *other than wage-reduction* were making for expansion or contraction.

A decrease of the average of the elasticities of demand (weighted as explained above) from 3 to $2\frac{1}{2}$ would cause the weighted average of the marginal revenues to fall by 10 per cent. and would offset the stimulating effect of a 10 per cent. reduction of wages. If the decrease in elasticities was greater than this, output in the wage-good industries would contract. If this contracted sufficiently and if real costs were on balance falling (*i.e.* rising as output contracted), the command over wage-goods accruing to employers might actually contract (Professor Pigou's K_2 on p. 73 would be less than K_1), and contraction in non-wage-good industries would ensue. Even if this did not happen, the contraction in wage-good industries might well be greater than the expansion elsewhere.

The burden of the foregoing criticism may be summarised as follows. 1. It is not certain that a money-wage reduction would entail a real-wage reduction. 2. It is not certain that the real wage appropriate to a higher level of output in the short period is lower than the real wage appropriate to a lower level. This would only be certain if conditions of perfect competition everywhere prevailed. 3. Whether a higher level of output requires a lower real wage or not, it is not certain that a real-wage reduction would cause the system to move to a higher level of output. If it is, in fact, the case that a higher level of output requires a lower real wage, the difficulties of 1 and 3 suggest that the possibilities of achieving this by means other than money-wage reduction should be sedulously explored.

It must not be supposed that I have attempted to replace Professor Pigou's affirmations by contrary negations. I only claim that the case for wage-reduction is not established by his reasoning. Nor must it be supposed that I have attempted to impugn the value of Professor Pigou's general analysis; for I have only singled out one strand in the great texture of his reasoning for consideration from one point of view.

His section on monetary factors (Pt. IV) is easier reading than the rest, perhaps because it is on more familiar lines. After a criticism of the concept of a " neutral " money, he proposes a standard monetary system, not wishing to imply that it is " better " than other systems but as a " reference model." It is, however, suggested, I understand, that its adoption would allow real forces to operate with the least possible friction. He writes: "I define the standard monetary system as one so constructed that, for all sorts of movements in the real demand function for labour or in real rates of wages, whether they last for a long time or a short, the aggregate money income is increased or diminished by precisely the difference made to the number of work-people (or other factors of production) at work multiplied by the original rate of money wages" (p. 205).

In this definition, by exception to the general rule in this volume, there appears to be some element of ambiguity. Ought not the words "due to real causes" to be inserted after "in the real rates of wages"? For it is possible to conceive of a fall in real wages, an increase of employment and an increase in aggregate money income, all associated together in such a way that the unamended definition of the standard system is fulfilled, but all are due to the infusion of new money. And surely Professor Pigou desires to rule such an eventuality out. A further difficulty remains. Suppose an improvement in productivity of Professor Pigou's "normal type" (p. 114) to occur in wage-goods industries such that, imperfect competition notwithstanding, the real demand for labour is increased; and suppose that on the instant the labourers demand such an increase of money wages, hoping to get a real increase of like amount, that the net effect of the two changes would be, if real wages were in fact raised by no more nor less than money wages, that employment was neither increased nor diminished. In these circumstances the monetary authority is to maintain aggregate money income unchanged. But if it does this, on normal assumptions, the price level will tend to fall and the real wage to rise more than was intended by the monetary increase. Unemployment will be generated in spite of the fact that the rise originally demanded by wage-earners was not of itself sufficient to generate it.

More generally, Professor Pigou, unlike Mr. Keynes, does not make it incumbent on the monetary authority to take into account what is actually happening in the world of wage negotiations when regulating their policy. This appears to be a weak point in his system. Another example may be given. Suppose a Trade Board set up in a sweated industry to raise wage rates there. If there was no change in the productivity functions or other surrounding circumstances, this might involve a rise in the average of real-wage rates in industry generally and a restriction of employment, and it would then be incumbent on the authority to reduce money incomes. Would it not be better, in the manner of Mr. Keynes, to allow a slight rise in prices, so that the action of the Trade Board might have no effect on the average of real-wage rates?

The general monetary analysis of Professor Pigou has a close family relationship to that of Mr. Keynes. This may be explained as follows. Professor Pigou's analysis bears to the Wage-Goods Fund theory the same relation that Mr. Keynes' equations bear to the Wages Fund theory proper. Mr. Keynes expects a dis-equilibrating force to be brought into existence, if entrepreneurs attempt to pay to wage-earners engaged on the output of non-consumable goods more or less purchasing power than is released by saving. Professor Pigou expects disturbance if entrepreneurs attempt to pay to wage-earners in the non-wage-good industries more wage-goods than non-wage-earners are prepared to set aside for this purpose out of the surplus not consumed by wage-earners in the wage-good industries (I leave aside complications connected with foreign trade). Just as the Wage-Goods Fund theory is complementary to and not contradictory of the Wages Fund theory proper, so the analysis of Professor Pigou may prove to be complementary to that of Mr. Keynes, and the standard system desired by the former to be identical with that desired by the latter. To trace the interconnections of the two methods of analysis would constitute an interesting piece of theoretical research. Which tool of thought is most helpful in application to practical problems can only be solved by experience.

Professor Pigou holds the principal weapon for maintaining the standard system to be the discount and open market policy of the central bank. But in times of deep depression the expedient of public loan expenditure should also be used. "In these circumstances attempts to uphold the standard monetary system, so long as reliance is placed on purely monetary defences, are bound to fail. If, however, at the same time that the banking system keeps money cheap the government adopts a policy of public works, the risk of failure is greatly reduced" (p. 213).

In more than one place Professor Pigou examines the effects of giving a subsidy to employment. His findings are on the whole favourable to the expedient. The most satisfactory method of using it would be to confine the subsidy to additional employment given in a certain period. He gives weight to the administrative difficulties connected with this method. In view, however, of the fact that economic experiments of doubtful merit in principle and of the most serious administrative difficulty are making and likely to continue to be made in this and other countries, it seems a pity that more serious public attention is not given to this particular expedient.

The *Theory of Unemployment* is a rich storehouse containing many and various treasures. It has only been possible to give some hints about a few samples of all that lies therein. Anyone who devotes patience and effort to exploring it will reap abundant profit.

R. F. HARROD

Christ Church,
Oxford.

[*Note.*—Prof. Pigou has asked the Editors to take advantage of this opportunity to make it known that he has prepared a printed slip of misprints in his *Theory of Unemployment* which have come to light since publication, and that the publishers, Messrs. Macmillan & Co., St. Martin's Street, London, W.C.2, will on application supply any owner of this book with a copy of this slip without charge.]

[2]

PROFESSOR PIGOU'S THEORY OF UNEMPLOYMENT

SUMMARY

Professor Pigou's Theory of Unemployment is one of the great books of recent years. Tho its perusal requires much time and effort, few books in economics will yield the reader greater returns. Its main features are the mathematical treatment, the emphasis of the real as against a monetary analysis, the derivation of the elasticity of real demand for labor and the reliance throughout on a wage-good theory. In returning to an approach reminiscent of the old wage-fund doctrine (sometimes, it seems, even too far) Professor Pigou advances further the movement initiated by Professor Taussig late in the nineteenth century, toward salvaging what was worth salvaging in the old wage-fund doctrine.

Of the numerous interesting problems raised by Professor Pigou, I limit myself to a discussion of the important ones which seem to require further elucidation. I shall do so with a detail that may appear wearisome, and this for two reasons.

One is that I hope the task of following the intricate reasoning will thereby be made easier for other readers, especially through the indication of short cuts, misprints, and occasional inaccuracies, which distract attention from the main course of the analysis. The other and more important reason is that the meaning of it all can not be grasped unless one attends with care to the details.

1. Elasticity of Demand for Labor in a Particular Occupation

In Chapter II of Part II, the analysis gets under way. I merely summarize its contents. Only in an ideally simplified world does there exist "a certain definite real demand function for labour in any period, such that to each rate of real wage asked for by workpeople there corresponds a definite quantity of labour demanded. . . . For very small — strictly for infinitesimal — differences in the real wage-rate asked for, the ratio

$$\frac{\text{proportionate change in quantity of labour demanded}}{\text{proportionate change in real rate of wage}}$$

is called the elasticity of demand for labour in respect of the initial quantity of labour or the initial real wage-rate. To determine this ratio for finite differences in the real wage asked for, it is not sufficient to know what the elasticity of demand in respect of the initial quantity, or initial wage is." (35) Pigou then shows that the relationship between proportionate changes in quantity of employment demanded and proportionate changes in wages can be calculated (when the changes are not infinitesimal) for constant elasticity and linear demand functions. He concludes that for "finite differences, as well as for infinitesimal ones, provided they are small, we may treat the elasticity of demand in respect of either of the two wage-rates under review as a rough measure of the ratio

$$\frac{\text{proportionate change in quantity}}{\text{proportionate change of wage.''}} \quad (37)$$

Finally Pigou comments on two difficulties of real life, one that the quantity of labor demanded is a function of the wage-rate which is expected to rule in the future (as well as that ruling in the present) and the second that $W=F(x,t)$ not $F(x)$. In respect of any assigned volume of employment, there is a whole family of elasticities with different members referred to different *time* (t) intervals. (39)

Chapter III of Part II treats of the problem of short-period elasticity of demand for labor in *particular* occupations in respect to a given real wage-rate, in conditions of free competition: the quantity of labor demanded at any given real wage is such that the value in terms of wage-goods of its marginal net product approximates to that rate of wage plus the employers' contribution of insurance.[1] $F'(x)$ is the wage-rate as defined above, x the quantity of labor employed in any occupation and, therefore, $\frac{F'(x)}{xF''(x)}=E_d$, the elasticity of real demand for labor in respect of a quantity X. Making numerous simplifying assumptions, the most important of which is the temporary neglect of the time factor,[2] Pigou then proceeds to set out the questions that must be answered if we are to determine the value of E_d. Now

$$W=F'(x)=\left\{\frac{d\Psi\{\phi(x)\}}{dx}-\frac{df\{\phi(x)\}}{dx}\right\}$$

if $\Psi'(y)$ is the demand price for y units of new output at works of finished product, and $f'(y)$ the supply price of y units of raw material and $y=\phi(x)$ where x is the number of units of labor that yield y units of processing. (42–43)[3] Then in order

1. For a criticism of this definition, see R. G. Hawtrey, "The Theory of Unemployment by Professor A. C. Pigou," Economica, 1934, pp. 148–51.

2. The result of postponing the discussion of the time element is that the final formula seems to have no meaning for processing undertaken at an early stage. Later, (56–60), however, Pigou finds that no correction is necessary when the length of the production period and the rate of interest are considered. He then, however, dodges one important issue, for he assumes that the raw material used is paid for at the time that the finished product containing it is sold; or, if not paid for, that the supply price is appropriately adjusted.

3. Mr. Hawtrey puts this more clearly, op. cit., p. 148, tho on line 12 of his discussion $\frac{dx}{df}$ should read $\frac{df}{dx}$.

$$w=\left(\frac{d\psi}{dy}-\frac{df}{dy}\right)\frac{dy}{dx}\text{ or }\frac{d\psi}{dx}-\frac{df}{dx}$$

to obtain E_d, $F'(x)$ is replaced by its equivalent in the equation for elasticity above $\frac{F'(x)}{xF''(x)}$ and $F''(x)$ is of course obtained by differentiating $F'(x)$, and from the resulting ungainly formula, by making ingenious use of the second differentials obtained, Pigou finally obtains the equation

$$\frac{1}{E_d}=\frac{1}{m-1}\cdot\left[\left\{\frac{m}{E_f}-\frac{1}{E_s}\right\}\frac{w}{q}\right]+\frac{1}{\eta}$$

where E_f is the elasticity of demand in terms of wage-goods, for new output at works of the finished product, E_s the elasticity of the supply of the raw material, η the elasticity of the productivity function of labor in respect of processing when x units are employed, m the demand price per unit of finished product at works divided by the price of the raw material used in it when $\phi(x)$ units are being produced. (43–44) For $\frac{x\phi'(x)}{\phi(x)}$, the marginal amount of processing done by x men multiplied by x and divided by the total quantity of processing done by x men, he substitutes $\frac{w}{q}$ where w is the money wage and q the money value of net output per head.

E_d, E_f and η are negative and $m>1$.[4] Therefore, E_d is (numerically) larger, the larger numerically is E_f; i.e., the more elastic is the demand for the finished commodity at works. The larger if positive, and the smaller, if negative, is E_s. The more elastic is the supply of the relevant raw material, the larger is m; i.e., the less important is the part played by the raw material in the cost of the finished product; the larger (numerically) is η and the smaller is $\frac{w}{q}$. (45)

By the application of this formula Pigou then attempts to determine the value of E_d for a group of workpeople engaged in a particular occupation; but the results are meagre. (45–51)

4. Mr. Harrod points to the possibility of a positive value for η under conditions of imperfect competition. R. F. Harrod, "Professor Pigou's Theory of Unemployment," Economic Journal, 1934, pp. 26–27. Pigou obtains a definite value for η, it may be added, only on the assumption that the function is linear or a constant elasticity function.

He, himself, allows that there are important difficulties in arriving at an estimate for E_f and E_s. One point here deserves special consideration. Write E'_f for the elasticity of the final buyer's demand for the commodity. Included as a rule in the final buyer's purchase price are payments for distributive services so that if the total value divided by the cost of distribution services equals $K, \frac{1}{k} \cdot E'_f = E_f$.[5] Pigou is not justified, however, to assume, even as a rough approximation, that the "proportion of the total value contributed by the cost of these services remains constant in the face of the short period variations in consumption that follow from changes in the wage-rate." (46) It is well-known that there is a relative constancy of monetary return for distributive services when wages and prices vary; and hence there is large variation in the proportion of the costs attributable to these services. The correction which Pigou allows should be made for E_f is therefore not an appropriate one. A similar difficulty arises in regard to m, for the assumption that m does not vary over short periods is a serious violation of the facts.[6] Consider the manner in which the proportion of the price for the final product accounted for by the receipts of farmers for raw material has varied from year to year and even from month to month since 1929.

A few additional difficulties remain. First, the appearance of $\frac{w}{q}$ $\left(\text{substituted for } \frac{x\phi'(x)}{\phi(x)}\right)$ in the final formula calls for comment, since Pigou has admittedly relegated the discussion of the time factor to a later part. For $\frac{w}{q}$ is the ratio of the

5. The assumption is made that there are no variations in stocks.

6. Pigou says that "the value of m, *ex hypothesi*, does not vary over short periods" (45), a statement not easy to understand. On page 43, he says that *ex hypothesi* one unit of raw material is always used in one unit of finished product. He has also postponed the discussion of the time element. It does not, however, follow that variations in the proportion of the price of the raw material relatively to the price of the finished product are thus eliminated.

return to labor (per head) to the net product per head. Second, and a more serious consideration, is that E_d depends on $\frac{w}{q}$ in such a manner that when $\frac{w}{q}$ is small, E_d tends to be large (numerically), altho common sense tells us that E_d ought to be larger, the larger is $\frac{w}{q}$. That is, a given reduction in wage-rates ought to lead to a greater increase in the demand for labor where the money wage is a large part of the money value of net output per head than when it is a small part. Third, it is very difficult, if not impossible, to make accurate corrections of E_f, the elasticity of demand of the final buyer, for variations in stocks.[7] Yet these variations over short periods, it need scarcely be added, may be of prime importance in determining the effects of a reduction in wages.

2. Employment in Non-Wage-Good and Wage-Good Industries

Having expressed E_d in equational form for individual occupations, Pigou proceeds in Chapters VI-VII to demonstrate that the functions for individual industries or centers are not independent and hence cannot be added for the purpose of arriving at the elasticity of demand for labor over all industries. In making his main point, he incidentally touches upon an issue which requires further discussion.

It relates to the effects on employment in wage-goods industries of additional employment in non-wage-goods industries. "Thus it is often argued that, if, whether as a result of reduced wage-rates there or of anything else, the number of men employed in road-making, or other sorts of capital construction is increased, without off-setting reductions in other non-wage-goods industries, a large mass of further employment will be created in the industries that make wage-goods by the expenditure of the newly employed men. . . . This argument, in the present connection, is invalid. *When the*

7. On the question of the periodicity of the accumulation and depletion of stocks, see A. C. Pigou, Industrial Fluctuations (2d ed.), 30–32, 113, and R. G. Hawtrey, Trade and Credit, 159–60.

real — not the money — rate of wages ruling in the wage-goods industries is given, the quantity of labor demanded in these industries is determined, subject to certain qualifications not here relevant, by the wage-rate in relation to their productivity functions and the rate of interest. . . . The money counterpart of this fact is simply that the thousand extra £s spent by the new employees taken on for road-making goes to buy wage-goods which would have been created anyhow and which if not so bought, would have employed other labour, have been consumed by non-wage-earners, have been exported by them or have been placed in store." (74–76)

This argument — really a criticism of the Keynes-Kahn wing of the Cambridge School — is not entirely tenable. In assuming that the wage-rate does not change and that the demand function is given by the productivity function, Pigou evades (or dismisses) part of the problem. When millions of additional men are put on pay rolls through public works, an additional demand is created for wage-goods. Given a wage-rate of 10 bushels per day, a rate of interest of 5 per cent and a value for η of —2, the volume of production is not uniquely determined; more goods may not only be taken off the market, but more goods may be produced if the authorities succeed in setting several million additional men to work. Pigou, himself, in Industrial Fluctuations[8] has been at great pains to argue that an improvement of prospects in the railroad industry would contribute to a marked improvement in the various wage-goods industries, and in a cumulative manner.

Pigou has quite rightly argued that the additional demand for wage-goods to be associated with the improved opportunities in the railroad industry may be satisfied by drawing on stocks, from the savings on unemployment dole and the like, as well through additional work in wage-good industries.[9] He then proceeds to discuss the process through which the effects are spread over all wage-good industries. In the

8. Pp. 59–64 and, especially, 114–16; also see The Theory of Unemployment, p. 235. The references here are to the first edition of Industrial Fluctuations. It is also necessary to consider the treatment of these subjects in the second edition (63–70, 111–13).

9. Industrial Fluctuations, 1st ed., p. 115.

second edition his position has changed, for he now points out that railroad entrepreneurs have railroad securities and not wage-goods to offer. The effects on employment may well be adverse. On the other hand, he concedes that in a monetary economy, real wages may be reduced and a favorable psychological reaction following the improvement in the outlook for the railroad industry may well contribute towards an increase in employment.[1] In his Theory of Unemployment, however, he brushes aside these considerations, thus minimizing the difference made in the final analysis by a consideration of fluctuations in the volume of monetary expenditures, movements in real wage-rates and prices, all factors as relevant to the problem as the elasticity of the productivity function. In his only substantial argument for public works, in his Theory of Unemployment (213), Pigou suggests their use as a means of driving up the "proper rate" of interest, i.e., the money rate which would maintain the Standard Monetary System, from a negative to a positive rate. It is to be pointed out, however, that the important effects on the "proper rate" follow not so much from the direct effects of expenditures on public works, but rather from the repercussions of these expenditures (through price and wage movements) on wage-good industries and other non-wage-good industries.

3. Elasticity of Discounting

Chapters VIII to X (Part II) are devoted to the problem of the elasticity of real demand for labor over *industry in general*. This is at once the most original, most difficult and most important analysis in the entire volume; and since the chapters are an excellent example of the type of analysis used by Pigou as well as of the manner in which he jumps from abstract hypotheses to problems of the real world, I do not hesitate to discuss this part of his book at some length. In the first of these chapters (VIII) on Elasticity of Discounting, the mathematics is not easy to follow.

The problem here is the effect on the elasticity of real de-

1. Ibid., 2d ed., 111–13.

mand for labor of a reduction in the real wage-rate which carries with it a rise in the rate of interest in terms of wage-goods units. The demand price of $\frac{x}{w}$ labor is expressed as $\left(\frac{1}{1+i}\right)^{k} \frac{dF\left(\frac{x}{w}\right)}{d\left(\frac{x}{w}\right)}$ where i is the rate of interest per day, K the length of the production period expressed in days, w the real rate of wages, x the total real wage-bill, $\frac{x}{w}$ the quantity of labor employed and $F\left(\frac{x}{w}\right)$ the total value in wage-goods of the embodied services of this labor that are due to emerge on the market at the end of the period of production. (78) The term $\left(\frac{1}{1+i}\right)$ is put as $f(x)$ for the rate of interest may be or is affected by the quantity of wage-goods that is set aside for engaging labor. Under conditions of competition this is necessarily equal to w. By algebraic manipulation and differentiation, he finally obtains the following:

$$-K\frac{xf'(x)}{f(x)}\cdot\frac{dx}{dw} = x\left\{-\frac{1}{w} + \left(\frac{\dfrac{d^2F\left(\frac{x}{w}\right)}{d\left(\frac{x}{w}\right)^2}}{\dfrac{dF\left(\frac{x}{w}\right)}{d\left(\frac{x}{w}\right)}}\right)\cdot\frac{d\left(\frac{x}{w}\right)}{dw}\right\} \quad \ldots (1)$$

He now proceeds to reduce this equation.

1. He calls $\frac{f(x)}{xf'(x)}$ the elasticity of discounting and names it e. It is derived of course as follows: $\frac{d(x)}{x} \div \frac{f'(x)}{f(x)}$. It

"measures the proportionate change in $\left(\frac{1}{1+i}\right)$ that is due, other things being equal, to a small proportionate change in x, divided by that proportionate change." (79)

2. The next task is to introduce E_d and get rid of $\frac{d\left(\frac{x}{w}\right)}{dw}$

$$``\frac{d\left(\frac{x}{w}\right)}{dw}=\frac{x}{w^2}\left\{\frac{w^2}{x}\frac{d\left(\frac{x}{w}\right)}{dw}\right\}=\frac{x}{w^2}E_d."$$

3. He then obtains E_d on the assumption that e is infinite, that is to say, on the assumption that there are no reactions through the rate of interest. This is called E_r, which by definition is the elasticity of the real demand in the absence of reactions through the rate of interest.

Professor Pigou thus obtains E_d (here E_r) on this assumption.

$$E_r=\frac{\dfrac{dF\left(\frac{x}{w}\right)}{d\left(\frac{x}{w}\right)}}{\dfrac{x}{w}\dfrac{d^2F\left(\frac{x}{w}\right)}{d\left(\frac{x}{w}\right)^2}}\ldots (2)$$

4. The next task is to dispose of $\frac{dx}{dw}$. Since $E_d=\frac{w^2}{x}\cdot\frac{d\left(\frac{x}{w}\right)}{dw}$ $=\left(-1+\frac{w}{x}\frac{dx}{dw}\right)$, it follows that $\frac{dx}{dw}=\frac{x}{w}(E_d+1)$.

5. "Hence, from equation (1) in the general case where e is not nil, we find $E_d=\dfrac{1-\frac{k}{e}}{\frac{1}{E_r}+\frac{k}{e}}$. (Corrected version) . . . (3)

From an inspection of the crucial equation $E_d = \dfrac{1-\dfrac{k}{e}}{\dfrac{1}{E_r}+\dfrac{k}{e}}$ it becomes evident at once that much depends upon whether e is positive or negative. For if e is negative, E_d must be negative, for E_r cannot be positive. "That is to say, in general, a reduction in the real rate of wages *must* lead to some increase in the quantity of labor demanded. That does not of course imply an increase in the quantity of wage-goods that is spent on labor. Whether that increases depends on whether $\dfrac{dx}{dw}$, namely E_d+1, namely $\dfrac{\dfrac{1}{E_r}+1}{\dfrac{1}{E_r}-\dfrac{K}{e}}$ is positive or negative which in turn depends on whether E_r is (numerically) greater or less than unity."[2] (82)

Unfortunately, errors are concealed in these conclusions. Pigou seems to be wrong when he argues that if e is negative, E_d must be negative. What is meant by a negative value for e? Simply that a small rise in x (the real wage-bill) carries with it a *decline* in $f(x)$, that is in $\dfrac{1}{1+i}$. A decline in $\dfrac{1}{1+i}$, it is to be noted, requires a *rise* in i, the daily rate of discount. It therefore seems unreasonable to expect that a rise in x following a reduction in real wages *must* be followed by a rise in employment *only* when e is *negative;* for e is negative (on the assumption of a rise in x) when the effects from the side of the

2. The sentence should read "negative or positive" and since $\dfrac{dx}{dw}=\dfrac{x}{w}(E_d+1)$, Pigou errs in substituting E_d+1 in (3) and not $\dfrac{x}{w}(E_d+1)$. The result, $\dfrac{\dfrac{1}{E_r}+1}{\dfrac{1}{E_r}+\dfrac{K}{e}}$ given in Pigou's correction (on his slip), is therefore wrong. Even assuming that $E_d+1=\dfrac{dx}{dw}$, Pigou's results seem to be wrong.

rate of interest are adverse, that is when the rate of interest rises, for when the rate of interest rises the value of the expression $\frac{1}{1+i}$, that is, $f(x)$, declines. Similarly, an increase in e (say from $\frac{1}{1+\frac{.06}{365}}$ to $\frac{1}{1+\frac{.05}{365}}$) should not account for a diminution in E_d; there ought to be a favorable reaction on E_d. Surely, Pigou would not argue that the effect on employment of a reduction in wages must be favorable only when an increase in the real wage-bill is accompanied by an adverse effect through the interest rate. (e is negative.)

"In view of these results it is very important to know whether and in what conditions the elasticity of discounting e is positive or negative. . . . Write y for the quantity of income devoted by non-wage-earners to immediate use, $\phi(y)$ for the marginal utility derived from this use by the representative non-wage-earner when y is devoted to it, and ϵ for $\frac{\phi(y)}{y\phi'(y)}$, namely the elasticity, in respect of this quantity, of the representative non-wage-earner's consumption-utility function. It is easy to see in a general way that, if Δy is withdrawn from the consumption use against future repayment, a burden is inflicted on the transferrer equal, on our assumptions, to $\Delta y\phi'(y)$ and that in order to induce him to make the transfer, $\frac{1}{1+i}$ must be diminished in a proportion equal to $\frac{\phi(y)}{\phi(y)+\Delta y\phi'(y)}$. Hence by a simple manipulation, we find $\frac{1}{e} = -\frac{\Delta y\phi'(y)}{\phi(y)} \cdot \frac{x}{\Delta x} = -\frac{\Delta y}{\Delta x} \cdot \frac{x}{y} \cdot \frac{1}{\epsilon}$. Now we know that $\frac{y}{x}$ is positive and that ϵ is negative. It follows that e is positive or negative according as Δy is of the same sign as or of the opposite sign to Δx." (83–4)

It is important to know under what conditions Δy and Δx are of opposite signs, and therefore when e (and hence E_d.) are necessarily negative.[3] The use of terms is rather confusing for Δy is positive when the income devoted by non-wage-earners to immediate use is *reduced*. I assume that this is true from the following: "In the very short period if there were no such thing as unemployment benefit and no possibility of adding to or subtracting from liquid stocks of wage-goods, Δy would always be equal to Δx and $\frac{\Delta x}{\Delta y}$ would always be equal to 1." (84) . . . "The existence of a system of unemployment insurance *must*, however, render Δy negative if Δx has a sufficiently small positive value, and may render it negative even when the positive value of Δx, consequent upon a reduction in the wage-rate by Δw, is fairly substantial." (85) Pigou then proceeds to estimate the net saving on unemployment benefit out of which Δx (the additional wage-bill) may be financed.

The net saving on unemployment benefit on the assumption of an unchanged wage-bill is $\frac{\Delta w}{w} \cdot \frac{x}{w}(r+t)$.[4] With Δx positive, there is an additional saving of $\frac{\Delta x}{w}(r+t)$. He finds total saving to be $\Delta x \frac{E_d}{E_d+1} \cdot \frac{r+t}{w}$. "Therefore Δy, and consequently e, is negative, provided that $\frac{E_d}{E_d+1} > \frac{w}{r+t} \ldots$" (85) In other words, the addition to the wage-bill (Δx) is then associated with an addition to the non-wage-earner's income available for consumption; Δx is positive and Δy is negative in Pigou's terminology. He calculates that Δy (and e) would be negative under the following conditions.[5]

3. If my interpretation is correct, E_d is necessarily negative when e is positive.

4. r = benefit paid per unemployed man and t the contribution per head to unemployment insurance of employed wage-earners. (22)

5. I should say that e would be positive.

$r+t$ *equal*	*Then* Δy *is negative*
1. w	1. for all values of E_d
2. $\frac{1}{2}w$	2. E_d with negative values <2
3. $\frac{1}{3}w$	3. E_d with negative values $<{}^3/_2$.

Let us summarize the discussion thus far. $\frac{1}{e} = -\frac{\Delta y}{\Delta x} \cdot \frac{x}{y} \cdot \frac{1}{\epsilon}$. The term $\frac{x}{y}$ is positive and ϵ is negative. Then e is positive or negative according as Δy is of the same sign or of the opposite sign to Δx. The elasticity of discounting e will then be negative if Δx is positive (the wage-bill increases) and Δy is negative, which on Pigou's definition means that the amount of income of non-wage-earners available for immediate consumption increases. This may clearly happen if the elasticity of real demand for labor is not too great and if the saving on the dole is large. The most troublesome element in the analysis is the assumption that only when e is negative, must the reduction in wages be followed by a rise in employment (E_d is negative). The truth of the matter is that a negative value for e when Δx is positive, entails a rise in the interest rate (i rises and $\frac{1}{1+i}$, namely, e declines) and, therefore, also entails an adverse effect on employment.

Pigou concludes as follows: In the conditions prevailing in this country reactions through the rate of interest "cannot in the very short period have an adverse effect if the elasticity would otherwise have been numerically greater than $-\frac{3}{2}$ or -2." (87) In respect of a period longer than the period of production of labor engaged in making wage-goods, the conclusion is: "Provided, therefore, that there exists a system of unemployment benefit with a benefit rate not less than one-quarter of the wage-rate, Δy, and, therefore, e must be negative[6] in all circumstances." (86) This conclusion rests on a *guess* that in the longer period three-quarters of the total extra wage-bill will be covered by the inflow of new wage-goods and claims to wage-goods.

6. So in Pigou's correction slips.

Pigou's brilliant analysis lays itself open to numerous criticisms. Unemployment insurance surely does not play the decisive part that he attributes to it; x may well be financed out of stocks, foreign borrowing and the like. Even in his treatment of the effects of the working of unemployment insurance, he makes (implicitly) assumptions that cannot be accepted. E.g., any savings on unemployment insurance do not inure merely to the benefit of non-wage-earners; the state and non-wage-earners are not identities; and an improvement in employment conditions may well induce an increase in the contributions to the unemployment fund by employers as well as a reduction of the *state's* contributions. Another important aspect of this problem is that additional employment following a reduction in wages may be provided at the expense of consumers in general, not merely at the expense of non-wage-earners. It is thus possible to obtain the means for providing x not only through savings on unemployment benefit and through direct contributions from income of non-wage-earners available for immediate consumption, but also through forced levies from *wage-earners* and non-wage-earners. Pigou's y is not sufficiently inclusive, for it includes only income of non-wage-earners available for immediate consumption. It is, moreover, wrong to assume that any drains on y or on wage-earner's income effected through forced savings will have effects on the rate of interest identical with those following from equivalent voluntary contributions by non-wage-earners. Finally, it is necessary to remind the reader that the assumption on which the whole analysis of movements in Δx and Δy is based (83), is the expectation of a constancy of taste and income on the part of non-wage-earners. In fact, a reduction in wages may well stimulate expenditures for investment. I conclude, therefore, that tho the analysis is brilliant and important and marks a large advance, difficulties still remain. Any application of these abstract results to actual conditions may easily mislead.

4. The Elasticity of Demand for Labor Over All Occupations

In Chapters IX and X of Part II, Pigou derives the elasticity of demand for labor over all occupations in terms of wage-goods and money. The argument begins with the assumption that x men are engaged in making wage-goods and exports the sale of which create claims to wage-goods from abroad. $F(x)$ = the output of these men in value of wage-goods and $F'(x)$ the general rate of wages. Then Pigou holds that $\{F(x)-(x+y)F'(x)\}$ is the trading surplus of wage-goods left over to non-wage-earners in the wage-goods and export industries. (89–90)[7] Let us call the elasticity of real demand for labor in the wage-good industries and the export industries together η, and the elasticity of the real demand for labor in the aggregate E_r.[8] Given the surrounding conditions, we are entitled to write $(x+y)=\phi(x)$. Then clearly we have

$$\eta=\frac{F'(x)}{xF''(x)} \text{ and } E_r=\frac{\phi'(x)}{\phi(x)}\div\frac{F''(x)}{F'(x)}=\frac{x\phi'(x)}{\phi(x)}\cdot\eta.\text{"} \qquad (90)$$

The short period demand function for labor in terms of wage-goods in the home wage-goods industries — which apart from reactions through the rate of interest, is identical with what in the chapter cited is called the productivity function — is likely to be highly elastic in respect of the output proper to a depression. (91) Pigou therefore concludes that η is certain to be (numerically) much larger than -1 and may well amount to -5 or more if one's starting point is low down in a depression. (91) This is no more than a guess.

The question may be raised whether the elasticity of real demand for labor over short periods is as favorable as Pigou has indicated. It is so only on the assumption that the productivity function is the demand function for labor. In the argument that follows I am criticizing Pigou's approach, which is based on this assumption.

7. This seems to be wrong for $(x+y)\ F'(x)$ are the wages paid in *all* industries, for y men are engaged in *other* industries.

8. The change of terminology is rather confusing. Cf. definitions of η and E_r in earlier discussion.

Excess capacity is available, of course. It does not follow that additional wage-goods produced after a reduction in wages will find a ready market. If consumption by wage-earners was well maintained in the previous period of unemployment and if non-wage-earners are not too optimistic concerning the use of wage-goods for investment purposes, the extension of production may not proceed so far as the productivity function may be supposed to indicate. Non-wage-earners will demand larger surpluses in the wage-goods industries, and wage-earners will refuse to work or will work less effectively, thus either creating unfilled vacancies or increasing real wages per unit of output. While wage-goods cannot depreciate in terms of wage-goods on Pigou's assumption of a single wage-good, they may become less valuable for the purchase of non-wage-goods and for use in investment.[9]

Pigou is concerned with the elasticity of the productivity function in the depths of the depression. But it is necessary in analysing the effects of a change in wages upon employment to go beyond the purely physical limits set by the productivity function. The following considerations are to be borne in mind. First, the prospects of increasing production without incurring large additional costs may seem bright for any one firm or industry, yet will not be equally favorable when all industries compete for available supplies of working capital. Second, plants are frequently allowed to run down in a long drawn-out depression, overhead charges being met with the savings thus effected. Third, a large reduction in real labor costs per unit of output is a reminder that tho the inefficient have been weeded out in the course of a depression, with revival they will resume operations. Fourth, the revival will also depend upon financial conditions, for industry cannot extend operations, whatever its plant capacity, if financial aid is not forthcoming. The first three points suggest that Pigou may be too optimistic concerning the value

9. Harrod presents brilliantly the issues involved when the assumptions of perfect competition and a *single* wage-good are removed. Op. cit., pp. 27–9.

of η, the fourth that the financial set-up is an important factor.

Having obtained a value for η, Pigou proceeds to obtain E_r. It is therefore necessary to obtain $\frac{x\phi'(x)}{\phi(x)}\cdot\eta$. His estimate for $\phi(x)$, that is, $x+y$, for Great Britain is obtained on the assumption that $y=\frac{1}{3}x$. He proceeds to the calculation of $\phi'(x)$, that is, the rate of change in $\phi(x)$, that is in $x+y$, which is to be associated with a given change in x, the employment in wage-goods and designated export industries. A lower limit is obtained for E_r by assuming that any surplus obtained by non-wage-earners from an increase in x is used, not in employing additional workers, but in increasing their consumption of wage-goods (directly or indirectly). Hence $\Delta x\phi'(x)=\Delta x$ or $\phi'(x)=1$. Employment in wage-goods and non-wage-goods industries together therefore increases only as much as in wage-goods industries alone. Another possibility is that non-wage-earners' demand for wage-goods is absolutely inelastic and therefore the surplus is used exclusively by non-wage-earners in putting men to work in non-wage-good industries. "In this case K being a constant $\phi(x)=\frac{F(x)-K}{F'(x)}$ for all values of x over the range relevant to our problem." (92) Pigou then proceeds to differentiate the above in order to get $\phi'(x)$ and the lower limit for E_r is thus found to be $\left\{\eta\frac{x}{x+y}\right\}$ $(\phi'(x)=1)$ while the upper limit is $\eta\frac{x}{x+y}-1$.[1] Therefore if $\eta=-1$, E_r is $-\frac{3}{4}$ to $-1\frac{3}{4}$ and if $\eta=-4$, E_r is -3 to -4.

1. The following may help the reader. $\phi'(x)=\phi(x)\left\{\frac{1}{\phi(x)}-\frac{F''(x)}{F'(x)}\right\}$. Now $\eta=\frac{F'(x)}{xF''(x)}$ and therefore $\phi'(x)=1-\frac{x+y}{x}\cdot\frac{1}{\eta}$.
But $E_r=\frac{x\phi'(x)}{\phi}\cdot\eta$ and therefore $E_r=\eta\frac{x}{x+y}$ when $\phi'(x)=1$ and when $\phi'(x)=\left\{1-\frac{x+y}{x}\cdot\frac{1}{\eta}\right\}$, $E=\left\{\eta\cdot\frac{x}{x+y}-1\right\}$.

The foregoing results are based on the assumption that unemployment insurance is not in effect. The initial employment in the y industries will be smaller with an insurance system in operation than in its absence, for part of the surplus will be absorbed in contributions by employers to unemployment insurance; and E_r will be larger where a system of unemployment insurance is in operation. Then $\phi(x) = \frac{F(x) - K - \{A - \phi(x)\} r}{F'(x)}$ where A is the would-be working population and r the benefit paid per unemployed worker. This is equal to $\frac{F(x) - K - Ar}{F'(x) - r}$. Differentiating in order to obtain $\phi'(x)$, substituting the result in the equation for $E_r = \frac{x\phi'(x)}{\phi(x)} \cdot \eta$, relying on some algebraic manipulation and substituting w for $F'(x)$, Pigou obtains $E_r = \eta \frac{x}{x+y} \left\{ \frac{w}{w-r} \right\} - \frac{w}{w-r}$. With $r = \frac{1}{3}w$ and $y^1 = \frac{1}{4}x$, and $\eta = -4$, E_r lies between $-3^1/_5$ and $-6\frac{1}{2}$. For periods longer than the production period of the generality of wage-goods, he concludes: "If, on the grounds given in Paragraph 5, we accept the view that in times of depression η is not numerically less than -4, it follows that at such times E_r cannot, on the least favorable assumption here suggested, be numerically less than -3 and may well be larger than -4." (96)

Pigou's analysis in these two chapters suffers from his overeagerness to draw positive conclusions; and these conclusions are not invulnerable. Thus, the values for η, ϕ (x) and the allowance for movements in the rate of interest cannot be accepted with much confidence; we are completely in the air as far as η is concerned. Numerous simplifying assumptions are made which remain when attempt is made to apply the analysis to actual conditions. For example, it is assumed that an unemployment insurance plan is completely established, wages being readjusted on the basis of contributions by the employer; it is also assumed, tho hardly justifiably, that the non-wage-earner makes the entire contribution to unemployment insurance.[2] The last point suggests a related one. The greater elasticity of real demand for labor with an insurance scheme in operation rests on the assumption that real wages will not rise when the contributions of the employer are reduced. Lastly, the operation of an insurance scheme will contribute towards additional employment with a cut in wages only if the improvement in the employment situation is of such significant proportions as to justify a reduction of the contributions from employers even in the face of a large state deficit.

5. Monetary Elasticity of Demand for Labor

In Chapter X Pigou inquires what changes in real rates are implied in given changes in the money rate of wages. The first possibility discussed is that E_m (monetary elasticity) $=0$ and $\frac{E_r}{E_m}=\infty$. The conditions for $E_m=0$ are satisfied when a change in money wages is accompanied by no change in real wages. Thus $E_m=0$ if, when money wages are reduced, prices of wage-goods respond immediately, and other incomes decline in proportion to the drop in prices and no changes in employment follow. He dismisses the possibility of this sequence of changes and contends that so long as income accrues to non-wage-earners, either real wages will be reduced or the value of non-wage-goods will rise with a reduction in money wages, and, therefore, additional laborers will be hired. The mathematical proof offered, however, fails to take account of the divergencies between income and expenditures and the movements of stocks. Harrod has criticized Pigou's position at this point, arguing that E_m may equal 0.[3]

2. Direct contributions by employed workers are excluded from consideration in order to avoid a further complication of the algebra. Other payments by wage-earners (taxes), payments by non-wage-earners as employers and as taxpayers, and contributions of entrepreneurs as against other non-wage-earners ought to be distinguished in this analysis.

3. Pigou's conclusion rests on the assumption to which Harrod objects, that non-wage-earners *maintain* their money expenditures. The latter's argument is that since non-wage-earners had not increased the *real* volume of their expenditures in the absence of a reduction in wages, it is not likely that they will do so merely because wages have been

In order to determine the value of E_m relative to E_r, it is necessary to make assumptions concerning the actual monetary system in operation. Pigou assumes that the aggregate money income I is some function of the real income of the community and so, for the short period, of the quantity of labor employed. Thus write $I = \Psi(x)$. It may be said parenthetically that if M (*money*) were made a function of X or better of T (transactions), the assumption would be more in accord with the facts.

On the author's assumptions, the money wage-rate in equilibrium is $\frac{\Psi(x)}{F(x)} \cdot F'(x)$ and hence $E_m = \frac{dx}{x}$[4] $\div \left\{\frac{d}{dx} \cdot \frac{\Psi(x) \cdot F'(x)}{F(x)} \div \frac{\Psi(x) \cdot F'(x)}{F(x)}\right\}$, that is, the money elasticity of demand for labor is given by a proportionately small change in employment divided by the proportionate change in the money rate of wages to be associated with the change in employment. Differentiating and substituting E_r for $\frac{F'(x)}{xF''(x)}$, he obtains $\frac{1}{E_m} = \frac{1}{E_r} - \frac{xF'(x)}{F(x)} + \frac{x\Psi'(x)}{\Psi(x)}$. If the wage-bill is $\frac{2}{5}$ of the national income, then $\frac{xF'(x)}{F(x)} = \frac{2}{5}$ and

$$\frac{1}{E_m} = \frac{1}{E_r} - \frac{2}{5} + \frac{x\Psi'(x)}{\Psi(x)}. \quad (103)$$

reduced. Harrod is undoubtedly justified in pointing out that assumptions concerning the level of expenditures of non-wage-earners other than that on which Pigou bases his argument, are reasonable. On the other hand, Pigou's argument is strong if the assumption of *some* increase in the volume of real purchases is justified and if his assumption is the most reasonable one possible under the circumstances. There are strong arguments for an increase in the volume of real purchases, following a reduction in money wages and prices. Non-wage-earners are guided by the monetary value of their purchases as well as by the real volume, and a reduction in prices is likely to stimulate the quantity of purchases. Furthermore, a reduction in wages is likely to result in additional outlays of wage-goods for investment.

4. In corrected version, $\frac{dx}{x}$ reads as $\frac{1}{x}$.

Pigou then proceeds to make certain assumptions concerning the nature of the monetary system. First, he assumes that the aggregate money income accruing per unit of time is held constant. Then $\Psi'(x)$ is nil, the element $\frac{x\Psi'(x)}{\Psi(x)}$ disappears and $E_m = \frac{5E_r}{5-2E_r}$. If $E_r = -4$, E_m is $-\frac{20}{13}$ and if E_r is $-\infty$, E_m attains its maximum value of $-2\frac{1}{2}$.

The assumption of a *constant money income* is made, let it be noted, tho the value for $\frac{1}{E_m}$ has been obtained on the assumption that $I = \Psi(x)$.

Other types of monetary system are possible, for example, one under which money income accruing per unit of time declines with the increase in real income. E_m would then be smaller relatively to E_r than under a system of constant monetary income. In Pigou's view a more likely system is one under which money income would increase with the rise in real income. Finally, Pigou says that "in a small country on the gold standard in a gold standard world the monetary system is of such a sort that internal changes leave the *price level* substantially intact; i.e., in my notation, $\frac{\Psi(x)}{F(x)}$ is constant. This implies that $\frac{F'(x)}{F(x)} - \frac{\Psi'(x)}{\Psi(x)} = 0$. Hence the formula of §6[5] reduces to $\frac{1}{E_m} = \frac{1}{E_r}$. (105) There is a confusion of *price* and *income* levels here: $\Psi(x)$ is the money *income* and therefore, under his assumptions, $\frac{\Psi(x)}{F(x)}$ would not be constant merely because prices are assumed to be stable. Second, aside from this $\frac{\Psi(x)}{F(x)}$ would be constant only on the assumption that there are no international changes in income and price levels.

5. Should read 5.

6. Factors Other Than Money Affecting the Level and Variations of the Real Demand for Labor

a. *Variations in the Demand for Durable Commodities*

Part III treats of the factors other than money affecting the level and variations in the real demand for labor. Unfortunately space permits only a discussion of five or six issues raised in this very interesting part. I begin with a discussion of a troublesome problem in Chapter III, namely variations in the demand for durable commodities.

Pigou proceeds as follows:[6] Let A = number of units of the durable commodity (capital or consumption) in use; nA normally needs to be replaced in a year and $\frac{1}{n}$ is, therefore, the life of the commodity. He then assumes that the commodity's service in demand rises 10 per cent. The new output demanded will then rise from nA to $nA + \frac{A}{10}$ and if $n = \frac{1}{5}$, the increase in demand will be 50 per cent (from $\frac{1}{5}A$ to $\frac{1}{5}A + \frac{1}{10}A$). (121) The stock in the next year becomes larger and if the demand for the total supply then returns to its former level, the demand for new production must fall below its old level. Thus, at the end of a year the stock stands at $A\left(1+\frac{1}{10}\right)$ when demand reverts to its original level. This implies that the demand for new production falls to $A - A\left(1+\frac{1}{10}\right)(1-n) = \frac{11n-1}{10n}$ times the normal amount.[7] (121–2) With $n = \frac{1}{5}$, this means a contraction of new demand below the normal of 40 per cent. Pigou concludes that "this line of

6. Also consult Industrial Fluctuations, pp. 107–10. His discussion of similar problems is, on the whole, better in Industrial Fluctuations.

7. An = normal amount. Therefore multiply and divide $A\left\{n\frac{11}{10} - \frac{1}{10}\right\}$ by n and we get $An\left\{\frac{11n-1}{10n}\right\}$ or $\frac{11n-1}{10n}$ times An, the normal amount.

thought goes far to explain the high variability of demand for labor in such industries as shipbuilding and also suggests that when a new durable commodity such as radios or gramophones is invented, the demand for labor to satisfy the first flood of demand for it . . . is likely much to exceed the subsequent demand for labor for making good wastage and satisfying the *stream* of wants of new customers."

Pigou's formula of demand for new production in year 2 (demand returns to normal) requires further consideration. The demand according to his analysis will be as follows: Let us assume that $A = 10{,}000$ (machines) and $n = \frac{1}{5}$ (the life of the machine is 5 years). Demand in year 1 rises by 50 per cent $\left(\frac{A}{10}\right)$. Then the question is, will $A - A\left(1 + \frac{1}{10}\right)(1 - n)$ give the demand for *new production* in year 2 when demand reverts to its original level. The formula gives a demand of 1200 machines in year 2 as compared to a normal of $\frac{A}{5} = 2{,}000$. With 11,000 machines in operation, this is clearly not a satisfactory solution; the fact that there are 1,000 additional machines in operation does not solve the problem for the owners of the 10,000 machines in operation in year 0; it is necessary to replace 2,000 machines in year 2 (and a larger number in later years.) The demand may of course fall below 2,000 because renewals may be postponed and some factories may close; but this is another problem and it is unlikely that the demand will fall to 1,200. Pigou, in short, errs in assuming that the 1,000 additional machines will be available to the owners of the remaining 10,000 machines who find it necessary to replace in year 2. All that can be said is that the new competition will deprive the owners of the old machines of some business, thus extending the life of the machines somewhat. The pronounced effect, however, will be a growth in excess capacity, altho over *several years*, the presence of these machines will have an appreciable effect on the demand for new output.

In leaving out of consideration the normal growth, Pigou

moreover, has omitted consideration of a very important aspect of the problem; for the annual purchases are not NA but are NA plus (or minus) the growth element.[8] The formula merely tells us the number of machines or automobiles that will be produced in year 2 on the assumption that the supply is that of year 0 and that the additional machines purchased in year 1 will provide part of the renewals required in year 2. They obviously cannot do so in so far as they have already been sold and put into operation by new firms or for new plants. So far as machines or ships are under consideration, a large addition of the number in use in year 1 may, of course, cut into the production necessary for normal growth in year 2. This is, however, not so safe a generalization for durable consumers' goods. The radio or the automobile serves an *individual* or a *family*, not a *market*. Large additional purchases of automobiles by individuals a_1 a_2 a_3 in year 1 are not so likely to discourage purchases by individuals b_1 b_2 b_3 in year 2 as large purchases of machines or ships in year 1 would depress the volume of sales in year 2.

I am not denying the significance of fluctuations in demand of durable goods for the problem of fluctuations in industrial activity. The emphasis is, however, to be put on the growth element, the distinction of demand for renewals from that for growth, the relation of *market* and *consumption* demand, and finally on the relation of new purchases and *payments* on old purchases.

b. Costs of State Stimulation of Employment

Pigou, in the next chapter, considers the effect of state stimulation of employment in particular occupations. (124–6) "A number of methods of stimulation are available, which, for the same effect on the quantity of labor demanded, involve very different expenditures by the state." Let r = rate of unemployment benefit and t = the rate of employed workpeople's contribution, E_d the number of men directly brought into employment and E_k the number indirectly driven out of

8. Cf. the excellent discussion in J. M. Clark, Strategic Factors in Business Cycles, pp. 33–40.

employment in other industries. Pigou argues that a guarantee of interest is the cheapest method of stimulation. The cost to the state is $-(r+t)\ (E_d-E_k)$, and this must be negative. The next cheapest is a bounty for each additional worker employed (let s be the rate of bounty required to produce the same effect on employment as above) — the cost to the state is $s.\ E_d-(r+t)\ (E_d-E_k)$. This may be negative. A less effective method is to pay the subsidy for all workpeople (A the number employed in initial position) — the cost is $s\ (A+E_d)-(r+t)\ (E_d-E_k)$. Even this may be negative. The most costly method is public works undertaken by the state. $E_d w-(r+t)\ (E_d-E_k)$ is the cost and if $r+t<w$, this cost cannot be negative.

This analysis is not adequate. Pigou fails to allow for the value of the public work which is constructed as well as for the outlay to be incurred later for any guarantee of interest. The cost of the first plan conceivably may be larger than that of the last. Moreover, throughout he apparently makes the unjustifiable assumption that the state derives the entire benefit from any saving on r and from additional receipts of t.

c. *Employment and the Supply of Wage-Goods*

The theme of Chapter IX (143–54) is that the amount of employment at a given wage-rate depends upon the volume of wage-goods available. Should a non-wage-goods industry be stimulated by an improvement in productivity or a state subsidy, a *net* improvement in employment at a given real wage-rate can be effected only in so far as the resulting rise in the rate of interest induces non-wage-earners to cut their consumption of wage-goods (C), reduce their stocks (S) or reduce their purchases of foreign non-wage-goods and securities (M) with their claims to wage-goods. The element $\{(A-E)r-Et\}$, the flow of wage-goods devoted to paying unemployment benefit to unemployed wage-earners minus the contribution towards this handed over by employed wage-earners, can only help if *some* contribution is made by the other items; it is not equal to the wage-rate and can provide additional employment only if contributions are also obtained from other sources.

This chapter is a challenge, hardly disguised, to all those who would improve the economic situation by the introduction of monetary or other measures that do not provide for the additional wage-goods necessary to increase the amount of employment at a given real wage-rate.[9] Pigou's treatment is a welcome reaction from the superficial treatment frequently offered by those who hold public works or monetary measures to be the cure-all. There are, however, weak spots in his discussion.

First, his concentration, also evident in other parts of the book, on the problem of increasing employment *at a given real wage-rate* leads to a bias in the handling of the subject. Economic practitioners are also interested in raising the *volume* of employment, even if at a somewhat lower real wage-rate; and to that end monetary measures may contribute. A higher volume of employment may be preferable even if the total wage payments are no larger; the argument holds *à fortiori* should the total wage-bill increase.

Second, had Pigou discussed *at this point* the problem of the stimulation of wage-goods industry resulting from additional investment in non-wage-goods industries, he could not but have gone on to a discussion of the possibility of providing additional wage-goods through additional production. Undoubtedly he would reply by referring to his earlier proposition that, given the real wage-rate, the productivity function and the rate of interest, employment in the wage-goods industry is determined. The trouble once more lies with his assumption that the productivity function and the demand function for labor are identical. The short-period supply curve may rise gently as it probably does in the depths of a depression; but how favorable this factor will prove will depend upon general demand conditions. Production will be pushed further should the government stimulate *net* expenditures than if the government refrains from interference.

9. In his Industrial Fluctuations, Pigou is much more optimistic concerning the elasticity of the supplies of floating capital. See especially 122–31, 315–19. For an attack on this emphasis on the elasticity of supplies of floating capital, see R. G. Hawtrey, Trade and Credit, pp. 178-84.

In other words, the amount of employment in the wage-goods industries is not uniquely determined if the values of the three variables given above are known.

Where did the additional wage-goods come from in the United States in 1933–34? Stocks (S) were large and some contributions were to be had from M, that is by reducing imports of non-wage-goods and of foreign securities. It is important to observe that surplus *world* stocks are available for those countries that introduce the appropriate policies and hence these stocks may be very large. In the same sense, M may be very large especially for creditor nations. Perhaps, even more important, contributions were to be obtained from C, the importance of which as well as of M and S, Pigou considerably underestimates. Moreover, a rise in prices (and a drop in real wages) may well stimulate production in wage-good industries, a consideration that a discussion on the assumption of an unchanged level of real wages misses. In Keynes' terms, unproductive consumption becomes productive and the rise in prices that makes possible a drop in real wages, and the rise in expenditures stimulates production in the wage-good industries. The favorable effects will be greater in proportion as the elasticity of the production function is more favorable.

d. Special Problems Relating to the Flow of Wage-Goods and the Amount of Employment

In Chapter X (154–7) Pigou treats a related problem, the effect on labor demanded of transfers of income between groups of non-wage-earners and also between wage-earners and non-wage-earners. He concludes that transfers between groups of non-wage-earners are not likely to have large effects on the aggregate demand for labor *the world over*, even if the beneficiaries are inclined to hoard or purchase foreign securities. For risks and other costs set a limit to the size of hoards, and purchases of foreign securities do not involve the using up of wage-goods for the world as a whole. He does admit, however, that the damage may be greater if the process involves a surreptitious rise in real wages. At this point once more the dangers of a *real* analysis are evident. Hoards in terms of money, not goods, are significant, for the risks and costs are not a deterrent for *monetary* hoards to the same extent as for real hoards. A much larger part of the national income may be kept in monetary hoards than in *real* hoards. It is the hoarding of the equivalent of goods *not produced*, not those already produced that requires emphasis. Large hoards of money account for the ensuing decline in prices which in turn explains the moderate volume of real hoards. That real hoards are kept at a low point is, paradoxically enough, the aftermath of the presence of large monetary hoards and may also be explained by the high costs of hoarding commodities. Unproductive consumption contributes to the diminution in the size of real hoards.

Later in this chapter Pigou takes what might be termed an anti-Keynes and anti-Roosevelt Administration position when he argues that "all gratuitous payments to poor people and all social services, in so far as they are financed at the expense of the richer non-wage-earning classes, whatever benefit they confer on the community in other respects, of necessity reduce *pro tanto* the quantity of labor demanded at a given real wage-rate." (155–6) The assumption is that wage-earners consume wage-goods only and non-wage-earners devote only part of their income to this purpose; these transfers therefore reduce the amount of wage-goods available for employment. Pigou's argument is a sane reaction from the purchasing power theories current today. But it still remains true that transfers to the wage-earners through their effects on hoards and purchasing power in use, and thereby on prices and real wages, *may* increase both the amount of employment and the volume of wage-goods available for employment.

Throughout the volume, Pigou is at pains to argue that the volume of employment depends on the amount of wage-goods used to put people to work. In Chapter XI (158–63) he discusses the possibility of increasing employment through an improvement in wage-goods industries or through a state subsidy (on wages) to these industries. This analysis is, however, seriously lacking in one respect. What will the *attitude* be of those who are asked to pay the subsidy? Pigou omits mention of this problem.[1] If the non-wage-earners' demand for wage-goods is inelastic, as he elsewhere argues, the taxes imposed or the loans issued for this purpose will have to be very large to provide the *wage*-goods that are necessary to increase employment.[2] Ultimately, adjustments may be made through movements of factors to wage-goods industries. Strangely enough, the possibility of transfers of this type occupies a minimum of Pigou's attention throughout the volume.

7. The Differences Made by Money

a. *Money and the Real Demand Function for Labor*

In Part IV Pigou jumps from his "real" analysis to reality. Unfortunately he minimizes the task ahead. "Everything that has been said is relevant to the actual world. All the influences of which an account has been given play their part there in the way that has been described. We have, in short, not assumed that there is no money, but simply postponed our discussion of its role." (185) On the other hand, he is not unaware that money does make a difference (especially 188, 212).

Pigou's concept of a standard monetary system with which he contrasts the monetary systems in operation, is colored by his real analysis. "*I define the standard monetary system as one so constructed that, for all sorts of movements in the real demand function for labor or in real rates of wages, whether they last for a long time or a short, the aggregate money income is increased or diminished by precisely the difference made to the*

1. He merely refers to the possibility of a tax which penalises the *production* of wage-goods.

2. A somewhat similar error is made in the discussion of the problem of the export and import trade in relation to the aggregate demand for labor. (Chapters 13 and 14, pp. 169–77.) It is not clear where the additional wage-goods necessary to carry on production of motor cars in Great Britain (instead of abroad) and to provide additional employment, are to be obtained, should the demand for wage-goods on the part of consumers of automobiles be highly inelastic.

number of workpeople (or other factors of production) at work multiplied by the original rate of money wages." (206)

Pigou does not pretend that the introduction of the Standard Monetary System will provide the world with an ideal economic system.[3] In his Industrial Fluctuations he has argued both that industrial fluctuations are an evil and ought to be removed if possible and that, even with the removal of fluctuations to be associated with money, large fluctuations would remain.[4] It is these monetary disturbances that his Standard Monetary System seems to rule out.

Altho the Standard Monetary System is based upon the real analysis in Part III, Pigou seems to emerge with results, particularly in relation to the supplies of floating capital, that are rather inconsistent with his earlier results, both in his Theory of Unemployment and in his Industrial Fluctuations. Thus, it is not necessary for entrepreneurs and the people from whom they borrow to forego consumption of wage-goods to the full extent of the additions to the wage-fund in order that money incomes rise *only* in proportion to the additional employment of the factors multiplied by the original rate of remuneration.[5] Stocks and unemployment contributions, for example, may provide additional wage-goods without adverse effects on prices in the short run. In short, in his Industrial Fluctuations he is optimistic concerning the elasticity of floating capital, both in a real and a money economy. On the other hand, in Part III of the Theory of Unemployment, he is not so optimistic concerning the elasticity in a real economy, and in presenting his Standard Monetary System here, he, by implication, further reduces the elasticity

3. Hawtrey is probably right when he argues that Pigou considers departures from his Standard Monetary System harmful. Economica, 1934, p. 162. On the other hand, Pigou also considers harmful the fluctuations in real demand for labor to which his standard system is to respond. He has in mind, tho he does not say so, fluctuations in real demand due to real causes. Harrod, op. cit., p. 30.

4. Industrial Fluctuations, Part I, Chapter XXII; Part II, Chapter I. The treatment of the effects of money upon the real demand for labor is similar to that in his earlier study. Cf. Ibid. 99–106, 132–39, 170–81, 210–19, with Theory of Unemployment, Part IV, Chapters IX-XII. The subject matter of Chapter XI is largely new.

5. See second paragraph on page 211.

in a *real* economy. The elasticity to be associated with monetary *disturbances* is, however, found to be as great as in his Industrial Fluctuations.

The trouble with actual monetary systems, according to Pigou, is that monetary incomes rise and decline *more* than in proportion to the rise and decline in the employment of the factors of production. The explanation is, he concludes, that industrialists and people from whom they borrow make inadequate sacrifices of consumption of wage-goods on the rise and do not increase their consumption adequately as they withdraw wage-goods from investment on the decline. But why should the responsibility for failure to consume be put exclusively on entrepreneurs and their creditors? Wage-earners, without jobs or anticipating unemployment, also cut their consumption; and in truth the entire public reacts in that manner altho the ensuing decline in prices makes possible additional consumption of an unproductive kind.

b. The Removal of Some Assumptions

In Part IV also, Pigou removes some of the assumptions on which the analysis of Part III was based. It was assumed that wages were the only direct cost and that real wages were fixed. The use of such assumptions is not objectionable; but it is wrong to argue that employment in wage-goods industries cannot be increased when in fact this is so only on the assumptions given above. In a monetary régime, the assumption of fixed real wages is especially far-fetched; and yet this assumption is not removed until Part V. He now also pays some attention to other primary costs; for he realizes that a fluctuating price level may, through the reactions on these other primary costs, affect the real demand function for labor. "The real demand function for labor being expressed in terms of wage-good units, it is evident that, in given conditions of productivity, this function will be lowered if the other elements of prime cost rise in value relatively to wage-goods; and that in converse conditions the real demand function will be raised. Now there enter into prime cost, or short period supply price, substantial elements of cost other than labor cost." (238)[6]

"The real demand function for labor will also be lowered if, other things being equal, the value at works of its product falls relatively to wage-good units; and in converse conditions will be raised." (239) What is relevant at this point is the lag of retail prices. "When prices are in process of falling, this time lag implies that the value of the marginal output *in terms of wage-good units* of *r* men at work in industry must be smaller than it was before the price movement began. Hence the quantity of labor demanded at any given real rate of wage, i.e. the demand function for labor, must be contracted below what it then was." (240) Pigou here assumes that the real wage-rate stipulated for will remain unchanged; but what is also significant is that the real wage-rate stipulated for by workpeople will be modified: they will stipulate for a lower real wage-rate, tho perhaps not to the full extent of the loss suffered as a result of the lag in the downward movement of retail prices.

c. *Intervals between Receipt and Expenditure of Income and between Latter and Reincarnation as New Income*

One other important point in his monetary treatment requires comment, for Pigou seems to have fallen into positive error here. (194–7) He represents annual income by *I* and relevant or active stock of money by M' and its income velocity per unit of time by V'. He then draws certain conclusions from estimates made by Keynes of the total active money, total money income, deposits used for income transactions and those used for business, finance and so on.

"If, then, we put total money income at about 4,000 millions, this implies that v' is equal approximately to 3; or,

6. This is one of the few references to the dependence of employment on working capital other than wage-goods. In a discussion of particular occupations, Pigou refers to the importance of the elasticity of raw materials; and in a discussion of tariff policy, he comments on the adverse effects on employment of a restriction of imports of raw material and machinery even if the result were the offer of wage-goods under more favorable terms. (45, 122–3, 176–7) These are exceptions, however.

in other words, that the average period that intervenes between the successive appearance of a representative £ of active money as income has in recent time for this country been about four months.

"Mr. Keynes has set out further figures, which can be used to split this period of four months into two parts, namely, (1) the average period between the receipt of money income and its expenditure, and (2) the average period between the expenditure of money income and its reappearance as somebody else's income. His guess is that there are held as a basis for income-transactions 275 millions of bank deposits, *plus* 225 millions of notes, and as a basis for business, finance and so on, 800 millions of bank deposits, *plus* 25 millions of notes. If these figures are roughly right, 5/13ths of our four months, i.e. about seven weeks, on the average is the interval between the receipt and the expenditure of a £ of income, and about ten weeks the interval between the expenditure of a £ and its subsequent reincarnation as new income." (196–7)

I pass over the difficulties of identifying income deposits as against other types of deposits. Even if the guesses were roughly accurate, they could tell us little concerning the length of these very important intervals. Thus if we assume, as we well may, that income deposits circulate slowly, then the time required to dispose of income is greater than is indicated by the relative magnitudes of the Income and Business (including financial) deposits. Again, the more rapid circulation of the latter may mean that the period between expenditure and reincarnation of income is less than that given by the relative size of the two groups of deposits. Finally, another factor requires consideration before any valid results can be obtained: the relative amount of work to be done by income deposits on the one hand and business and financial deposits on the other.

8. Causation of Unemployment

"Finally in Part V the results obtained are brought together and utilized in a direct discussion of the causation of unemployment and its fluctuations." (Preface) What are some of the conclusions relevant to British conditions of today? Without offering much evidence of the interdependence of the long-term real demand for labor and the real wage stipulated for, Pigou concludes that "when once any given state of demand has been fully established, the real wage-rates stipulated for by workpeople adjust themselves to new conditions." He draws the inference that long run government policies, tho they make the state of labor demand permanently better or worse than it otherwise would have been, are not either causes or remedies for unemployment. (248–9) The persistence of a large amount of unemployment despite the improvements of demand for labor over a period of sixty years before the War is the evidence offered of an interdependence of real demand and wage-rates stipulated for. One ought not to infer from the persistence of unemployment, however, that workers did not take part of the gain in a very large increase in the amount of employment. That there is some interdependence between demand and wage-rates can hardly be doubted; and Pigou, pointing to this interdependence, quite rightly minimizes the significance of statistical correlation between real wage-rates and the amount of employment: real wage-rates and other factors relevant to employment not being independent of one another. (299–300)

In this part, for the first time, he seriously considers the problem of short run shifts in the real rate of wages that occur "automatically and not merely as a response to shifts in demand conditions." (272) In Chapters VI and IX Pigou makes the admission of the invalidity of an assumption of constant real wages: "These factors of inertia, which, in an economy where wage rates are always contracted for in kind, would tend to keep real wages stable in the face of a changing demand, in a money economy tend to keep money wages stable." (294) The trouble is that actually "downward price movements go with contractions in the real demand for labor and upward price movements with expansion. The reason is that variations in the real demand function for labor due to changes in desires and expectations about capital goods and other non-wage-goods take place on a much larger scale, and play a much larger part in short-period economic movements than variations due *solely* to changes in the productivity of wage-goods industries. Hence, in general, the transition of inertia from real wage-rates to money wage-rates causes real rates to move in a manner not compensatory, but complementary, to movements in the real demand function." (295–6)

It is not exactly clear from this whether the transition from a real to a money economy is the dominant factor or whether it is the relatively large fluctuations in the capital goods industries that would apparently occur even in a real economy. What Pigou fails to note *at this point* is that the fluctuations in the capital goods industries would not be nearly so large under a real economy, for much larger transfers of floating capital upon which the capital boom depends, are possible under a monetary economy than under a real economy. The transition to a money economy influences the size of fluctuations for this reason as well as through its effects on real wages.

A feature of the treatment of numerous problems in Part V is the consideration of the difference made on the assumption of mobility and immobility of labor. In general Pigou's conclusion seems to be that mobility of labor is desirable. In a discussion of the effects of a rise in wages stipulated for (Chapter IV) in one of two centers, he does, however, point out the possibility that mobility may do positive harm; for workers may now move into the high wage center, thus possibly creating unfilled vacancies in the low wage center and not obtaining more employment in the high wage center. In a discussion of compensatory swings of demand (Chapter VIII), he points out that should the wage system be perfectly plastic, then also there would be less employment when workers move freely than when they do not move at all; perfect mobility is possible but not instantaneous mobility. Where wage-rates are rigid, free movement of labor (Chapter VII) helps on the upward swing only when unemployment exists elsewhere and on the downward swing if unfilled vacancies exist elsewhere. Pigou, therefore, concludes that it does no good to move coal miners and shipbuilders when unfilled vacancies are not to be found elsewhere. Despite these reservations he seems to prefer mobility. Thus, wage rates are not plastic in Great Britain and therefore less unemployment will result when demand in one center declines if the pressure to reduce wages can be exerted widely; for a small drop in real wages generally enforced probably would be accepted by the workers; but a large reduction in one center will be refused and hence a large measure of unemployment will result. A perfectly plastic wage system (Chapter VIII) or perfect and instantaneous mobility (wage-rates rigid) will on the assumption of this chapter prevent unemployment; the latter is, however, to be preferred because it assures the optimum distribution of labor. Furthermore, in discussing the state of employment (Chapter XI), he concludes not only that the size of the pool of unemployment and unfilled vacancies will be at a maximum when workers do not move and at a minimum when they move freely, but he also infers from British conditions that there is more unemployment in the pool than unfilled vacancies, the explanation being the superior strength of the workers who prefer high wages and unemployment. Mobility, in short, reduces unemployment when wage-rates are rigid.

Conclusion

Professor Pigou has written one of the few truly great books that have appeared since Marshall's day. Making hardly any use of the findings of others, and striking out on lines of his own, he has contributed more to our science in this book than in any of his earlier ones. He has brought attention to methods of analysis that promise solutions to problems hitherto held insoluble. That he has isolated for us the variables requiring consideration for a concrete meaning to the concept of real elasticity of demand for labor, and has suggested the tools and manner of analysis, alone constitutes a great contribution.

It is in his search for positive results that Professor Pigou lays himself open to attack. In his guarded moments, he draws attention to the type of analysis rather than to the positive results; but in unguarded moments he claims too much for the latter. When the method of analysis is presented by itself, as the thing, the neglect of some variables, even tho they be relatively important, is not disastrous. But when Professor Pigou announces that the real elasticity of demand for labor is —4, one may quite properly object to the omission from consideration of this or that variable and may with reason object to the wild guesses made in attaching values to each variable. Nor can we find much satisfaction in the thought that the analysis might lead to positive results if the variables that have been neglected were given adequate attention. For the analysis, tho restricted to a relatively small number of variables and tho put in mathematical form, is most involved and difficult, and the introduction of a few more variables might well alienate the relatively few economists who have plodded through the book thus far. The great need now is to put the theory in such form that the test of completeness and simplicity of presentation may be met; then, and only then, will positive results be attainable and the results easily available to economic practitioners. Our only hope in attaining both completeness and simplicity must be in the use of mathematics, and Professor Pigou has contributed to the advance of economics in adding his name to the list of those economists who urge the use of these tools, so sharp both for purposes of analysis and exposition.

Professor Pigou's second great service seems to me to consist in his emphasis on the *real* analysis. The world today needs a shift of emphasis back to real considerations. In these days of technocracy, economists are too prone to take economic resources for granted and to argue as tho the monetary policy or volume of expenditures alone determines the economic situation. The Classicists, on the other hand, undoubtedly erred in underestimating the difference made by the money to the results obtained under barter conditions. It may well be necessary to rewrite the whole theory of value and distribution in terms of a monetary economy. Hence a widening of the domain for monetary theory may also be desirable, tho it does not follow that the real analysis becomes invalid at every point where monetary considerations are introduced. Professor Pigou, on the other hand, may justly be criticized at times for making an insufficient allowance for the difference made by money. If this is error, it is error in the right direction, being as an offset to the excessive influence of inflation and purchasing power theories. It is refreshing these days to be reminded by Professor Pigou that employment does depend upon wage-goods, the production function, the interest rate, and wage-rates, and that transfers from the rich to the poor may cut employment.

S. E. Harris.

Harvard University.

[3]

ARTHUR CECIL PIGOU, 1877–1959

WHEN I first "went up" to Cambridge, in 1945, Pigou was already a living legend. The survey lectures on economic principles which he had given for so many years were now being given by his successor in the Chair, D. H. Robertson, and all that remained of his presence was the comment, deeply pencilled into one of the desks at Mill Lane by some departed undergraduate, "Pigou mumbles." Because of the post-war influx of students, however, he was for the first time in his life supervising undergraduates for King's College, and sometimes one of them—George Clayton, Frank Davidson, Robin Marris, I. G. Patel, Eric Russell—would repeat some particularly penetrating comment or suggestion he had made on an essay paper. Beyond that, he was a tall, straight figure, eccentrically garbed, glimpsed occasionally walking about the countryside or, when the warm weather returned, reclining in a deck chair on the grass by the porters' lodge inside King's front court.

Later, during my six years as a Fellow of King's College, I naturally saw much more of him; but I never got to know him well. For one thing, he hated to talk shop, an antipathy for which retirement gave an added excuse; I can recall only one such conversation with him, when the *London and Cambridge Economic Service Bulletin* looked like ceasing publication, in which he deplored the loss of the long series which it published. (The only other conversation I recall is one in which we agreed on the demerits of a trashy American "shocker" which we had both borrowed from the Combination Room.) He disliked above all being asked to meet visiting economists (though he was extremely gracious to Alvin Hansen and his wife); and I soon learnt not to try to introduce strangers, no matter how eminent, to him after Hall dinner. On one such attempt, I remember, he dismissed us with "I don't know anything any more; I'm gaga." (This was, of course, a pose; not the least remarkable thing about him was his ability to turn out economic analysis of a respectable quality long after his retirement.) Nor did he attend College meetings, or take an interest in College affairs, with the notable exception of his membership of the Electors to Fellowships (on which he served forty years in all). The full extent of his aversion to ceremonial of all kinds was displayed by his discovery, several months in advance, of a previous engagement which prevented his attending the Service in Commemoration of the Restoration of the Windows of King's College Chapel, an event graced by the presence of the King and Queen and Princess Margaret and preceded by a magnificent luncheon. And he lived up to his reputation for sartorial economy, appearing at the Marshall Library one day in the fifties proudly wearing a suit bought before the First World War.

Nevertheless, he was a familiar and respected figure in the College; and he played an important part in its life, not only as a Fellowship Elector, in which capacity his judgment carried great weight, but much more through his friendships with and interest in the undergraduates, parties of whom he would take to his cottage in the Lake District, and for whom he would organize chess matches. (It was also his doing that the three noisy Chinese geese on the Backs became known to the undergraduates by the names of the three most talkative members of High Table.) It was always interesting to sit near him at dinner—he had the knack of stimulating entertaining conversation. (He always came in late, which had the dual advantage of avoiding grace and enabling him to pick his company.) My last memory of him in the College is of his presiding over the election of a new Provost following the unexpected death of Provost Glanville—a duty which devolved on him as Senior Fellow—and describing the outcomes of successive votes, not altogether to the pleasure of the Fellows, in the horse-racing terms which he sometimes affected.

Arthur Cecil Pigou was born on November 18, 1877, eldest son of an officer in the 15th Regiment. From Harrow, where he was Head of the School in 1895, he won a Scholarship to King's, where he read for the Historical Tripos, taking a First in 1899. That same year he won the Chancellor's gold medal for English verse, with an ode on Alfred the Great; the last few lines of this ode reflect the idealism which, under the inspiration of Alfred Marshall, led him on to the study of economics:

Hear ye King Alfred's voice, sons of my blood;
Not mine to trace the secret of the years;
I know not what they bring; but this I know;
I would not that King Mammon held my seat;
For things there are more worthy praise than gold
And temples grander than the ordered mart;
And O! far off, as the long centuries roll,
I pray to heaven some voice more clear than mine
May lead this people far from the black slough
Of soulless greed, into more generous paths
Onward and upward, following Truth's bright star
And Reason's light, and that diviner gleam
That dwells a mystery in the hearts of men.

(It was characteristic of his generosity that the medal was sold after the First World War for the relief of starving Georgians.)

In 1900 he took a First in Part II of the Moral Sciences Tripos, with special distinction in Advanced Political Economy. It was typical of the breadth of his interests that in 1901 he won the Cobden Prize for an essay on "The causes and effects of changes in the relative values of agricultural produce in the United Kingdom during the last fifty years," and the Burney Prize for an essay on "Robert Browning as a religious teacher." The latter, Pigou's first published work, is characterized by a certain cool contempt for Browning's philosophical inconsistencies, combined with a genuine admiration for his poetry. It failed to win Pigou a Fellowship in 1901, but he was successful in 1902 with the Cobden Essay, and remained a Fellow of King's until his death on March 7, 1959. In 1903 he won the Adam Smith Prize for an essay on "The Principles and Methods of Industrial Peace," which became the basis of the Jevons Memorial Lectures he delivered at University College, London, in 1903–4 and of his book of the same title (1905). During this time he was also taking an active speaking and writing interest in the controversy over tariff reform, and produced two short books on the subject of tariffs.

Meanwhile, the Cambridge Economics Tripos had been established in 1903, and Pigou, who had been lecturing on economics for the Moral Sciences Tripos since 1901, was appointed to the Girdlers' Lectureship in 1904. When Marshall retired in 1908 Pigou, who was carrying much of the teaching load, was appointed his successor to the Chair, though he was barely thirty at the time. His Inaugural Lecture, "Economic Theory in Relation to Practice," contained a powerful statement of his own version of the Marshallian view of what economics is about—that it is for its fruit-bearing and not for its light-bearing qualities that economic knowledge is worth pursuing. "If it were not for the hope that a scientific study of man's social actions may lead . . . to practical results in social improvement, I should myself . . . regard the time devoted to that study as misspent. . . . If I desired knowledge of man apart from the fruits of knowledge, I should seek it in the history of religious enthusiasm, of passion, of martyrdom and of love; I should not seek it in the market-place."

How far Pigou's life-work conformed to the ideals laid down in his Inaugural Lecture, and reiterated on later occasions, is one of those questions which it is unkind to ask and difficult to answer fairly in an obituary. His major work on the economics of welfare undoubtedly carried those ideals into practice, in the sense that it created the apparatus required for, and largely carried out, the exploration of cases in which the operation of the competitive system offered scope for improvement by wisely designed social intervention. But his intellectual bent, and the chronological drift of his work (in method, at least), was towards a mathematical formalism whose justification is easier to make out in terms of light than of fruit. It is somewhat ironical, too, that the reports of two of the three bodies of public inquiry on which he served—the (Cunliffe) Committee on the Foreign Exchanges (1918–19), and the (Chamberlain) Committee on the Currency and Bank of England Note Issues (1924–5), the third being the Royal Commission on the Income Tax (1919–20)—paved the way for the restoration of the gold standard at the pre-war parity, that act of blind traditionalism which did so much to aggravate Britain's economic and social problems in the inter-war period.

Towards the end of his life, indeed, he became disillusioned with his original methodological position. In his presidential address to the Royal Economic Society in 1939 after a scathing description of the abandonment of free trade in 1931 he concluded: "In view of these things, the hope that an advance in economic knowledge will appreciably affect actual happenings is a slender one. It is not likely that there will be a market for our produce. None the less, by a sort of reflex activity, we cultivate our garden. For we also follow, not thought, but an impulse—the impulse to inquire—which, futile though it may prove, is at least not ignoble." The fact that protection was the proximate cause of his disillusionment is revealing, both by contrast with the other features of the 1930's which younger economists found much more disturbing, and as an indication of the ardour with which he had defended free trade in writings and speeches thirty years before.

From the problem of industrial peace, Pigou moved on to a study of the cause of unemployment, a study which soon expanded to embrace the whole problem of economic welfare. The result was *Wealth and Welfare* (1912), which contained the essence of his major contribution to economics. In this work, Pigou defined economic welfare as depending on the size, distribution, and variability of the national dividend, and systematically analysed the ways in which the competitive system fell short of the ideal, the methods by which improvement might be achieved, and their economic effects, inventing for the purpose the fruitful concept of divergence of marginal private and marginal social net product, and deploying in the argument a mass of institutional information.

The remainder of Pigou's long working life can be regarded as largely occupied with strengthening the foundations laid in *Wealth and Welfare* and elaborating the superstructure erected on them. As to the foundations, the passage from welfare as states of consciousness to economic welfare to the national dividend is fraught with philosophical difficulties, and the notion of national income itself is beset with conceptual problems, to which the dozen pages devoted to these topics in *Wealth and Welfare* gave scant recognition; in later versions, much more space was taken up with elaboration, though without fundamental concessions. In addition, the book contained a major theoretical error, the proposition that both increasing and decreasing returns create a divergence between marginal social returns in different industries, requiring bounties in the one case and taxes in the other. The nature of the error—the confusion of rent with real cost—was pointed out by Allyn Young in 1913, but with characteristic stubbornness Pigou did not accept the criticism until the second edition of the *Economics of Welfare*. The problem of the laws of return continued to bother him—he returned to it in articles in the late twenties—but he played virtually no part in its solution through the elaboration of the theory of the firm, his own concept of the "equilibrium firm" being simply an evasion of the issues. (Incidentally, the impression widely held among American economists that Pigou was willing to accept correction only from English, that is, Cambridge or King's College, economists, is erroneous. He was unwilling to accept correction from *anyone*—perhaps because he got his Chair so early—but when finally convinced that his critic was right, as with Young and later with Keynes, he admitted it unreservedly.)

Wealth and Welfare was followed in 1913 by a book on *Unemployment*, the problem from which Pigou had started. Then came the war. For Pigou, as for all that pre-war generation of Cambridge men, the war was a shock, and a source of intense personal strain. He remained at his post in Cambridge, carrying more and more of the lecturing load as well as part-time responsibilities at the Board of Trade, the recipient of offensive letters urging him to join up and let Foxwell (his rival for the Chair in 1908) take over his professorial duties while the war was on; but he spent most of his vacations in voluntary ambulance work at the front, first in France and Belgium and then in Italy, and what he saw sickened him. There can be no doubt that this experience was responsible for transforming the gay, joke-loving, sociable, hospitable young bachelor of the Edwardian period into the eccentric recluse of more recent times. In the words of his colleague and life-long friend C. R. Fay, "World War I was a shock to him, and he was never the same afterwards." On the professional side, war turned his attention to problems of war economics, and especially war finance.

After the war, Pigou rewrote *Wealth and Welfare* into the first edition of

The Economics of Welfare (1920), incorporating in it not only a great deal of material and ideas accumulated during the war, but also large selections from his pre-war work on labour problems. The incorporation took the form of the addition of two new parts to the earlier structure, one on "The National Dividend and Government Finance" and the other on "The National Dividend and Labour." The former became *The Political Economy of War* (1921) and later *A Study in Public Finance* (1928), being dropped from the second edition of *The Economics of Welfare* (1924); the part entitled "The Variability of the National Dividend," one of the three pillars in the architecture of *Wealth and Welfare*, was also dropped, in anticipation of the completion of *Industrial Fluctuations* (1927). The third (1928) and fourth (1933) editions of *The Economics of Welfare* differed in no important respects from the second.

In the 1930's, Pigou turned his attention once more to the problem of unemployment. His *The Theory of Unemployment* (1933) was one of the main objects of Keynes's derision in the *General Theory*; Pigou was deeply offended by the *General Theory*, more on Marshall's account than on his own, and in his *Economica* review hit back strongly against "this macédoine of misrepresentations," at the same time professing to find little positive merit in the book ("We have watched an artist firing arrows at the moon"). But this assessment changed radically with the passage of time, though he continued to deplore the tone of Keynes's criticisms of his predecessors. In the Preface to *Employment and Equilibrium* (1941) he recognized that Keynes had "rendered a very great service to economics by asking important questions"; in *Keynes's General Theory: A Retrospective View* (1950) he admitted that his original review had failed to grasp the significance of Keynes's conception; and in *Alfred Marshall and Current Thought* (1953) he concluded that Keynes's error lay in attacking the long-run analysis of the *Principles* rather than the short-period analysis of the *Evidence* where Marshall "would, I like to think, have agreed that Keynes had detected him in a serious mistake." His own methods of monetary analysis became identifiably Keynesian, except that he continued to use velocity rather than liquidity preference; and his writings, especially *Employment and Equilibrium* and *Lapses from Full Employment* (1945), helped to elucidate the substance and the limitations of the Keynesian Revolution. Indeed, to many young economists, Pigou is famous chiefly for his contribution of "the Pigou effect" to the counter-revolution.

The foregoing account of Pigou's life and works has perforce concentrated on the main stream, without reference to the many subsidiary inlets and branches along the way. No complete bibliography of his work exists, but the King's College Library catalogue lists nearly thirty books and over a hundred pamphlets and articles. Of these, mention should perhaps be made of the *Memorials of Alfred Marshall* (1925) compiled with filial devotion to his master, and of *Socialism versus Capitalism* (1937), which weighed the balance more heavily in favour of the former than he perhaps intended. The very volume of this output, maintaining such a high average standard over such a long period, entitles him to recognition as one of the giants of the Cambridge School and a formative influence on modern economics. Beyond that, *The Economics of Welfare* was an important contribution in its own right; as F. H.

Knight remarked in his review of the first edition, it shifted the argument from the choice between conflicting systems of economic organization to the methods of improving on the existing, functioning system. That was at once its originality, in the period when Pigou first developed it, and its obvious limitation during the troubled inter-war period which followed its publication. Now that the Keynesian Revolution has been digested, and the political divisions of the thirties and forties have been reconciled in a system of welfare capitalism, economists are becoming increasingly occupied with policy problems of the kind with which Pigou was concerned, and in whose analysis he was the pioneer.

Harry G. Johnson

[4]

PIGOU AND THE "PIGOU EFFECT": RENDEZ-VOUS WITH THE AUTHOR[1]

JACQUES MELITZ

Tulane University

INTRODUCTION

The "wealth effect" is generally considered as A. C. Pigou's basic reply to J. M. Keynes concerning possible "unemployment equilibrium" under flexible money wages. But a scrutiny of Pigou's major writings soon gives rise to a number of suspicions regarding this interpretation of his stand. For example, it is curious that in the one section of his 1943 article on "The Classical Stationary State"[2] dealing with the impact of a general wage reduction on unemployment as such, he ignores the "wealth effect" and concentrates on a different argument. It is also odd that later in this article and throughout the 1947 companion piece on "Economic Progress in a Stationary Environment,"[3] in treating the way in which the "wealth effect" eliminates an excess supply of commodities, Pigou assumes that there would be no unemployment in the first place if money wages were flexible downward. In addition, wherever the question of the impact of money wage reductions on unemployment occurs in Pigou's late writing, there is not the least allusion to the "wealth effect." He utilizes this effect strictly in order to analyze the case of a general overproduction of commodities at a theoretical minimum interest rate.

I will attempt to show here that Pigou does not rely on the "wealth effect" in his attack on the doctrine of "unemployment equilibrium" with flexible money wages (a doctrine which, incidentally, he never considers clearly Keynesian). Instead, he depends on a form of "substitution effect," hinging on a change in the "convenience yield" on money relative to the yield on physical capital. This particular line of thought is much closer than the "wealth effect" to the sort of reasoning concerning stock adjustments to differences in yields which has become popular today.

In this view of Pigou's position, the principal mechanism in his work for restoring full employment under flexible wages is the "substitution" rather than the "wealth effect" of wage-price reductions. It is important, therefore, to be clear at the start about the difference between these two effects, both of which pertain to an influence of a change in real money. The "substitution effect" requires a mere rise in the ratio of real money to real wealth, whereas the "wealth effect" hinges on a rise in total wealth. An increase in real balances necessarily raises the ratio of real money to total wealth (thus producing a movement in the relative yields on different assets), but may not augment total wealth. The reason is that, in a wage-price fall, private real indebtedness to the monetary sector may increase as much as the value of money balances, thus keeping total wealth the same. Therefore, though a "substitution effect" necessarily follows a

[1] I would like to thank the Social Science Research Council and the Tulane University Faculty Research Council for their support during the period of this study. I am also grateful to Professor William J. Baumol, and my colleague, Professor Seymour S. Goodman, for helpful comments.

[2] Arthur C. Pigou, "The Classical Stationary State," *Economic Journal*, LIII (1943), pp. 343–51.

[3] Pigou, "Economic Progress in a Stable Environment," *Economica*, New Series, XIV (1947), pp. 180–90; reprinted in A.E.A. *Readings in Monetary Theory* (Homewood, Ill.: Richard Irwin, 1951), pp. 241–51. All future references to this article will relate to the A.E.A. volume, which shall be cited as A.E.A. *Readings*.

wage-price reduction under constant money, there may be no "wealth effect."

Further, the two effects must operate, at least in part, in different markets. In the immediate aftermath of a real balance change, the "substitution effect" cannot occur in the consumption goods market. Any influence on consumption requires a movement in the general yield on wealth relative to consumption, whereas initially, a rise in real balances only affects the yield on a few particular assets. Consequently, immediately after a real balance change, if tastes and productivity are unchanged, all movements out of assets into consumption (as opposed to movements between assets) must be attributable to a variation in total wealth. On the frequent assumption of no "budget restraint" among firms, furthermore, there never can be a "wealth effect" on the demand for physical investment. In accord with these distinctions Pigou relates the "substitution effect" to the demand for investment goods but not desired saving, while strictly applying the "wealth effect" to the consumption demand in the commodities market.

Still the issue may appear to be basically of historical interest. There is, however, an important analytical question involved. One major assumption of the Keynesian debate, still thriving in many quarters, is that the so-called "liquidity trap" leaves no room for any legitimate criticism of Keynes besides the "wealth effect." If so, Pigou's "convenience yield effect" is an invalid objection to Keynes's theory under the "liquidity trap." *Per contra,* however, I will try to show that Pigou's argument holds in this case. On this view, the dramatic postwar emphasis on the "wealth effect" respecting Keynes has been much exaggerated.

First in order of presentation will be Pigou's famous 1943 and 1947 contributions to the *Economic Journal* and *Economica,* which have been the center of attention thus far. Next we will also examine the evidence from Pigou's other writings. In the final section, the focus will be on the validity of Pigou's treatment in the context of Keynes's peculiar interest rate floor.

MAIN TESTAMENTS

As Pigou makes clear in the first few pages of "The Classical Stationary State," this article is a response to a few critical passages in Alvin Hansen's *Fiscal Policy and Business Cycles,*[4] which develop the important yet secondary theme of the *General Theory* that highly industrialized countries have a secular tendency toward a position of "unemployment equilibrium." According to Hansen, the classicists were right in arguing that there is a long run tendency toward zero net investment, but they were wrong in supposing that this "stationary" equilibium position is necessarily one of full employment. Due to the strength of saving habits, "stationary equilibrium" might be attainable only at levels of output far below those which the economy has the capacity to produce. Consequently, the "classical stationary state" might involve large-scale unemployment.

In reply, Pigou first explains that under usual classical conditions, which require equality of the rate of interest and the marginal rate of time preference in equilibrium, the interest rate mechanism would suffice to bring about equilibrium in the commodities market. He maintains, however, that this classical view hinges on the assumption that people save only for the sake of future income receipts. Contrary to this view, though, Pigou considers that people save partly for safety reasons and for purposes such as prestige. In the light of these further motives, equilibrium can be said to hold only when the marginal rate of time preference equals a certain "amenity yield" plus the market rate of

[4] Alvin Hansen, *Fiscal Policy and Business Cycles* (New York, 1941), p. 288. See also pp. 334–35.

return.[5] Saving then may be positive at a zero rate of interest, since at this rate the "amenity yield" on saving might outweigh the positive marginal rate of time preference (favoring consumption). Therefore, a position of "stationary equilibrium," where desired saving and desired investment are zero, may require a negative rate of interest. A negative rate of interest, however, is impossible, because saving always can be made in the form of money, which Pigou regards as a sure means of earning a zero market rate of return.[6] This brings Pigou to the central problem of his discussion: the possibility of an excess of desired saving over desired investment at all positive or zero interest rates.

Before tackling this problem, however, Pigou turns briefly to Hansen's contention of the possibility of unemployment under flexible money wages in the stationary state, which he dismisses at the opening, saying: "It is not necessary to examine it [Hansen's argument] at any length."[7] Since Pigou's argument on this point forms a central pillar of my revision, I may quote him at length:

> With any known type of banking system, and equally under an arrangement in which the stock of money is rigidly fixed, money income must be a function of the rate of interest, being lower or higher according as that rate is lower or higher. This follows from the fact that, for equilibrium, the convenience and so on yielded to the representative man by the marginal unit of resources held in the form of money must be equally attractive with the interest yielded by the marginal unit invested in real capital. For the degree of this convenience is greater or less according as real income divided into the real value of the stock of money is less or greater; i.e., according as money income divided into the stock of money (i.e., the Marshallian k, which is the inverse of the income velocity of money), is less or greater, i.e., when the stock of money is given, according as money income is greater or less.... Thus, monetary arrangements being given, money income cannot fall unless the rate of interest falls. Since, however, in our supposed less-than-full-employment stationary state, the rate of interest is already at the minimum admissible level, it cannot fall any farther. Therefore the acceptance of lower money wage-rates by wage-earners cannot cause money income to fall. Therefore, with given employment, it cannot cause prices to fall. It follows that by cutting money wage-rates workpeople *can* cut real wage-rates, and so *can* expand employment above the amount proper to any less-than-full-employment stationary state.[8]

To recapitulate, Pigou reasons that given unemployment and a fixed stock of money, a fall in money wages, by reducing money income, would raise k. This in turn would cause the "convenience yield" on money to fall, hence further leading to a switch out of money into other forms of wealth in order to equalize yields.[9] But if, corresponding to Pigou's previous dilemma, "the" interest rate—meaning the yield on physical capital—is "already at the minimum admissible level," then implicitly no further fall in the "convenience yield" on money is possible. Therefore no rise in the ratio of money to income, or k can result. As money is constant, this means that money income cannot fall and hence that any drop in the money wage rate must raise employment and not merely lower commodity prices. In short, as long as the rate of interest on assets in general can fall, reductions in money wage rates increase the demand for investment goods through a "convenience yield effect," while once the rate of interest no longer can fall,

[5] Pigou's first statement of this point in the Keynesian debate may be found in *Employment and Equilibrium. A Theoretical Discussion* (London, 1941), pp. 105, 126. The identical wording appears in the more readily available 1949 revised edition of this work (London), pp. 111, 130–31.

[6] Cf. *ibid.*, 1941, pp. 118–26, 1949, pp. 123–31; and Pigou, *Keynes's "General Theory": A Retrospective View* (London, 1950), pp. 33–36.

[7] Pigou explicitly views this section as a diversion. See "The Classical Stationary State," *op. cit.*, sec. 8, l. 1 (p. 347), and sec. 10, l. 4 (p. 349).

[8] *Ibid.*, pp. 348–49 (author's italics).

[9] Cf. Pigou, "The Value of Money," *Quarterly Journal of Economics*, XXXII, (November 1917), pp. 38–65; reprinted in A.E.A. *Readings*, pp. 162–83, especially 166–68; *The Veil of Money* (London, 1949), pp. 77–81; and *Keynes's "General Theory," op. cit.*, pp. 16–19.

reductions in money wage rates must directly raise employment.

Next, Pigou returns to his main dilemma of a possible excess supply of commodities at full employment "at the minimum admissible rate of interest." In this section, he explicitly assumes "that we are dealing with full employment," thus expressly abandoning his concern with the impact of money wage reductions on employment. Indeed, he simply supposes, as his preceding argument implies, that if money wages are downwardly flexible, falls in commodity prices do not induce unemployment. It is under circumstances of this sort, where wages are flexible and there is no unemployment, that in 1943 Pigou introduces the famous "Pigou effect." His attendant reasoning is more fully developed in the later and better known article, "Economic Progress in a Stable Environment."

There, he divides the case of commodity excess supply at a minimum, or zero interest rate in two parts. First, Pigou supposes money wages to be perfectly rigid. On this assumption, he reasons that the fall in commodity prices, by causing falling employment, will cut real income, thereby reducing the desire to save, and in this fashion eventually bring about commodity market equilibrium at a low level of employment.[10] Accordingly, equilibrium will be achieved independently of the "wealth effect." But since workers are not likely to admit any low level of employment by refusing to accept wage cuts, Pigou proceeds to the second assumption, namely, that money wages are too flexible downward to permit sizeable unemployment.

On this assumption, at last Pigou introduces the "wealth effect." That is, if falling prices merely lead to falling wages, Pigou views that the influence of rising values of cash balances on private wealth explains commodity market equilibrium.[11] Clearly, the "wealth effect" does not enter this reasoning to explain the supposed tendency of reductions in money wages to equilibrate the labor market. In fact, the 1947 essay, unlike the 1943 piece, offers no reason for this tendency.

A SYSTEMATIC EXPOSITION OF PIGOU'S ARGUMENT

A more systematic presentation of Pigou's argument is possible at this point with the aid of Figure 1. Let us suppose that physical capital and money are the only two types of wealth present. Suppose also that the market rate of interest on money is uniformly zero. This means, of course, that a "convenience yield" of some sort is necessary to explain why any money is held at a positive rate of interest on physical capital. A problem of dimensions occurs in regard to this "convenience yield" on money, since it must be viewed as a percentage, while the denominator in the fraction, money, has an accounting value, but the nominator "convenience," viewed in the abstract, can be understood only as measured in terms of utility. What I propose to do in order to overcome this objection, without any precedent in Pigou, is to assume higher transaction costs on physical capital than money and no difference in risks between the two. This results in a conceptually unambiguous "convenience yield" on money as an economy in transaction costs per unit of money per time period (r_t). In line with Pigou, I will assume this yield, r_t, to be a negative function of the ratio of money to income, or the Cambridge k. In equilibrium, it then can be said, the return on investment, r, must equal r_t. In order to avoid unnecessary further complications, I will suppose no difference in transac-

[10] This point was stated clearly in *Employment and Equilibrium, op. cit.,* where no mention was made of the "wealth effect." The corresponding passage in the 1949 edition is on pp. 133–34.

[11] Pigou, "Economic Progress in a Stationary Environment," A.E.A. *Readings,* pp. 248–51.

tion cost per unit of consumption and net investment (positive or negative) in real or money terms. Hence, in equilibrium r also must equal the rate of discounting future satisfactions as adjusted for the positive amenity yield on saving (ρ).

In regard to the net investment demand and saving functions, Pigou's presentation can be essentially followed with minor modifications (which will be indicated in footnotes). Let the demand for net investment (I) be a function of the existing stock of capital (C) and the yield on money (r_t).

(1) $$I = \phi(C, r_t),$$

where

$$\frac{\partial I}{\partial C} < 0,$$

and

$$\frac{\partial I}{\partial r_t} < 0.$$ [12]

Let desired saving (S) be a function of total private wealth (W), the rate of interest on desired net investment (r), and the yield on human capital (Y) (which will be referred to hereafter as "real income").[13]

(2) $$S = f(W, r, Y),$$

where

$$\frac{\partial S}{\partial W} < 0, \frac{\partial S}{\partial r} > 0,$$

and

$$\frac{\partial S}{\partial Y} > 0.$$

The form of the first function is governed by the marginal productivity of investment; the form of the second by the rate of discounting future satisfactions as offset by the amenity yield on saving. The only relevant equilibium conditions, omitting others which will be assumed to hold whenever these do, are:

(3) $$S = I;$$

(4) $$L = N,$$

i.e., quantity of labor demanded equals quantity supplied; and

(5) $$r = r_t = \rho.$$

One other major point in Pigou's exposition is the assumption of a lower limit to r_t at zero, *i.e.*, $r_t \geqslant 0$.

In Figure 1, r and r_t are measured along the vertical axis, while I_0 and $I_\prime$ illustrate two particular schedules of desired net investment as a function of r_t at two different levels of capital, C_0 and $C_\prime$. Since r_t cannot fall below zero, I_0 is the lowest net investment demand schedule along which a non-negative net investment solution is possible. On the saving side, three different schedules as a function of r are shown. All three are associated with the same level of wealth, W_0, but different levels of real income. S_0 is the saving schedule for the full employment level of output (Y_f). This schedule is deliberately shown as positive at $r = 0$ so as to correspond with Pigou's problem. $S_\prime$ and $S_{\prime\prime}$ pertain to two levels of real income below Y_f, involving successively higher employment. Pigou's argument now can be readily presented.

Assume that the physical stock of capital is $C_\prime$, wealth is W_0, real income is Y_u', and we are at point A. The relevant saving and investment functions are therefore $S_{\prime\prime}$ and $I_\prime$ and equilibrium exists in the commodities market while there is unem-

[12] Pigou considers I as a function of r, the rate of return on physical investment, but should have treated it instead as a function of r_t, since r depends crucially on I through the productivity function.

[13] There is some small difference in Pigou's definition of the saving function. If we take the 1943 article as our basic text, Pigou first presents S as a function of the physical stock of capital, the rate of interest on investment, and real income. When the general wealth-saving relation comes in view, he then includes real money balances as a fourth variable in the equation.

ployment. Now, if the money wage rate falls in response to the unemployment, commodity prices will fall. This will lower the convenience yield on money (represented by r_t), which in turn will enhance the quantity of net investment demanded, and thereby bring more labor into employment and raise real income. In terms of Figure 1, therefore, the outcome of the fall in the money wage rate will be a shift rightward in desired saving. Through such repeated shifts, the saving function will attain S_0, and downwardly flexible wages eventually will bring about equilibrium at $r' = r_t' = \rho$ and net investment of OC. This particular solution only will hold, however, if we neglect the expansionary influence of the wage-price reduction on private wealth, since a rise in wealth would inhibit, and possibly altogether reverse the rise in desired saving, thus yielding commodity market equilibrium with full employment at a rate of interest above r' and a level of investment below OC. As Pigou neglects the "wealth effect" in this part of his argument, the r'-OC solution can be said to agree with his exposition.

The next position to be considered is at the origin, O, with income Y_u, capital C_0, and r_t and r, of course, zero. I_0 and S_I then are the relevant functions. Once again, there is unemployment coupled with commodity market equilibrium. But in this position, a fall in r_t is not feasible. With M constant, it is then impossible to entertain the possibility of any fall in commodity prices. Therefore, a fall in money wages must produce a proportional fall in real wages at first, leading to higher employment and real income, which then permits some fall in commodity prices. Eventually this process will lead to the elimination of unemployment at income Y_f. We will then arrive at position B on the S_0 saving schedule. However, this will leave us with an excess supply of commodities OB. Therefore, wage flexibility would not have taken us very far; or to repeat Pigou: "The logical outcome is that in circumstances where a full employment stationary state is impossible a less-than-full-employment stationary state is also impossible; in other words, that no position of long-run equilibrium can be attained."[14] What is the "escape from this impasse"?

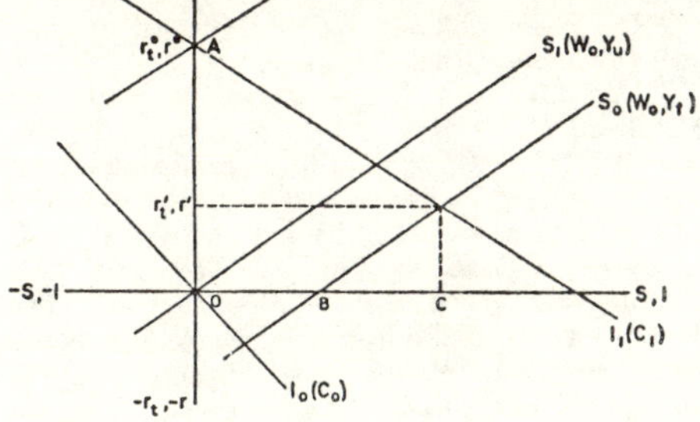

FIGURE 1

Given the full employment but oversupply of commodities at position B, if commodity prices fall and money wages stay rigid then, of course, we will simply return to point O at the origin, attaining commodity market equilibrium through the positive income-saving relation but at the expense of unemployment. However, if at position B, money wages are permitted to fall in proportion to commodity prices, the current level of employment will hold. Then the influence of falling prices and wages on real balances, thus on private real wealth, will afford the mechanism yielding commodity market equilibrium. As wealth rises, the saving function will fall, real income staying at Y_f, until full equilibrium is attained at point O. (The saving function which illustrates this equilibrium, involving Y_f and some W above W_0, is not shown on the diagram.) This completes Pigou's argument.

[14] Pigou, "The Classical Stationary State," *op. cit.*, p. 349.

One point that Pigou overlooks in this exposition is that his grounds for rejecting falling commodity prices after a fall in money wages, given unemployment at point *O*, apply with equal force given full employment but excess supply of commodities *OB* at point *B*. At the latter point, as at the former, a fall in commodity prices is ruled out since the fall would lower the convenience yield on money, which is already zero and cannot fall. Yet without a fall in commodity prices there can be no "wealth effect." This simply shows the awkwardness of conducting the analysis at the lower mathematical limit of a yield on money and other assets of zero.[15] With the "convenience yield" on money at zero, and no other source of market or subjective return on money, additional money ceases to be a good. Thus we cannot consider the yield on money at the level zero. It is best therefore to proceed on the assumption that the rate of interest, in general, has fallen very low but not quite to zero. From this position it is quite clear that both the "wealth effect" and the "convenience yield effect" are immediately relevant under unemployment, overproduction, or both.

This points to another problem in Pigou's exposition; namely, that there is no logical basis for his apparent division of functions between the two effects, according to which the "convenience yield effect" explains full employment under flexible wages while the "wealth effect" explains commodity market equilibrium under wage-price flexibility. Whether unemployment or an excess supply of commodities initially is present simply determines whether the wage level or the price level falls first.[16] Given a price level fall, barring exceptional circumstances, both effects immediately come into play. This division of functions probably stems largely from a polemical concern. Most likely, he did not wish to use so novel an argument as the "wealth effect" in order to defend classicism on the important traditional issue of full employment.[17]

The main source of error in interpreting Pigou has been the failure to observe his distinction between unemployment and commodity overproduction. This mistake is evident in the essay which has played the largest part in the development of the current conception of Pigou's reply to Keynes: Don Patinkin's 1948 article, "Price Flexibility and Full Employment."[18] In the early parts of this article, Patinkin defines Pigou's opposition to Keynes basically in terms of equilibrium in the commodities market, as we might expect any

[15] Because of possible inflation, this value is not necessarily the lower mathematical limit in the general case. For another relevant consideration, see Pigou, *Lapses from Full Employment* (London, 1945), p. 22.

[16] It may be noted, in this connection, that some pre-Pigouvian presentations of the classical reply to Keynes clearly stressed the "wealth effect" in regard to unemployment under flexible money wages. See Tibor Scitovsky, "Capital Accumulation, Employment, and Price Rigidity," *Review of Economic Studies*, VIII (Feb. 1941), pp. 69–88, reprinted in *Papers on Welfare and Growth* (Stanford, 1964), pp. 40–68; and Gottfried Haberler, *Prosperity and Depression* (revised and enlarged 3d. ed., Geneva, 1941), pp. 491–503, esp. 499–500. It is important to observe that the cited pages in Haberler's *Prosperity and Depression* belong to a section which does not appear in the first, 1937 edition, or the second, 1939 edition. In the earlier editions, Haberler's argument is consistently formulated, it seems to me, in terms of changes in the *distribution* of private wealth in the form of liquidity rather than changes in *aggregate* private wealth due to variations in total liquidity.

[17] Cf. Pigou, "The Value of Money," *op. cit.*, A.E.A. *Readings*, esp. pp. 166–68.

[18] Don Patinkin, "Price Flexibility and Full Employment," *American Economic Review*, XXXVIII (1948), pp. 543–64, reprinted with revisions in A.E.A. *Readings*, pp. 252–83. See also Lloyd Metzler, "Wealth, Saving and the Rate of Interest," *Journal of Political Economy*, LIX (April 1951), p. 94; and Gardner Ackley, "The Wealth-Saving Relationship," *ibid.*, p. 154. For a more cautious treatment of Pigou's position, though still adhering to the same general view, see Haberler, "The Pigou Effect Once More," *ibid.*, LX (June 1952), pp. 240–46, esp. 240–41.

close textual rendition of Pigou to do.[19] In the same process, he subsumes the question of unemployment beneath that of commodity market equilibrium, making reference to full employment saving and investment functions. That is to say, Patinkin simply assumes that Pigou's equilibrating mechanism in the commodities market explains full employment too. Now, while Pigou might have reasoned in a corresponding fashion without falling into any error, the fact is that he did not. Moreover, Patinkin's association of equilibrium in the commodities and in the labor market in the 1948 essay, uncharacteristic of later work, is rather simplistic—too much so to do credit to Pigou on any construction of his stand.

OTHER SOURCES

Further collaborating evidence for the preceding interpretation of Pigou may be found in his other writings dating from the appearance of the *General Theory*.

These other writings confirm the previous distinction in Pigou's thinking between the doctrine that money wage reductions may not influence unemployment, and the idea that an excess supply of commodities may exist under full employment at the theoretical minimum interest rate. The first of these two doctrines Pigou never attributed to Keynes, and indeed seemed on the whole to consider non-Keynesian; the second he viewed as Keynes' main challenge to classicism. This distinction appears already in Pigou's 1936 review of Keynes' *General Theory*.[20] In this work, Pigou questions that Keynes actually had meant to deny that money wage reductions would lower unemployment if the aggregate demand for commodities otherwise were constant. He interprets Keynes to argue that reductions in money wages are ineffective if the aggregate demand for commodities is *falling independently*. Consequently, he finds no fundamental disagreement between himself and Keynes on the issue of money wage reductions, though mentioning some differences regarding the process through which equilibrium comes about.[21] Later, in his 1943 *Economic Journal* article, Pigou goes so far as to say: "[The argument that] it is out of the power of wage-earners to make cuts in the rate of wages for which they ask, and so to secure employment, because every cut in money wage-rates will automatically bring about an equiproportionate reduction in prices . . . is sometimes found in popular expositions of what the expositors mistakenly believe to be Lord Keynes' views." [22] Though subsequent writings reveal some doubts in Pigou as to whether Keynes actually had argued for the possibility of large-scale unemployment *strictly* on orthodox classical grounds of downwardly rigid wages,[23] he never attributed any other position to his fellow pupil of Marshall. It is noteworthy, in this respect, that in his important 1943 contribution he always considers the tendency toward full employment under flexible wages in regard to Hansen rather than Keynes, while in his 1947 piece he does not entertain this question at all.

[19] Note that all of Patinkin's figures pertain to the commodities market.

[20] Pigou, "Mr. J. M. Keynes's General Theory of Employment, Interest, and Money," *Economica*, New Series, III (May 1936), pp. 115–32. See pp. 127–30 in particular.

[21] "Though, if I am right, the results which Mr. Keynes and I forecast are the same, the processes by which we respectively look for them to be brought about are entirely different." Pigou, *ibid.*, p. 128.

[22] Pigou, "The Classical Stationary State," *op. cit.*, p. 348.

[23] See, in particular, Pigou, *Keynes's "General Theory," op. cit.*, p. 50. In his *Lapses from Full Employment*, pp. 22–25, containing probably his fullest discussion of Keynes's position on the influence of money wage reductions, Pigou may seem to admit that Keynes viewed money wage reductions as ineffective in reducing unemployment. The relevant pages, however, must be interpreted carefully. Pigou envisages a situation where due to a drying up of investment opportunities, a considerable excess supply of commodities is present, leading to falling commodity prices.

The 1936 review already contains a clear definition of the problem, upon which Pigou later lavished much attention, that at full employment an excess supply of commodities may exist at all positive or zero interest rates. If this problem holds, Pigou understood Keynes to say, equilibrium may settle in the commodities market only at a low level of income involving large-scale unemployment. It is this possible low-employment market equilibrium that Pigou referred to in 1936, 1941, and once again in 1947, as Keynes's "vision of the Day of Judgment."[24] Though inadequately explicit in 1936, he evidently attributed the Keynesian unemployment in this state to downwardly inflexible wages.

Subsequently, Pigou addressed a 1937 article, "Real and Money Wages in Relation to Unemployment," to the question of the impact of general wage reductions on unemployment.[25] This article would seem at first to be aimed against Keynes, though Pigou does not mention him. Nevertheless, a reply by Pigou to a note by Nicholas Kaldor[26] casts serious doubt on this interpretation. Commenting (by footnote) on a note by Keynes preceding the one from Kaldor,[27] Pigou says: "I have not been able to follow the reasoning of Mr. Keynes' short note.... But what is said in the following paragraphs about the interrelations of money wage-rates, employment and the rate of interest is much closer to his general view than the argument of §10 of my previous article."[28] Section 10 of Pigou's previous article had concerned an aspect of the equilibrium process through which money wage reductions supposedly eliminate unemployment in the case of perfect competition. The subsequent paragraphs of the comment, which Pigou suggests, are likely to suit Keynes better than Section 10 of the original, retain the essential conclusion that money wage reductions are effective in achieving full employment. It would seem, therefore, that Keynes was not the essential culprit whom Pigou had in mind, but leaves open the question of the identity of this, or these culprits. On this issue, the published evidence permits no answer. While evidently suspecting the accuracy of various interpretations of Keynes, it is obvious that Pigou himself was consider-

In this context, if the interest rate already is at its minimum, he supposes Keynes to say that a fall in money wages will only produce an "equivalent" (equiproportional) fall in commodity prices, and thus fail to prevent unemployment. However, this must be interpreted in a dynamic sense, I believe, as concerning the question whether, given a prior fall in the demand for labor, falling money wages can avoid the occurrence of unemployment in disequilibrium. Pigou considers Keynes's answer negative on this point. But this does not mean that in a condition of unemployment and no downward pressure on employment, Pigou would understand Keynes as saying that a fall in the money wage rate would fail to raise employment under classical assumptions. This interpretation of Pigou seems to me supported by his agreement with Keynes in the particular case concerned that "owing to the inevitable lag in the first wage reduction, employment must be cut down." Yet it must be admitted that this entire passage does not accord fully with anything else Pigou wrote on the subject of Keynes, and that no particular interpretation, including my own, seems fully satisfactory. For a later interpretation of Keynes's stand by Pigou, in full harmony with the 1943 and 1947 articles, see *Employment and Equilibrium,* 1949, pp. 133–36. The corresponding pages in the first (1941) edition (pp. 129–32) differ on small, yet significant points. Another interesting passage, but also somewhat difficult to interpret, is in Pigou, "John Maynard Keynes; Baron Keynes of Tilton 1883–1946," *Proceedings of the British Academy,* XXXII (1946), pp. 408–11, esp. 410–11.

[24] Pigou, "Mr. Keynes' General Theory of Employment, Interest, and Money," *op. cit.,* p. 129; *Employment and Equilibrium,* 1941, p. 129; and "Economic Progress in a Stable Environment," A.E.A. *Readings,* p. 249.

[25] Pigou, "Real and Money Wages in Relation to Unemployment," *Economic Journal,* XLVII (1937), pp. 405–22.

[26] Nicholas Kaldor, "Prof. Pigou on Money Wages in Relation to Unemployment," *ibid.,* pp. 745–53.

[27] John Maynard Keynes, "Prof. Pigou on Money Wages in Relation to Unemployment," *ibid.,* pp. 743–45.

[28] Pigou, "Money Wages in Relation to Unemployment," *Economic Journal,* XLVIII (1938), p. 134, n. 1.

ably uncertain about Keynes's exact meaning. Unfortunately, Keynes's brief response to his 1937 article would not have resolved these doubts.

On the question of unemployment, Pigou's argument in the 1937 writing significantly corresponds to the one in his 1943 article discussed above. The essential difference is that the 1937 argument never entertains the possibility of a fall in the interest rate, whereas the 1943 one does. But given a constant interest rate, the two arguments amount to different ways of saying essentially the same thing: namely, that if money stays constant along with the interest rate as money wages fall, a fall in commodity prices while output is the same, implying a fall in V (a rise in k,) is out of the question, and therefore the fall in wages must lead to some rise in employment and output. Significantly, the failure of V to fall, in both arguments, derives not from a general postulate of constant V, but rather from the fact that the interest rate is supposed not to go down. Kaldor's criticism of Pigou's article, in fact, was directed mainly at the alleged constancy of the interest rate. He maintained that under the conditions Pigou stipulated, the interest rate must fall with the drop in money wages since any rise in output would lead to greater saving. Subsequently, Pigou completely accepted this criticism in his comment on Kaldor's note. Still, he held that even if the interest rate should not fall due to the absence of any relation between desired saving and the rate of interest, a fall in the wage rate would increase employment on the previous grounds.[29] Therefore he surrendered nothing of substance in his earlier position vis-à-vis Keynes.

Pigou returned again twice to the question of the influence of wage flexibility on employment after the 1943 article: first in 1949, in *The Veil of Money*,[30] and more formally in 1950, in *Keynes's "General Theory": A Retrospective View*.[31] On neither occasion did he mention the "wealth effect" in regard to this last question. Instead, he pressed the aforementioned argument that a fall in money wages given unemployment, by inducing lower commodity prices, must yield a drop in the interest rate on assets in general, thus leading to higher demand for output and employment. He chose not to raise the question of a possible floor on the interest rate in these writings. After 1943, in general, he considered the "wealth effect" only in connection with the resolution of a possible excess supply of *commodities* at the theoretical minimum interest rate.[32] If Keynes's basic challenge is to be viewed, therefore, as the doctrine that unemploy-

[29] "Our main conclusion that, within the framework of our model, a cut in money wage rates will lead to a new equilibrium situation in which employment is larger, and the rate of interest lower, than before, depends, it will be understood, on the *factual* proposition that the representative man's rate of time-preference falls as aggregate real income increases. If it were independent of aggregate real income, a cut in money wage rates would increase employment, while leaving the rate of interest unchanged." *Ibid.*, p. 138 (author's italics). Still, Lawrence R. Klein claims in his *Keynesian Revolution* (New York, 1949, 3d. printing; 1st ed. in 1947): "One of the most important points to recall from this debate [the present exchange between Kaldor and Pigou] is that Pigou admitted that money wage cuts will not increase employment unless interest rates are reduced as a result of the cut" (p. 108). Klein was generally amiss in his report of Pigou's position in the 1937 article, maintaining, contrary to the very crux of Pigou's message in 1937, that in order to establish that money wage cuts would lead to more employment Pigou "made use of the proposition that the main influence of the wage cut would be on interest rates" (p. 107). This description contrasts with Pigou's closing statement of his stand in the relevant section of the 1937 article: "Its is enough for my purpose to show that a money wage cut is not simply a piece of ritual that enables the real cause of employment expansion—a fall in the rate of money interest—to take effect" (*op. cit.* p. 411).

[30] *Op cit.*, pp. 75–111, esp. 104–11. The preface to this book, though, is dated October 1947.

[31] *Op. cit.*, pp. 49–50.

[32] Apart from the 1947 article, I refer to Pigou, *Lapses from Full Employment*, p. 24; and *Keynes's "General Theory,"* p. 36.

ment may not be resolved by flexible money wages under classical conditions, the evidence would indicate that the "wealth effect" is no fundamental part of Pigou's reply.

CONCLUDING OBSERVATIONS ON PIGOU'S STAND

The essential problem remaining for contemplation is whether Pigou's "convenience yield effect" is valid under the conditions of interest rate downward inflexibility which Keynes postulated as contingent in a state of widespread unemployment. It may be noted, first, that this "convenience yield effect" is not tantamount to the "Keynes effect," which clearly is ruled out under the "liquidity trap." The "Keynes effect" pertains strictly to a movement between money and securities. Keynes's writing does not make it plain whether this movement is supposed to derive from a change in the yield on money relative to other assets or a change in aggregate wealth or both. By contrast, however, Pigou's "convenience yield effect" concerns a movement between money and physical capital due to a change in the yield on money relative to capital. If we suppose, on Keynesian grounds, that there is no advantage in converting extra money assets into securities, thus foreclosing the "Keynes effect," nothing is to prevent the "convenience yield effect" from causing shifts of new money into investment goods.[33]

Another objection to Pigou's "convenience yield effect," though subordinate, is that the conversion of money into investment goods could be undertaken only by firms, which suggests that this effect is confined to the business sector. However, this criticism is lighter than it may appear. A fall in the yield on money relative to capital, theoretically speaking, not only may induce firms to convert cash balances into investment goods, but also may induce households to transfer money into business accounts. In the case of individual proprietorships and partnerships, this may entail, *pari passu,* an expansion in desired investment. In the instance of corporations, though, admittedly increases in households' equity would require a purchase of shares, and therefore involve the mediation of securities. Even then, it is questionable that Keynes's argument for an indefinite "speculative demand" for money applies. In line with frequent observations, by "the" rate of interest Keynes usually meant the rate of interest on long-term bonds; and as Joan Robinson has suggested, the expectation of rising yields on long-term bonds is quite compatible with anticipation of capital gains on stocks.[34]

It can be easily surmised at present that the only possible obstacle to Pigou's "convenience yield effect," as I have termed it, is a higher expected yield on money than all non-money types of wealth. Therefore the sole serious challenge to Pigou's position under the "liquidity trap" is the interpretation of this "trap" as a zero rate of return on all non-money assets. In a condition of pervasive zero returns, if money bears utility, money is necessarily more attractive than any alternative form of wealth. Indeed, at a zero rate of interest on assets in general, including a zero "convenience yield" on money, which is the only similar case that Pigou considers, he abandons his "convenience yield effect" argument. Instead he relies on an inconsistency in the view that a fall in money wages would lead strictly to a fall in commodity prices.

But apart from the conceptual difficulties which this zero-yield hypothesis involves,

[33] On this point and with respect to the general previous emphasis on the distinction between yields on different assets, cf. James Tobin, "Money, Capital and Other Stores of Value," *American Economic Review Paper and Proceedings,* LI (May 1961), pp. 26–37.

[34] Joan Robinson, "The Rate of Interest," *Econometrica,* XIX (1951), pp. 92–111; reprinted in *The Rate of Interest and Other Essays* (London, 1952), pp. 3–30, esp. 21–23.

the previous interpretation of the "liquidity trap" has little textual basis. The spectre of a zero interest rate appears in Keynes only in the course of a discussion of the possible—admittedly not too distant—future. Yet as widely recognized, his fundamental theory, relating to the short run, pertains to a condition of positive yields (even if we abstract from costs of negotiation, which enter into Keynes's discussion). That is, by common understanding, the "liquidity trap" arises in Keynes due to fears and expectations of adverse price movements cancelling a positive contractual return on *securities alone*. On this view, implying non-positive returns nowhere but on securities, Pigou's "convenience yield effect" is a perfectly suitable reply to Keynes in the case of his particular interest rate floor. Only in the rarefied atmosphere of the Keynesian "Day of Judgment" does the "convenience yield effect" lose its vitality.[35]

But in this "Day of Judgment" the "wealth effect" is also fully infirm. If the rate of interest on all assets, including the "convenience yield" on money is zero, the price level cannot fall since the "convenience yield" on money already is at a minimum. Therefore, a "wealth effect" cannot occur. Alternatively, with the "convenience yield" on money at zero, there is no reason for anyone to accept money in trade for any other good, since short of anticipations of deflation, money provides no source of return or satisfaction. As additional money is not wealth, rises in money cannot produce a "wealth effect."[36] Moreover, the hypothesis of a zero yield on all assets is fundamentally weak, since on any sensible view of the economic universe, such a condition can be only approximated, but never reached.

The outcome of these deliberations, therefore, is that Pigou's "convenience yield effect" of wage-price reductions is true under relevant Keynesian conditions. If we admit a certain set of other circumstances, which deviate sharply from Keynes's short-run theory, this effect does not hold. But then the other principal argument for full employment through flexible prices in this state is equally untenable. Perhaps the best course to follow in a zero-yield world and unemployment is that of trying, like Pigou, to prove an inherent inconsistency in the situation if money wage reductions are supposed not to raise employment.

It appears that Pigou made a more sizeable contribution in his reply to Keynes than has been observed in the past, requiring some reassessment of the previous Keynesian debate. Pigou's persistent effort in later writings to establish the post-Keynesian viability of Marshallian thought may be subject to criticism. But there is little doubt that in his 1943 and 1947 writings, he performed this task more skillfully than former accounts of his position would convey.

[35] The textual basis for Pigou's general preoccupation with the "Day of Judgment" is almost exclusively to be found in Keynes's Chapter XVI, "Sundry Observations on the Nature of Capital" *The General Theory of Employment, Interest, and Money* (London, 1936), pp. 210–21. Apart from this chapter, I believe that it would be quite difficult to relate Pigou's treatment of the *General Theory* to Keynes's text.

[36] A similar conclusion follows if the yield on money is supposed to be positive and all other yields are zero, though the reasoning is somewhat different. While the price level can fall in this case, and thus raise wealth, the subsequent "wealth effect" must consist entirely of an increase in the demand for real money assets. Thus, there is again no "wealth effect" in the commodities market.

[5]

THE APPOINTMENT OF PIGOU AS MARSHALL'S SUCCESSOR*

R. H. COASE
University of Chicago Law School

In the course of an extremely interesting article on the part which British economists played in the Tariff Reform Campaign of 1903, Professor A W. Coats suggested that "there is reason to believe that the events of 1903 may have directly influenced the choice of Pigou as successor to Marshall at Cambridge, a decision that ensured the pre-eminence of economic theory at the leading academic centre of British economics."[1] And later, he put the same point in the form of a hypothetical question: "Is it, then, too much to suggest that but for the tariff reform debate of 1903, the election of 1908 might have gone differently . . .?"[2] H. S. Foxwell, who was a candidate for Marshall's chair, seems to have believed that this may have been the case.[3] It is, however, my belief that, in the events which led to the selection of Pigou instead of Foxwell in 1908, the roles which they played in the tariff controversy were relatively unimportant. The decision to appoint Pigou would, I believe, have been the same had the tariff controversy of 1903 never occurred. The purpose of this note is to explain why I hold this view.

Alfred Marshall was not one of the electors for the Professorship in Political Economy, but it is obvious that his opinion about who should be appointed as his successor would carry great weight. In fact, Marshall apparently did everything in his power to ensure that Pigou was selected. I would not wish to suggest that the electors, left to themselves, would not have selected Pigou

* I would like to acknowledge and to express my thanks for the assistance I received in the research leading to this note from Mr. Piero Sraffa and the staff of the Marshall Library in Cambridge, to Mr. James Claydon of the Cambridge University Library and to Mr. K. Carpenter of the Kress Library of Business & Economics in the Harvard Graduate School of Business Administration. I am grateful to Mr. Paul Sturges of the Institute for Historical Research in London for drawing my attention to the diaries of J. N. Keynes, now in the Cambridge University Library. I am indebted to Professors George J. Stigler and Aaron Director for comments on an earlier draft of this note.

1 A. W. Coats, Political Economy and the Tariff Reform Campaign of 1903, 11 J. Law & Econ. 181, 225 (1968).

2 *Id.* at 228.

3 See Audrey Foxwell, who was no doubt expressing her father's opinion, in Herbert Somerton Foxwell: A Portrait, 9 (1939) (Harvard Graduate School of Business Administration, Kress Library of Business & Economics).

—they might well have done this—but Marshall's active support for Pigou must have told heavily in his favour.

Marshall was, of course, deeply concerned about the future of economics, and particularly Cambridge economics, and, given his temperament, it is unthinkable that he would not exert himself to the full to secure the election of the candidate who, in his view, would do most for Cambridge economics. If we study the relations of Marshall with Pigou and Foxwell, it seems to me that the events before 1903 and in the years after, form part of a continuous story with no trace of any change brought about by the tariff controversy. Marshall's preference for Pigou is clearly foreshadowed before 1903. If the events of that year had any effect on Marshall, it could only have been to strengthen an opinion already formed.

Foxwell was, of course, an old colleague of Marshall's at Cambridge (he had in fact been one of the electors when Marshall was appointed to the chair of Political Economy in 1884). Pigou did not enter the picture until about 1899. On December 11, 1899, John Neville Keynes records in his diary that he and his wife (Florence) "dined with the Marshalls meeting Carter of Oxford, the Ryles and Pigou of King's." Pigou was then a student and it seems probable that one of Marshall's aims in arranging the meeting was to draw J. N. Keynes' attention to Pigou. In this Marshall was no doubt successful but in other respects the meeting was less happy. J. N. Keynes adds in his diary (a very typical reference on his part to Marshall): "Marshall is the most exasperating talker I know. He will agree with nothing you say & argues & dogmatises so as to drive one wild. He is a pro-Boer & kept making innuendoes, but without success, to draw us into argument on the subject. Florence said she agreed with absolutely nothing he said all through the evening."

Marshall had for some time felt the need for a young lecturer who would give an introductory course on economics. In a letter to J. N. Keynes written early in 1899, after referring to other problems, he said: "After these the most urgent need for the Board—& may become the most urgent of all—is, in my opinion, the need for a young lecturer on economics, who has time and strength to do drill work for men of medium ability. I cannot do that without neglecting other work that is more important; and it is not done. If such a man could be had, I should cease to give a general course, and give more specialized advanced courses."[4] Three months after the disastrous dinner, Marshall revealed his intentions with regard to Pigou. He said in a letter to J. N. Keynes: "When the Moral Science Board was discussing its needs at the last meeting, I was

[4] Letter from Alfred Marshall to J. N. Keynes, Feb. 2, 1899, on file in Marshall Library, Cambridge, as Keynes 1 (letter no. 115). [Letters in Marshall Library are hereinafter cited by file name and letter number.]

under the impression that a movement for raising the Fellowships of Professors under the new statutes at St. Johns to £200 had fallen through. So I urged the Board to represent that another lecturer in addition to Foxwell was needed. But to my surprise I heard yesterday from the Bursar that he had paid £200 into my account. So I am at once reviving old schemes for action, on my own hook, wh(ich) I had set aside." What Marshall had in mind was that, instead of asking the University to pay for another lecturer, he would pay the salary of the lecturer himself (as, in fact, Marshall did for several lecturers over a number of years). The lecturer he had in mind was Pigou: "I am now inclined to think that the ideal man is at hand:—Pigou. But he would hardly be ripe for lecturing in 1900-1: and I have not said anything to him about it yet. I have some thoughts of asking Bowley to give a course of about ten lectures on statistics and statistical method, with special reference to his own subject—U.K. wages. His work in that seems to grow in excellence and in general favour. But as the loose cash has been jingling in my pocket for less than 24 hours, I am not ready to 'say something and stick to it'." The letter ends with another reference to Pigou: "I had Pigou in my mind at last Board meeting: but I had not then seen much of his papers. I have seen a good deal since then; & I think he is thoroughly satisfactory."[5]

Foxwell did not approve of Marshall's intention to ask Pigou to give introductory lectures and does not seem to have welcomed the proposal that Bowley should lecture. At any rate, it was difficult to make arrangements which were satisfactory to Foxwell. J. N. Keynes apparently wrote to Marshall, relaying an objection from Foxwell to the proposed hour at which Bowley was to lecture since Foxwell was himself lecturing at that hour. Marshall replied, asking that his letter should be passed on to Foxwell: "The choice of hours for Bowley's lectures was very difficult, and was long and often discussed before a final decision was taken. Twelve o'clock seems best for lectures designed, as Bowley's are, to catch some men who are not reading economics for any Tripos. On the whole it is best for Historical men, who will form his largest single contingent in all probability, and unless my untrustworthy memory has played me another trick, Foxwell agreed that Bowley should clash with his 12 o'clock than with his 11 o'clock lectures. . . . So though I much regret the clashing, I do not see how to change except for the worse. Taking account of everything, I see no reason for thinking that the conclusion originally reached with so much pains, could ever have been improved on; & change now would be an evil in itself."[6]

Marshall's letter (and also one from Bowley) were sent to Foxwell. He

[5] Letter from Alfred Marshall to J. N. Keynes, March 4, 1900, Keynes 1 (116).

[6] Letter from Alfred Marshall to J. N. Keynes, Oct. 6, 1900, Keynes 1 (121).

replied to J. N. Keynes: "Many thanks for the trouble you have taken. I did not expect much success with Marshall; his arrangements are always the best possible & the result of infinite calculation!". But later in the letter Foxwell indicates his fear that Bowley's lectures might draw off the better students from his own course and he also refers to Pigou's new course: "It is perfectly true that I should prefer Bowley to lecture at 12 rather than at 11 on those days. But it is not the case that I only get beginners at my general lectures: & I much prefer a salting of the better class of men: but I almost fancy that Marshall does not like them to come to me: for we have had a good many differences on these matters: culminating in his having engaged Pigou to deliver an elementary course: a man, of all I have known, least qualified to deal with a general class, as he is such a prig!".[7]

It will not come as a surprise to learn that making the arrangements for Pigou's lectures proved to be even more troublesome than it was for Bowley's. J. N. Keynes records in his diary for May 20th, 1901: "Marshall is putting on Pigou as a Lecturer in Political Economy and the relations between him & Foxwell are very strained. I am having rather lengthy letters from Marshall on the subject." The character of this correspondence can, I think, be gathered from an extract from a letter sent by Marshall to J. N. Keynes, two days after this diary entry: "My own view is that there is some, though not great, harm in Pigou's lectures clashing with Ward's; & there is no real harm at all in their clashing with Foxwell's course. But if I propose it, I shall be told again that I am 'making an attack on him'. Time does not diminish

[7] Letter from H. S. Foxwell to J. N. Keynes, Oct. 6, 1900, Keynes 1 (40). Foxwell's unfavourable view of Pigou never seems to have changed. In a letter to W. R. Scott, Nov. 24, 1926 (in Kress Library of Business & Economics), Foxwell said, with reference to Pigou's election to the British Academy: "As to Pigou, I promised to vote for him, much against my principles, for he is the last Economist I wish to see in any position where he could influence economic study. He has ruined it at Cambridge where complaints are incessant and you have probably seen the letter of Benn in the Times. Let someone nominate him who believes in him: it is bad enough for me to swallow the necessity of a vote agst (against) my deepest convictions."

The "letter" (actually article) of Sir Ernest Benn had appeared in The (London) Times, November 17, 1926, at 15-16, under the heading, "The Teaching of Economics, Examples from Cambridge, Issues Ignored". He complained of a lack of concern with the factors determining production and claimed that teaching concentrated on "distribution, division, taxation, or confiscation". He said that Universities were "led by the nose by the Socialists." This led to an angry letter from Pigou denying political bias (The (London) Times, November 19, 1926, at 15): "In the University of Cambridge, when a man is appointed to teach, enquiry is not made into his political opinions. . . . It is his duty to discover and teach what is true. . . . Where there is a difference of opinion among competent authorities it is his duty to let students know that this is so, and to put the issues fairly before them. These things are our duty at once to our University and to the spirit of science. For an outsider, ignorant of our practice and an amateur in our subject to charge us with violating it is an impertinence." So far as his colleagues were concerned, the charge was "untrue".

my feeling of soreness. It seems to me the story of the wolf & the lamb. Foxwell refused for 15 years to set papers, though he knew his not doing so was regarded by me as a great oppression. Then when at last I had got arrangements wh(ich) would (i) free me from a disagreeable position (ii) enable the better sort of beginners to have a systematic general course from which people who want quick & really advanced teaching wld (would) be excluded & (iii) enable a proper advanced course to be given; wh(ich) has never been done yet—then he instantly cuts in before Pigou & duplicates in anticipation a part of the course wh(ich) he knows the Mo(ral) Sc(ience) Board accepted with [and?] heartily approved a year ago, & wh(ich) Pigou has been preparing himself to give. Of course, they will not duplicate one another. Pigou could not duplicate him & he has never done what I hope Pigou will ultimately do. Pigou and I care for the men: & I think I may truly say for the men only. Foxwell does not seem able to understand this sort of aim, & hunts for some other."[8]

In the light of these events in 1900 and 1901, it is hardly possible to date Marshall's breach with Foxwell from 1903 (the date of the tariff controversy). The fact is that Marshall's conception of economics and his views on economic teaching were very different from those of Foxwell as he explained in a letter to Foxwell in 1906. Marshall had previously suggested that Foxwell should lecture on economic history and that Macgregor should take over some of Foxwell's economics lectures.[9] To this Foxwell apparently replied at length, defending his methods and declining to give the economic history lectures. Marshall replied, in part, as follows: "I have always known you to be a most excellent expositor. I have heard you speak many times; and have thought your method, your style, your lucidity and your geniality most attractive to your hearers, and most effective on behalf of the cause you were advocating. And everything I have heard from others, whether young or old about you has been in the same direction. . . . Of course our ideals in economics are different. I have noticed that when a book or a pamphlet pleased you greatly you describe it as 'scholarly' whereas I am never roused to great enthusiasm about anything wh(ich) does not seem to me thoroughly 'scientific' . . . . I think it is very important that there should be considerable diversities of temperament among the teachers of any subject, and especially of one of which the past and the present are so meagre, and the future is so uncertain as economics. . . . It seems to me that our differences in temper causes you to lay greater stress upon accuracy as regards facts, & me to insist more on their wrestling with difficult analysis and reasoning. . . . That you lay

[8] Letter from Alfred Marshall to J. N. Keynes, May 22, 1901, Keynes 1 (124).

[9] Letter from Alfred Marshall to H. S. Foxwell, Feb. 7, 1906, Marshall 3 (48).

what seems to me insufficient stress on what, from my own particular point of view, is at once the most arduous, the least attractive and the most essential duty of the lecturer, is the *only* objection wh(ich), as far as I am aware, I have ever raised to your lectures. I regard your lectures as a most important part of our scheme; and I should regard your being displaced by young men as a great calamity. . . . I do not wish to urge you to undertake anything for wh(ich) you were not inclined. And I trust that we may agree finally on some plan that provides fuller introduction in economics for Freshmen, and enable you to do only what you wish and that in your own way, wh(ich) I quite recognize as being excellent of its kind."[10]

Marshall did not share Foxwell's antipathy to theory[11] or his enthusiasm for the historical approach in economics. And Foxwell's speciality, the history of economic thought, was to Marshall a subject of secondary importance.[12] Pigou, with his analytical approach to economic problems, his evident ability and high potential, was bound to appeal to Marshall. Given Marshall's views, and the seriousness with which he held them, it is inconceivable that he could have preferred Foxwell to Pigou as his successor.

The election of Marshall's successor took place in 1908. The electors were: A. J. Balfour (who took no part in the proceedings); Lord Courtney; F. Y. Edgeworth; J. N. Keynes; J. S. Nicholson; R. H. Inglis Palgrave; V. H. Stanton; W. R. Sorley. It is possible to form some notion of the events surrounding the election from the entries in the diary of J. N. Keynes:

April 30, 1908. Interview with Marshall on the subject of the Election to the Political Economy Professorship. He speaks in the highest terms of Pigou and

10 Letter from Alfred Marshall to H. S. Foxwell, Feb. 12, 1906, Marshall 3 (49).

11 Foxwell's comment on Allyn Young (who had been responsible for arranging for the purchase of his second main book collection by Harvard University, now in Kress Library of Business & Economics) made after his death in a letter to W. R. Scott, March 8, 1929, (in Kress Library of Business & Economics) affords an example of his point of view: ". . . I have seldom met anyone with whom I was in more general agreement. He perhaps attached more importance to pure theory than I should: but it was clear that his interest in it was steadily diminishing."

12 See letter from Alfred Marshall to J. N. Keynes, Dec. 13, 1908, Keynes 1 (137), in which he refers to Keynes having perhaps "a higher opinion of the importance of Foxwell's speciality to Cambridge than I have." Earlier in 1902, Marshall had argued against making the paper on the history of economic theory compulsory in the Economic Tripos. "As to the position of the paper on history of economic theory, it is not necessary to argue now. The time for that will come when the details of a scheme are being elaborated. In Germany even academic students have almost abandoned the study of the history of economic theory: wh(ich) I think goes to the opposite extreme. But, knowing the tone of your mind, I feel sure that if you had been through what I have been through during the last twenty years, you would not wish to make it compulsory." Letter to J. N. Keynes, Feb. 6, 1902, Keynes 1 (126).

is clearly most anxious that he should be elected. He very distinctly does not want Foxwell to be elected. I very much wish that I were not an Elector.

May 24, 1908. (Sunday). Next Saturday's election is hanging over me.

May 27, 1908. Another interview with Marshall about the Political Economy Professorship.

May 28, 1908. Palgrave has come to stay with us until Saturday.

May 29, 1908. Today Nicholson has arrived to stay until Monday. Dinner Party—Palgrave, Nicholson, Dr. & Mrs. Tanner, Miss Jones, Dr. & Mrs. Bond, Florence, Margaret and myself. Edgeworth (who is staying with Marshall) arrived at 9:30 to discuss tomorrow's election. We gathered that he had been sent by Marshall. Nicholson is intensely annoyed at what he thinks Marshall's unfairness to Foxwell.

May 30, 1908. 10. V.C. [Vice Chancellor] 12-1.45 Political Economy Professorship Election. V.C., Lord Courtney, Palgrave, Edgeworth, Nicholson, Stanton, Sorley, and myself. Balfour did not come. The candidates were Ashley, Cannan, Pigou, Foxwell. Pigou was elected. I am extremely sorry for Foxwell. The whole thing has worried me very much. We dined with the Marshalls. Nicholson tells me that Marshall did not speak to him the whole evening.

May 31, 1908. Palgrave left yesterday. Nicholson will stay till tomorrow. We have enjoyed having them both & Margaret is full of admiration for Palgrave. I think Palgrave thoroughly enjoyed his visit, and even enjoyed the election, which I certainly did not. . . . Nicholson went in to see Foxwell. N is very severe on Marshall's manoeuvring, & I certainly do not think that Marshall has come out of the whole thing well.

June 1, 1908. Foxwell has expressed his intention of no longer lecturing in Cambridge. At the request of Dickinson & Pigou I went in to see him & to try and persuade him to reconsider the question. But I knew of course that he would not. It was one of the most painful interviews I have ever had. He had felt so confident of being elected that he had even begun to write his introductory lecture. He was quite cordial to me personally, but he was very excited, & at one time I thought he wd (would) break down. I felt and still feel exceedingly grieved on his account. He is very bitter against Marshall, and at this I do not wonder.

June 2, 1908. Foxwell told me yesterday that Marshall wrote him a very fulsome letter. Foxwell seems to have written rather frankly in reply.

June 14, 1908. I am a little tired. Perhaps I have not yet recovered from the Political Economy Professorship Election & all that it has brought in its train. It has been like a black cloud throwing its shadow over the whole of the term.

Marshall's "fulsome" letter was preserved by Foxwell:

My dear Foxwell

Pigou is in my opinion likely be recognized ere long as a man of quite extraordinary genius: and I hoped that he wd (would) be elected to the Professorship. But I have just written a letter to the Master of Peterhouse expressing my gratitude to the Economics Board in general, & to him in particular, for his kindly treatment of me, & for their recent most generous resolution. And I should like to add a word of special gratitude to you, the oldest of my colleagues. We differ in opinion a good deal, and in temperament perhaps even more: so that some things, for which I cared much, seemed of little importance to you. But so far as these differences permitted, you have cordially, heartily, and generously supported and furthered my poor endeavours: sometimes even your genial friendship has perhaps induced you to go a little further in the direction in which I was working, than your own unbiassed judgment would have prompted. For all this I shall ever feel myself your debtor: I shall ever look back on our association with pleasant & grateful memories.

I am sure that the University as a whole cherishes feelings of high regard for your whole hearted & very poorly remunerated services to it. I have not heard very much about it: the proceedings of the election between 12 and 2 yesterday have been kept absolutely secret; but I have heard no one, not even among the most enthusiastic supporters of Pigou's claims, who is not deeply pained by the thought that it has not been possible to crown your long and trusty work by a high reward.

Please do not answer this just now: for you must be feeling sore. But I wish you to know that though I think the Electors, acting as trustees, did their duty, I share with all of them to whom I have spoken a deep sorrow on your account and an affectionate gratitude towards you.

Yours in sympathy,
Alfred Marshall[13]

After the election, Henry Higgs, a pupil and friend of Foxwell, and at that time holding a position in the Treasury, suggested that money should be raised to provide a Professorship for Foxwell. Marshall's attitude to this

[13] Letter from Alfred Marshall to H. S. Foxwell, May 31, 1908, Marshall 3 (56).

proposal may be gathered from the following letter which he sent to J. N. Keynes:

Dear Keynes,

There has been much more correspondence with Higgs. Its chief items on my side are

(1) a letter on the 9th resuming that part of my earlier letters which is entirely free from personal references, with an intimation that he may show it to any one

(2) a letter in continuation of that, written two days later to the effect that after consideration I have decided to urge him to enter into direct communication with you, on the grounds that:—"Keynes has perhaps a higher opinion of the importance of Foxwell's speciality to Cambridge than I have: he has not committed himself, as I have for the last forty years, to the opinion that Professors ought as a rule to resign at the age of sixty: partly for that reason he does not rate as highly as I do the evils which might arise from the precedent that would be set by founding a temporary Professorship on the understanding that Foxwell should be elected to it". I add other reasons connected with your personal qualities and your access to the Council by means informal as well as formal.

(3) Some letters marked "private" in which I have explained—in answer to his continual urging as to the importance of Foxwell's experience and judgment—that in my view the speciality of Cambridge teaching is to develop faculty, and to leave judgment to be formed later: and that a lecturer, who imposes his own judgment on youth, is not acting up to the best Cambridge tradition.

[I did *not* add that as Foxwell's judgments while always confident, are apt to turn in opposite directions at six months notice, I have a fear of his judgments. On Finance in particular, one of the subjects proposed for him, I think his judgment is extraordinarily bad. He seems never to see more than one side of any complex question.]

In Higgs' last letter but one he half asked my opinion as to the danger of there being "two Kings in Brentford". I replied that—though I had not mentioned the matter to Pigou—I felt sure there wd(would) be no trouble on that side: but that recent events had made me a little anxious on the other side. And I lifted the veil which covers those events so far as to say "Foxwell wrote to me in June declaiming against electors, who had set aside the claims of friendship. I shuddered. I did not answer: but that was the forerunner of trouble."

Holding the opinions which you do, I think you would be right to provide(?) Higgs' scheme, provided it is so worked as not to undercut the expected appeal of the Cambridge Association on behalf of the Economic school. But at most I can be "benevolently" neutral. And if, as is possible, the question is raised whether a second Professorship—should there be one —should go to Clapham or Foxwell, I *must* speak for Clapham. I know you have not come much in his way, & do not have my eager admiration for him. But you must have heard rumours of his success as a lecturer. And I, who have seen a good deal of him, would always go to him as counsellor of the first weight in any difficult matter of judgment. I think his achieved work is of a very high order, full of individuality and strength. Even if Foxwell were still in his prime, I should hesitate to put him on the same intellectual level with Clapham.

I now leave the matter in your hands. For the sake of auld lang syne, I will stretch my academic conscience as far as it will go. But it has a stiff neck. It may be well that you should have learnt at an early stage how far my benevolent neutrality towards Higgs' proposal is likely to reach. I am clear that I cannot *actively* support it in its present form.

Yours very sincerely,
Alfred Marshall[14]

Whether because of the lack of any active support from Marshall or for some other reason, the Professorship for Foxwell was not established.

So far I have concentrated on Marshall's views and actions. But, as I have indicated, it seems quite possible that Pigou would have been selected had Marshall not engaged in any "manoeuvring". A modern appointments committee would not have had any doubt, assuming that the choice was one between Foxwell and Pigou.[15] Pigou's writings (excluding writings in non-

[14] Letter from Alfred Marshall to J. N. Keynes, Dec. 13, 1908, Keynes 1 (137). How far Foxwell knew about these efforts or of Marshall's views, particularly his preference for Clapham, I do not know. Foxwell later attempted to get Higgs elected to the British Academy and was disappointed that he did not succeed and particularly that Clapham was preferred to Higgs, as is shown in the following extracts from letters to W. R. Scott (in Kress Library of Business & Economics): "I am surprised to hear of the apathy about Higgs. There is no living economist more brilliant, & none to whom *English economics is more profoundly indebted*." (Letter, Nov. 18, 1927); "[Higgs] is really a born scholar, with a touch of genius added. That such a common-place & in some respects objectionable person as Clapham should have been preferred to him is the greatest blow I have received since Marshall got me rejected at Cambridge & harder to understand. It seems to me that those who really devote themselves to public service, & do the real work, get laughed at for their pains, & only earn the familiarity that breeds contempt." (Letter, June 10, 1928).

[15] I have discussed the selection procedure in terms of a choice between Foxwell and Pigou, which was, I believe, the actual situation. However, a modern appointments committee would have found Edwin Cannan a strong candidate. His publications, among others, were Elementary Political Economy (1888, plus two subsequent editions in 1897 and 1903); The History of the Theories of Production and Distribution in English Political Economy from 1776 to 1848 (1893, plus a second edition in 1903); The History

professional journals and book reviews) up to and including 1908, consisted of the following articles, all in the Economic Journal: "A parallel between economic and political theory" (1902); "A point of theory connected with the corn tax" (1902); "Some remarks on utility"(1903); "Pure theory and the fiscal controversy" (1904); "Monopoly and consumer's surplus" (1904); "Professor Dietzel on dumping and retaliation" (1905); "The unity of political and economic science" (1906); "The incidence of import duties" (1907); "Social improvement in the light of modern biology" (1907); "Equilibrium under bilateral monopoly" (1908). In addition, during this period the following books by Pigou had been published: Robert Browning as a Religious Teacher (1901); The Riddle of the Tariff (1903); Principles and Methods of Industrial Peace (1905); Protective and Preferential Import Duties (1906); The Problem of Theism, and other essays (1908). During this same period, Foxwell's published work consisted of an introduction of just over a page to the printing of a letter from Malthus to Ricardo in the Economic Journal (1907) and an article on "The Goldsmiths' Company's Library of Economic Literature" in Palgrave's Dictionary of Political Economy (1908).

J. N. Keynes does not tell us how the various electors voted. He is indeed silent about his own preference and although it seems probable that he supported Foxwell's candidature, it is by no means certain that he did not, in the end, vote for Pigou. Pigou was a close friend of his son, Maynard Keynes,[16] he was a visitor at his home, and although there is only one comment in the diary indicating an opinion about Pigou (on March 25, 1905), it is laudatory: "Yesterday and today I have been putting together questions in political economy for the Economics Tripos. Pigou has sent me his questions and I think them excellent."[17]

---

of Local Rates (1896); his edition of Adam Smith's Wealth of Nations (1904) as well as numerous articles in the Economic Journal and elsewhere. But Cannan was not a Cambridge man and his interests in economics and his approach (not to mention his connection with the London School of Economics) would not have commended him to Marshall and I do not think he received serious consideration as Marshall's successor.

[16] It was at Pigou's suggestion that Marshall wrote to Maynard Keynes on April 3rd, 1908, about the possibility of him returning to Cambridge to lecture on economics. And one of Pigou's first acts after being appointed Professor of Political Economy was to invite Maynard Keynes to lecture, an offer which was accepted. Pigou paid the salary of £100. Marshall's letter was cautiously worded since Pigou was then still a candidate for the Professorship. Marshall said that the proposal for Maynard Keynes' appointment would be made at the Economics Board on "(probably) June 3", that is, after the election. He felt obliged to add that this was "subject to some reserve in the case of one possible election to the Professorship", that is, if Foxwell was appointed instead of Pigou. Marshall's caution led J. N. Keynes to say, in a letter dated April 23, 1908: "Is not Marshall's letter in some respects very vague? I am glad you have not committed yourself at present." See 15 Collected Writings of John Maynard Keynes, 13-15 (Elizabeth Johnson ed. 1971).

[17] This is a sharp contrast to the references to Marshall in the diaries, which are uni-

Unless Nicholson's attitude simply represented annoyance at Marshall's efforts to influence the electors, it would seem that he supported Foxwell's candidature.[18] But, as against Nicholson, Edgeworth obviously supported Pigou.[19] It seems to me that no selection committee could have failed to be swayed by the fact that the Professors of Political Economy at both Oxford and Cambridge were agreed that Pigou should be appointed. Even if Marshall had not taken steps to make his views clear, it seems improbable that the electors would not have wished to discover what they were.

Foxwell's daughter, in a passage to which Professor Coats refers, does not go beyond saying that Foxwell, "partly as a result [of the tariff controversy], was not chosen as a successor to Marshall."[20] In fact, Marshall had many reasons for preferring Pigou to Foxwell, and their respective roles in the tariff controversy must have been one of the least important. Mr. C. W. Guillebaud, in his obituary of Foxwell gives what I consider to be a correct assessment of the position: "A bimetallist and protectionist, an anti-Ricardian with a profound suspicion of abstract economic analysis on classical lines, Foxwell was opposed to much for which Marshall pre-eminently stood.

formly hostile. Thus, in the month before the reference to Pigou, we find an entry (Feb. 1, 1905) noting a meeting of the Economics Board which reads: "I really have not time to be on a Board of which Marshall is a member." This antagonism to Marshall should be borne in mind when interpreting J. N. Keynes' account of the election and Marshall's part in it. But it would be wrong to assume that this antagonism extended to Pigou. Nonetheless, I am inclined to accept as correct Foxwell's account of the voting given in the letter reproduced by Coats in his comment (see A. W. Coats, The Appointment of Pigou as Marshall's Successor: Comment, 15 J. Law & Econ. 493 (1972)), which indicates that J. N. Keynes did in fact support Foxwell.

18 Nicholson's attitude tends to weaken somewhat the view that Foxwell's opposition to the "Professors' Manifesto" was an important element in the decision, since Nicholson was himself a signatory of the Manifesto.

19 Edgeworth had a high regard for Pigou as an economist. In his review of Pigou's book, The Riddle of the Tariff, he said: "The power with which he wields the organon of economic theory is of the highest promise. One who had observed the early work of Clerk Maxwell remarked: 'it is impossible for that man to go wrong in physics.' For 'physics' substitute what Jevons called the 'mechanics' of industry and trade, and the dictum might be applied without extravagance to the author of the analysis that we have mentioned." 14 Econ. J. 65, 67 (1904). Compare also, Edgeworth's discussion of some of Pigou's contributions in his Appreciations of Mathematical Theories, 17 Econ. J. 221-226 (1907), reprinted in 2 F. Y. Edgeworth, Papers Relating to Political Economy 321-326 (1925). Professor Austin Robinson has described Pigou's method in his book, Principles and Methods of Industrial Peace, published in 1905: "He applied to economics the method of the philosopher, clarifying the issues, dissecting them and analyzing them, trying to see how different assumptions regarding the material might modify conclusions—the analytical method applied with great precision to an essentially qualitative argument." Article on Arthur Cecil Pigou, in 12 International Encyclopedia of the Social Sciences 91 (1968). It is easy to see that such an approach, handled with skill, would greatly appeal to Edgeworth.

20 Audrey Foxwell, *supra* note 3, at 9.

It was understandable therefore that when Marshall retired from the Cambridge Chair of Political Economy in 1908, he should have favoured the candidature of his own pupil, A. C. Pigou."[21]

An account of why Pigou and not Foxwell was chosen to succeed Marshall draws attention to Foxwell's weaknesses. But it should be recorded that if Foxwell was an anti-Ricardian, he was also a champion of Jevons. He had a most extensive knowledge of economic literature. His assembling of the books which formed the basis of the Goldsmiths' Library in London and the Kress Library at Harvard, has put all scholars of the history of economic thought in his debt. Foxwell was not a negligible figure. And his reservations about Pigou proved, in the event, to have some substance. It seems clear to me that Pigou did not fulfil the high hopes which Marshall had of him.[22] In many respects his influence on the development of economics has been bad. He seems to have lacked any feeling for the working of economic institutions.[23] But this does not mean that I consider the electors wrong in preferring Pigou to Foxwell. The difficulty that they faced in choosing a successor to Marshall was that there was no-one comparable to Marshall that they could have chosen.

My criticism of what was, in the context of Professor Coats' article, a minor point, does not affect his main argument or detract from the significance of his findings. Professor Coats' study shows that the entry of the economists into the tariff controversy did not raise the quality of the debate, brought economics into public disrepute, was devisive within the academic community and weakened the professional *esprit de corps* of economists. I agree with him that "one of the general lessons to be drawn from this example is that such quasi-political activities pose a threat to the economics profession." Nor would I wish to disagree with his surmise that "few economists would conclude that this is too high a price to be paid for the opportunity of shaping policy," although for most economists the word "illusion" should probably be substituted for "opportunity."[24]

[21] 49 The Eagle, No. 218, at 275 (St. John's College, Cambridge, 1935).

[22] That Marshall had reservations about the character of Pigou's work is clear from his comments on "Wealth and Welfare". See Krishna Bharadwaj, Marshall on Pigou's *Wealth and Welfare*, 39 Economica 32 (1972).

[23] Compare Austin Robinson's comment on Pigou: "He was never, as an economist, quick to see intuitively the order of magnitude and the potential dangers of economic forces, and he was never a person to whom colleagues turned instinctively for advice in the sphere of economic policy making." *Supra* note 18, at 94. For my own criticisms of Pigou, see R. H. Coase, The Problem of Social Cost, 3 J. Law & Econ. 1, 28-42 (1960).

[24] A. W. Coats, *supra* note 1, at 229.

[6]

THE APPOINTMENT OF PIGOU AS MARSHALL'S SUCCESSOR: COMMENT

A. W. COATS

The University of Nottingham

PROFESSOR Coase's effort to dispose of the counterfactual conditional proposition advanced in my 1968 article rests on the answers to two factual questions: How did the individual electors vote on May 30, 1908; and why did they vote as they did? Unfortunately, in the present state of our knowledge, the first question cannot be answered definitively; and given the complexity and obscurity of human motives, the second question is hardly even conceivably answerable. Yet it is worth reconsidering the situation not only because of its intrinsic importance to the history of British economic thought, but also because of the new evidence contained in John Neville Keynes' diaries, which were not available when I undertook my research six or seven years ago.

Before going into matters of detail, it is worth emphasising two major points. The first is that Marshall took the fiscal controversy very seriously indeed, so much so that on several occasions he broke his customary rule of abstaining from public declarations on controversial policy issues.[1] And there

[1] On July 14, 1903, Marshall wrote to W. A. S. Hewins, as follows: "If I really thought there was any danger that the scheme which you advocate would be put into practice, I should feel bound to break through my rule against taking active part in the discussions in the market place." Letter from Alfred Marshall to W. A. S. Hewins, July 14, 1903, Hewins papers, now at the University of Sheffield. By August he evidently viewed the prospect differently, for he signed the so-called "Manifesto of the Fourteen Professors" which was published in The Times (London), August 15, 1903, and he completed the first version of his Memorandum on Fiscal Policy of International Trade for C. T. Ritchie, the Chancellor of the Exchequer (Gt. Brit., Parl., H.C., Sessional Papers 1908, vol. 107, No. 321). Two months later he (presumably) allowed the Secretary of the Unionist Free Food League to publish in The Times (London), November 23, 1903, his letter of November 19, which contained the following passages: "I deeply regret that I am unable to cooperate in the great work which the [anti-Chamberlainite] Unionist Free Food League is doing, for I have ever acted on the principle that academic economists should avoid joining leagues and should belong to no political party unless, indeed, they give themselves largely to politics, as Professor Fawcett did. . . . About 30 years ago I became convinced that a protectionist system, if it could be worked honestly as well as wisely, might on the whole benefit countries in a certain stage of industrial development, and that set me on the inquiry whether a free trade policy was wholly right for England. I have pursued that inquiry ever since, and have gradually settled down to the conclusion that the changes of the last two generations have much increased the harm which would be done to England by even a moderate protective policy, and that free trade is of more vital necessity to England now than when it was first adopted."

is no doubt that he deplored the fact that the economists had exposed their disagreements to the public, and had encountered considerable opposition and even ridicule in the process.[2] The second point is that Marshall was so eager to secure Pigou's election that he intervened actively in a manner that earned him the disapproval not only of Foxwell's supporters, but also of moderates like J. N. Keynes and J. S. Nicholson. In view of his well known scepticism about the value of pure theory, is it sufficient to explain Marshall's remarkable enthusiasm for Pigou simply in terms of that young man's analytical ability? Is it not more reasonable to regard Pigou's ardent espousal of the free trade cause and his outspoken defence of the professional economist's authority[3]—both of which were of great concern to Marshall—as significant additional reasons for Marshall's support? Marshall's undignified behaviour prior to the election reveals his state of anxiety about the outcome; and it was not unusual for him to become excited about matters he regarded as important. J. N. Keynes, a calm and temperate man and a shrewd judge of char-

[2] In view of Foxwell's bitterness after Pigou's election one may legitimately question his retrospective account of Marshall's reaction: ". . . Bonar and I are profoundly disagreed on Free Trade, on which B is a fanatic. It was he who induced Marshall agst M's better judgment, and after M had twice refused, to sign the Professors' Manifesto. It was just because he felt his signature was a blunder, that he was so angry with me for attacking it. He came to my room scolding violently for an hour: finally said 'You were lying, and you knew it'. When I had to tell him that I was too busy to sit there listening to talk of that kind, and wished him good evening. He went out, and came back next day to apologize: but he never forgave me, and did everything in his power to set people against me, though I did not realise how persistent he had been till Nicholson told me." Letter from H. S. Foxwell to W. R. Scott, February 18, 1930, in Harvard Graduate School of Business Administration, Kress Library of Business & Economics [hereinafter cited as Kress Library]. However J. N. Keynes' diary appears to confirm L. L. Price's story that "at the Cambridge meeting of the British Association in 1904 . . . Marshall chid me like an irate dominie flogging a naughty schoolboy, for my support of Tariff Reform. I imagine that he had not liked the ridicule in the Times of the damning pontifical Manifesto of the Free Trade professors against Chamberlain, and had nursed his wrath." See L. L. Price, Memories and Notes on British Economists, 1881-1947, ch. 2, at 14-16 (Typescript in Brotherton Library, University of Leeds, 1946). In his diary, on August 19, 1904, Keynes recorded: "Rather a heated discussion between L. L. Price and Marshall" at the Economics Section Committee—Fiscal Question. He himself considered "the issue of the manifesto unwise and likely to injure the authority of professional economists." J. N. Keynes, Diaries, August 20, 1903, in Cambridge University Library. The Times (London) had mentioned him as a non-signatory of the Manifesto, but he added "It assumes wrongly that all the non-signatories are supporters of Mr. Chamberlain."

[3] According to Cambridge gossip, dating from the 1903-1908 period, Marshall was said to have declared that a man who refused to support free trade could not be a *bona fide* professional economist. I am not at liberty to give the source of this report, but this hearsay evidence adds piquancy to Pigou's statement that "nearly all economists would subscribe to a remark which one of the most distinguished of them once made in the presence of the writer, that any one who advocates Protection for England now does not know how Protection works." See A. C. Pigou, Free Trade and its Critics, 73 Fortnightly Rev. 547 (1903).

acter, was frequently exasperated by Marshall's conduct in Cambridge university affairs, referring to him in his diary as "silly," and, at another time, "ridiculous."[4] Professor Coase considers it "unthinkable that he [Marshall] would not exert himself to the full to secure the election of the candidate who, in his view, would do most for Cambridge economics." But this is not to say that his judgment was balanced and unprejudiced, or that it was based on purely scholarly or scientific considerations.

A substantial part of Professor Coase's argument turns on the personal relationship between Marshall and Foxwell. This is far too involved a subject to be dealt with adequately in a few paragraphs. It is quite true that the "breach" between them cannot be dated precisely from 1903; but this is not a decisive consideration. Undoubtedly they disagreed on a number of significant pedagogical, methodological, theoretical, and policy issues, and some of these disagreements extended at least as far back as the early 1890s.[5] But despite these "family quarrels," they were staunch allies against the historians, moral philosophers (including Keynes), psychologists, and others in their lengthy campaign to establish economics in its rightful place in the Cambridge curriculum. Moreover, there is no reason to doubt Marshall's sincere regard for Foxwell, even as expressed in his "fulsome" post-election letter, for it is consistent with earlier correspondence. For example, in 1897 he wrote to J. N. Keynes:

> Your news about H.S.F. is startling. I wd like his library to remain in E'land. But I am even more anxious that he shd. remain at Cambridge;

and he went on to explain the increasing need for "many teachers who can keep abreast of modern work and movements."[6] Almost four years later he was concerned that Foxwell might move to the new chair of Commerce at the University of Birmingham, and his letter to Keynes deserves to be quoted

[4] J. N. Keynes, Diaries, *supra* note 2, at May 29, 1902; Oct. 15, 1902. See also *id.* at Feb. 1, 1905, and the letter cited in R. F. Harrod, The Life of John Maynard Keynes 117 (1951).

[5] It would be wrong to suppose that the differences between the two men can be summed up as a contrast between "scientific" and "scholarly" standards, to quote Marshall's words, or to regard Marshall as the spokesman for economic analysis and Foxwell as the advocate of applied economics. Marshall himself claimed that the principal task of future generations lay in dynamic, statistical, and empirical studies. Memorials of Alfred Marshall 301 (A. C. Pigou ed., 1925); also T. W. Hutchison, Review of Economic Doctrines, 1870-1929, at 22, n.1 (1953). And there were times when Foxwell and Keynes joined forces to persuade Marshall that he had underemphasized analysis by declaring publicly that "Economics is an inductive science." Letter from Alfred Marshall to J. N. Keynes, Jan. 30, 1902, in Marshall Library, Cambridge, Eng.

[6] Letter from Alfred Marshall to J. N. Keynes, Aug. 30, 1897, in Marshall Library, Cambridge, Eng.

in extenso as it seems to imply that Marshall then regarded Foxwell as the logical successor to the Cambridge chair.

Foxwell's affairs trouble me. He is not framed for living on a small income; and even the sale of his books would not set him up for good without some permanent source of income. He has some notion I think that he may go to Birmingham: but even if that post be open to him—and of course there are hitches in the way—it would not be well that he should leave Cambridge. He came to me on Sunday to talk about a letter he had had from Chicago about his books. And all the time the thought was in my mind that it would be a great thing if a post for him could be found here: it may have been in his mind too more or less; but no allusion of any sort was made to it. As to the future of the Professorship here I should retire if I could afford to. But I cannot. If I did I should have an income of only about £150 a year exclusive of the rental equivalent of my house, and sundry checks from Macmillan.

I propose, if I can get the right man as Pigou seems to be for the present, to continue to pay £100 a year in order that there may be one general course of lectures suitable for high-class beginners, and treated from the scientific as distinguished from the historical and Literary point of view. That together with the Adam Smith Prize and other sundries exhausts what I can afford to contribute to the progress of economics.

It is therefore out of the question for me to attempt to get up a private subscription to provide a post for Foxwell here. If anything is to be done, it must I think be an appeal to the University to found a Readership (not necessarily perpetual) for him. Do you think there is any chance of such an appeal meeting with response? If so how should it be started? Should the matter be brought before the MO:Sc: Board?

I had thought he would be well provided for in London, books and all. But what he said on Sunday implied that he was not likely to get an adequate salary in London. This is the new point in the situation. If it had arisen before I should have gone to Sidgwick to lay the matter before him. As it is I think you are clearly the person whom I should approach first about it.

There is no hurry: any steps should be deliberate. Will you think over it at your leisure. Perhaps we may later have a talk about it.

Yours sincerely,
Alfred Marshall

P.S. Since writing this Foxwell's face has again come in at the door; but this time more cheerful. He has had better news about his books. As it is not very relevant to the main issue; and as I could not ask him for leave to tell it to you, without giving some reason, I had better not go into detail. It is an additional reason for taking no active steps for a fortnight or so: if I had not already written this letter I think I shd have put it off. As it is I will send it.[7]

[7] Letter from Alfred Marshall to J. N. Keynes, Jan. 8, 1901, in Marshall Library, Cambridge, Eng.

In the last resort, interpretations of Marshall's motives are hardly less speculative than attempts to guess the electors' motives. Nevertheless in my view it is unnecessary to maintain that the events of 1903 marked a sharp breach in his relationship with Foxwell. For one thing, their continued co-operation was essential to the success of the new Economics Tripos, for which they had battled so valiantly for so long. But the fiscal controversy may well have marked the end of Marshall's willingness to view Foxwell as a suitable successor, for as Professor he would have become the leading spokesman for Cambridge economics. The heated public controversy among the professional economists had, admittedly, died down during the middle years of the decade. But the tariff question was still at the centre of current politics both in Cambridge and in the country at large. Like Pigou, the young Maynard Keynes was an active spokesman for the Free Trade cause,[8] and his friend, the historian G. M. Trevelyan, has recorded that "Joseph Chamberlain's Protectionist campaign aroused my Cambridge and London friends to an active interest in political affairs which they had not previously felt. They were nearly all of them Free Traders."[9] More important still, perhaps, is the testimony of W. T. (later Lord) Layton, who began lecturing on economics at Cambridge in 1908, under Pigou's regime. Layton recalled that "The academic year 1907-8 ended with Professor Marshall's resignation. As the Free Trade controversy was still a central issue in British politics, the question of Free Trade and Protection inevitably affected the discussion of a successor. But it happened that Arthur Balfour, the ex-Prime Minister, was one of the electors and tho' he sat on the fence in 1906 in the fight for protection, his influence was thrown on the side of a young don, A. C. Pigou of Kings, who had been very active on the Free Trade side. Balfour's support was decisive, and at thirty-two years of age Pigou became the youngest professor at Cambridge."[10]

Lord Layton's testimony is intriguing, but difficult to assess. He was a young man at the time, and just about to begin his academic career, and there is no reason to assume that he had 'inside' knowledge of the election. We know that Balfour did not attend the election; but he probably did respond to the Vice Chancellor's request for his opinion,[11] and it is possible —though distinctly unlikely—that he exerted his influence on Pigou's behalf.

[8] R. F. Harrod, *supra* note 4, at 96, 98, 108, etc.

[9] G. M. Trevelyan, An Autobiography and Other Essays 30 (1949).

[10] W. T. Layton, Dorothy 32-3 (1961). Pigou was only 30 at the time of the election.

[11] A. W. Coats, Political Economy and the Tariff Reform Campaign of 1903, 11 J. Law & Econ. 181, 227-28 (1968). It is curious that Balfour mentioned only three candidates—W. J. Ashley, Foxwell, and Pigou—whereas J. N. Keynes' diary also includes Edwin Cannan.

However Layton's recollections do support the contention that the free trade issue was still important to Cambridge economists in 1908.

Although Marshall appears to have done his utmost to ensure Pigou's success, this does not necessarily mean that his influence was decisive. He had no vote, though he may have been consulted, if only as a matter of courtesy; and there have been occasions when an over-eager outgoing professor has overplayed his hand, thereby damaging his favourite's chances. Indeed, this may have been the effect of Marshall's behaviour on Nicholson and Keynes; though for various reasons it seems certain that Edgeworth voted for Pigou, for he is known to have been deferential to Marshall's authority. Nicholson's position is complex and tantalising, for he was an independent-minded man, who is said to have been anxious to limit the influence of Marshallian economics. He had, of course, signed the 1903 'Manifesto,' and might therefore be regarded as a committed free trader. However in the year after Pigou's election he published *A Project of Empire* which, though chiefly concerned with Adam Smith's ideas, could be interpreted as displaying some sympathy for moderate tariffs on lines resembling Chamberlain's proposals.[12]

J. N. Keynes' position is even more significant, for as Registrary of the University he was a key figure in its administration and his judgment probably carried great weight with the non-economist electors. He had close personal associations with the economists and some claim to expertise in the field; moreover he had worked closely with another elector, Professor W. R.

[12] The following letter from George Unwin, the economic historian, to Lord Courtney, is of interest in this connection. He describes Nicholson's book as "an exposition of Adam Smith emphasising some aspects wh. Prof. N. regards as over-looked, i.e. the economic primacy of the home market, the Nationalist feeling of A.S. (re Navigation Acts etc.)! and the suggestion for Imperial Federation. Prof. N. has never been a purely deductive Free Trader, and he considers it desirable—and indeed the only safe method—to base Free Trade on arguments of expendiency. He thinks that an uncompromisingly doctrinaire attitude creates a grave risk of leaving Free Trade defenceless when it breaks down.

Academically I agree with him. Politically and in the present crisis I am as uncompromising as McCulloch or any Conscript Father of the P.E.C. [Political Economy Club].

But Nicholson is also (like many Liberally inclined Scots) a Nationalist and wants a scheme of Imperial Defence supported by a 5% duty.

Out of these elements he has produced his book which is quite sincerely as cross-benched as it professes to be, and is *not* meant to bridge over his way to Tariff Reform. But in reading the proofs I saw it was certain to be interpreted in this way by his party critics (and told him so).

Most unfortunately the Manchester Guardian and Nation have both taken this line—*very* injudiciously—as N is sensitive. Profs. Chapman and Bastable are very indignant at the M.G. (they think it is L. T. Hobhouse or Hirst). I heard from Owen that Hobson had said Nicholson had *gone over*. I write this so that you may contradict any rumours." Letter from George Unwin to Lord Courtney, Feb. 13, 1910, in Courtney Collection, London School of Economics.

Sorley, on the Moral Sciences Board, and had served with the Vice Chancellor both on the University Senate and on the Board of Indian Civil Service Studies.[13] In politics he was probably a liberal, and most likely a free trader; but as Marshall believed him to be sympathetic to Higgs' scheme to establish a second Professorship,[14] he may conceivably have voted for Foxwell.

Of the other electors, apart from Lord Courtney, we know nothing relevant to the main issues. Courtney was a staunch free trader, and may be assumed to have voted for Pigou.[15] On the whole it seems likely that the election was close—which may account for Foxwell's bitterness, since he claimed to know the division of the votes.[16] Foxwell's own version of the proceedings was given in a remarkably explicit and detailed letter written approximately one week after the election to one of his London disciples, Clara Collet.[17]

> I fell pretty sick of things in general. This election puts a stop to my Cambridge work, the work I have enjoyed most—and I feel as if I had nothing further to do but to scrape together a few pence for my bairns.
>
> It was regarded here as a moral certainty that I should be elected. 15 to 1 was Macgregor's estimate. I did not know that Marshall as an elector afterwards told me was moving heaven and earth to prevent my election, and raking up every conceivable thing that he thought might prejudice me. Ever since October I had been preparing for the reorganisation of the school here. I had got Fay elected to a fellowship, and had most cordial promises of help from tutors, and some prospect of money for additions to the staff. The V.C. was doing all he could for me.
>
> Well Courtney, Edgeworth, Sorley and Stanton voted against me: Nicholson Palgrave and Keynes for me. Balfour refused to come, on the ground that it seemed to turn on politics: a curious ground for a party leader to take. If he had come and had voted for me I should have got in, in spite of Marshall, for the V.C. would have given me 6 casting votes if he had them.
>
> This is Marshall's rather savage revenge for a letter I wrote in 'The Times' a

[13] J. S. Reid, Memoir of the Rev. Ernest Stewart Roberts [reprinted from The Caian (1913) in Cambridge University Library]. Roberts is described as being uninterested in "passing political problems. . . . The clash of parties was distasteful to his temperament. . . . He became more conservative and more reserved about political subjects as he grew older, and some of his earlier opinions were changed." *Id.* at 37.

[14] "Holding the opinions which you do, I think you should be right to provide (sic) Higgs' scheme. . . ." Letter from Alfred Marshall to J. N. Keynes, Dec. 13, 1908, in Marshall Library, Cambridge, Eng.

[15] See G. P. Gooch, Life of Lord Courtney 485 (1920). Unfortunately the Courtney papers contain only one brief unrevealing reference to the election.

[16] L. L. Price, *supra* note 2, at 15.

[17] Miss Collet was a student of Foxwell's at University College, London, and the initiator, and later Secretary, of the Junior Economic Club. See her obituary notice, Professor Foxwell and University College, 46 Econ. J. 614 (1936); also her Supplementary Note, 50 Econ. J. 558 (1940). Her career is described in Clara Elizabeth Collet, in 111 J. Royal Stat. Soc. 252 (1948).

propos of the ridiculous professorial manifesto. He writes a hollow letter, extolling Pigou's extraordinary genius, saying he is glad P. was elected, and thanking me for "hearty, cordial and generous support", extended even to cases where his policy did not commend itself to my judgment: The bare truth. The Webbs, on the other hand, with whom I have had many a difference, write in the kindest possible manner.

Nicholson came here on Sunday, and paced up and down my garden for two hours abusing Marshall. A member of the Council told Olive yesterday that wherever he went in the University there was "universal execration". Cunningham's verger told my servant that he had never know[n] C. so upset and so indignant. C. referred to the business in his sermon yesterday!

Well, as Caldecott and two other men have written to me, it is, so far as I am concerned, an irretrievable disaster. It was the one piece of work I wanted, and which I have been encouraged to believe I could do well.

If I had not trebled the members of the school in five years, I would have readily resigned. There are only 13 in for economics as against 167 for history! This is entirely due to Marshall's restrictive and repressive influence.

Pigou is a brilliant man and personally an excellent fellow. He has been particularly kind and delicate in his communications with me. But he is young, even for his age (30 or 31): and has been an extreme agitator on a side not popular either here or among influential people in the country. A member of Council writes me that "this election will condemn the Cambridge school of economics to the same level of impotence to which Edgeworth has reduced the Oxford school." I hope not. Keynes is doing what he can, but he takes a gloomy view of the outlook.

I hope things are better with you.[18]

It would obviously be naive to accept Foxwell's account *in toto*. In an excited and embittered state of mind he was hardly a reliable witness, and much of his information may have been derived from gossip supplied by disappointed supporters. Yet in a close-knit academic community like Cambridge it would have been difficult to keep secret the details of such a *cause célèbre*, and we cannot entirely rule out the possibility that Foxwell's principal informant was Nicholson, one of the electors.[19] Parts of Foxwell's letter are

[18] Letter from H. S. Foxwell to C. E. Collet, June 8, 1908. I am most grateful to Mr. Paul Sturges, Research Assistant on the Guide to Archive Sources for the History of British Economic Thought, who reminded me of this letter which I originally saw some years ago. It is now in the possession of Mr. W. R. Collet of Northwood, Middlesex, who has kindly consented to its publication.

Among the persons mentioned in the letter, D. H. Macgregor and C. R. Fay were young Cambridge economists; Olive was Mrs. Foxwell; Archdeacon William Cunningham, the distinguished economic historian, was a long-standing critic of Marshall; and Alfred Caldecott, a student and Fellow of St. John's College, Cambridge, was Professor of Logic and Mental Philosophy at King's College, London.

[19] Such a suggestion, of course, implies that Nicholson was guilty of disclosing the confidential proceedings of the electors' meeting. There is no direct evidence for this suggestion; but Unwin's opinion of Nicholson may be relevant in this connection. "I don't often see Prof. N. but continue to like him personally. There is a curious incalculable

confirmed by other sources—for example his explanation of Balfour's absence,[20] his account of Nicholson's reaction, and his paraphrase of Marshall's letter of condolence. His description of Marshall's behavior is consistent with other evidence, and his estimate of the voting, though uncorroborated, is quite plausible—especially in the cases of Courtney and Edgeworth. There is no reason to doubt that Cunningham was furious, and Pigou tactful; nor is it wholly unlikely that Nicholson and Keynes supported Foxwell.

Nevertheless, after all the conjectures have been assembled, the matter still remains in doubt, and there is no point in prolonging these speculations. In judging the outcome from this distance in time it is important not to be influenced by our present-day assessment of Pigou and Foxwell, even though most qualified persons nowadays would probably agree with the electors' choice. At the time Pigou was remarkably young and comparatively inexperienced as a teacher, despite his impressive list of publications. In the early years of this century publications carried less weight in the ancient English universities than they do today, and in assessing the importance of Foxwell's long and loyal service to the university we should not necessarily join Marshall in shuddering when Foxwell protested that the electors had "set aside the claims of friendship."[21] For it has been said of the greatest Cambridge economist of this century, that "Throughout his life the claims of friendship came first with Maynard."[22] Some of the electors, most of whom had known Foxwell for many years, may have felt the same. Indeed, this largely explains why J. N. Keynes found the whole matter so distasteful.

---

strain in him (I have noticed it in other philosophers of partly Celtic blood) which might deflect his judgment from its natural course on occasion." Letter from George Unwin to Lord Courtney, Feb. 7, 1909, in Courtney Collection, London School of Economics. In view of J. N. Keynes' comments on Nicholson's reaction to the election, perhaps this was just such an "occasion"?

[20] See A.W. Coats, *supra* note 11, at 227.

[21] Letter from Alfred Marshall to J. N. Keynes, Dec. 13, 1908, Marshall Library, Cambridge, Eng.

[22] R. F. Harrod, *supra* note 4, at 32. See also J. N. Keynes' reference to this point in his obituary of Foxwell: Herbert Somerton Foxwell, 46 Econ. J. 590 (1936).

Marshall on Pigou's *Wealth and Welfare*[1]

By Krishna Bharadwaj

As Marshall's favourite pupil and successor, Pigou is considered to have confirmed and extended Marshall's conclusions on the question of maximum satisfaction under free competition. In the words of Keynes:[2] "Marshall's proof that *laissez faire* breaks down in certain conditions, *theoretically* and not merely practically, regarded as a principle of maximum social advantage, was of great philosophical importance." But, as Keynes adds, Marshall did not pursue this argument in all its ramifications, and it was Pigou who worked out fully its consequences for social policy.

While Pigou looked upon his early work as being "merely supplementary"[3] to that of Marshall, there has been no direct evidence as to how Marshall viewed the extension of his method by Pigou. Marshall's manuscript notes in his own copy of Pigou's *Wealth and Welfare*,[4] published here for the first time, reveal that Marshall had strong reservations concerning Pigou's conclusions in that book which, however, he did not intend to disclose "for the present", even to Pigou himself.[5]

It is notable that Marshall's comments, dated October 10, 1914, were made more than two years after the publication of Pigou's book. It is probable that the comments were occasioned by the attack on marginalism made by J. A. Hobson in his *Work and Wealth: A Human Valuation*, published in 1914. Hobson noted that Pigou, by showing that the supply price and the "marginal supply price" of an industry diverge excepting under constant returns, had virtually admitted the failure of marginalism to establish that competition ensures *maximum satisfaction.*[6] Marshall refers twice to this passage of Hobson in his

[1] I am grateful to Piero Sraffa for suggesting this topic to me and for all the invaluable discussions we have had during the course of preparing this article. Thanks are also due to M. Dobb, P. Garegnani, L. Pasinetti and Joan Robinson for their helpful comments.

[2] J. M. Keynes, "Alfred Marshall, 1842–1924", *Economic Journal*, vol. XXXIV (1924).

[3] A. C. Pigou, "Producers' and Consumers' Surplus", *Economic Journal*, vol. XX (1910), p. 366.

[4] A. C. Pigou, *Wealth and Welfare*, 1912.

[5] Marshall's library (including the Pigou volume) was given to the University of Cambridge after his death. The volume was withdrawn by Mrs. Marshall when the Librarian of the Marshall Library, Mr. P. Sraffa (incautiously, as he realized too late) drew her attention to the notes. After her death the volume was returned to the Library, but was kept in reserve during Pigou's lifetime.

[6] "Professor Pigou (*Wealth and Welfare*, p. 176) though adopting the general position of marginalism, makes a concession, as to its applicability, which is a virtual admission of its futility. For, by showing that only in 'industries of con-

comments (see §§1 and 11 below). He agrees with Hobson if only to the extent that he himself considers Pigou as overrating "the possibilities of the statical method".

Marshall's manuscript notes are presented in Section I in the form of 16 numbered comments.[1] Where appropriate, the relevant passage from *Wealth and Welfare* or a summary of the relevant portion of the text is presented (in smaller print) before the comment itself. Abbreviations used by Marshall are expanded in square brackets. Asterisks are reproduced as placed in the text by Marshall. Underscorings by Marshall are noted in the footnotes. The page reference at the beginning of each comment is to the appropriate page in *Wealth and Welfare*. Explanatory notes are provided in the footnotes.

In Section II of the article we discuss differences between Marshall and Pigou in the light of the Comments in section I; we have also drawn upon other unpublished supporting evidence in the Marshall Papers.

I. Marshall's Comments on Pigou

§1

On the front end-paper of *Wealth and Welfare*, Marshall makes the following general comment.

10.10.1914.

I incline to think that the marginal supply curve Part II Ch. VIII has no reality; I think he overrates the possibilities of the statical method, and so far I agree with Hobson's criticism of marginalism, *Work and Wealth* p. 174,[2] though most of what J. A. H[obson] says on the subject seems to me invalid.

In this I may be wrong. For I can't follow all that A. C. P[igou] says: and it is possible that he has some recondite meaning. Anyhow I incline not to controvert him, even under 4 eyes, for the present. When he translates his W[ealth] & W[elfare] into realism, then I may perhaps raise a question, if I still cannot follow him. But on the whole I incline

---

stant returns' are 'supply price' and 'marginal supply price' equal, and that in industries of 'decreasing' or of 'increasing returns' there exists a tendency to exceed or fall short of the 'marginal net product yielded in industries in general' he virtually endorses the criticism that 'marginalism' assumes a statical condition of industry. For only in a statical condition would all industries be found conforming to constant returns: the operation of increasing or diminishing returns means nothing else than that changes in volume or methods of production are raising or lowering productivity and remuneration above or below the equal level which 'marginalism' desiderates." (Hobson, *Work and Wealth*, p. 175, n.)

In Marshall's copy of Hobson's *Work and Wealth*, which is now in the Marshall Library, the passage quoted here is marked with an asterisk. He writes in the margin: "See my pencil note on this passage", which presumably refers to the pencil annotation on Pigou's *Wealth and Welfare* (§11 below; see also §1).

[1] Some incidental comments of Marshall on transportation, economies of large scale and joint costs, etc. have been omitted on the suggestion of the Editors.

[2] See p. 32, n. 6, above.

to keep my[self] close to Pr[inciples] (especially in regard to the limitations of the statical method) in [Book] IV.[1]

§2

(p. 17)

Pigou contrasts Marshall's definition of national dividend, as comprising the whole of the gross dividend minus such part as would suffice to maintain the country's capital intact, with that of Irving Fisher. "Professor Fisher, on the other hand, placing in the forefront of his argument the proposition that the savings are in no circumstance income, claims unequivocally to identify the national dividend with those services, and those only, that enter directly into consumption."

This is a definite unit; but I do not think "income" is the right name for it.

§3

(p. 18)

"When . . . we are concerned, not with an imaginary stationary state, but with the condition of affairs that actually exists, the mere maintenance of the physical efficiency of our plant is no longer obviously equivalent to the maintenance of our capital intact. Machinery that has become obsolete because of the development of improved forms is not really left intact, however excellent its physical condition; and the same thing is true of machinery for whose products popular taste has declined. If, however, in deference to these considerations, we decide to make an allowance for cases of obsolescence, we are exposed to the retort that this concession logically implies the recognition of the value, and not the physical efficiency, of instrumental goods as the object which is to be maintained intact."*

* I do not follow this. I regard an obsolescent machine as I do a horse that is "ageing" perhaps prematurely. On the other hand, in so far as invention etc. cause the efficiency of plants to increase relatively to its cost I take the addition to be included in my main statement. I am however aware that I have made no attempts to supply suggestions for avoiding double entry in so far as (i) an improved machine and (ii) its (improved) product are both entered. I do not think such subtleties are appropriate in a broad statement.

§4

(p. 149)

"By the 'social net product'[2] is meant the aggregate contribution made to the national dividend; by the 'private net product'* the contribution made to the earnings of those responsible for the industry under review".

[1] The sixth edition of Marshall's *Principles* was the latest in print when Marshall wrote this comment. Chapter XIII of Book IV of that edition included the section, "Correlation of the tendencies to increasing and to diminishing return".

[2] The word "net" is underscored and the words "i.e. Net product" written in the margin by Marshall.

* i.e. private net product is the "remuneration" of the worker whether it comes in the form of wages or in the price of the product or service wh[ich] he makes and markets on his own account.

§5

(pp. 172–173)

"In respect of any industry, construct a demand curve DD . . . Construct, secondly, a supply curve SS_1 of the ordinary type, a curve namely, such that, if a perpendicular PM be drawn from any point P upon it to cut the base line in M, PM represents the price which, in the long run, tends to maintain an annual output OM. Finally, construct a curve of marginal supply prices SS_2, such that, if a perpendicular QM be drawn from any point Q upon it to cut the base line in M, QM represents the difference made to the aggregate expenses of the industry*[1] concerned by the production of the OMth unit of output. Let the curve of marginal supply prices cut the demand curve in Q. Then in order that equality may be established between the marginal net product of resources in our selected industry and in other industries, it is necessary that the output of our industry be OM units".

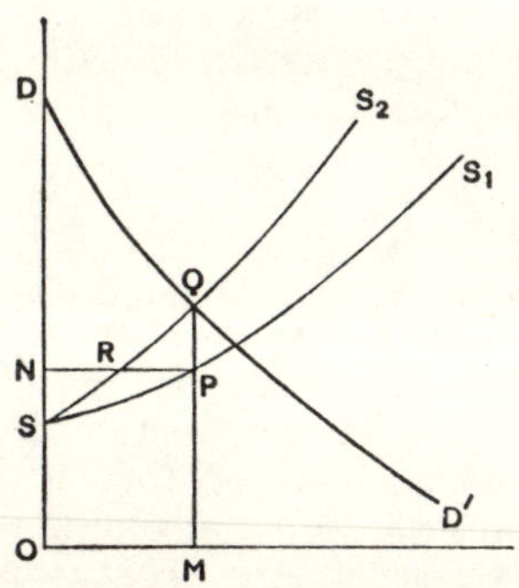

I rather think that QP is (neglecting influences on the technical economies of farming caused by increased production) not a real expense but an extra charge wh[ich] landlords will be able to put on producers, in consequence of the increased value of land. I understand this to be implied by F. Y. E[dgeworth]'s statement, Ec[onomic] J[ournal] 1913, p. 210[2] (mag[azine]s[3] Transport 1914, No. 10) that area OMQS= OMPN, i.e. SPQ=SPN.

* I do not understand "the aggregate expenses of the industry". If all economies appertaining to an increased scale of prod[uctio]n were

[1] Marshall underscores "aggregate expenses of the industry".

[2] In "Contribution to Theory of Railway Rates—IV". The statement is: "If the ordinate of any point of the abscissa, M, intersects SS_1 at P and SS_2 at Q, the area OMQS is equal to the area OMPN. But the area OMPN represents the total expenses incident to the production of quantity OM; inclusive of rent (the area PSN) and of entrepreneur's remuneration . . .".

[3] "Magazines" are volumes of articles from periodicals bound together, for Marshall, according to subjects. These are now in the Marshall Library.

"internal" to particular firms, then I think one sh[oul]d look to the expenses of an increased production (not hurried) of a "representative" firm. But as in fact increased economies in shipbuilding depend in part on correlated economies in the manufacture of plates there seems to me to be no one point at which the "aggregate expenses" act as a specific motive force.

§6

(p. 173, footnote)

"It must be carefully observed that 'the difference made to aggregate expenses' by the production of the OMth unit of output, means the difference between the aggregate expenses of an industry when it is producing and is fully adjusted to producing x units and when it is producing and is *fully adjusted to* producing $(x+\Delta x)$ units. . . . This . . . may be illustrated from the facts of railway transportation. . . . The loading of all trucks will be different according to the total quantity to be carried. The next step after 40 overloaded trucks would not be 40 overloaded trucks *plus* one truck containing one parcel but 41 lightly loaded trucks".[1]

I think he means that if the demand for such trainloads had been anticipated as permanent the trucks w[oul]d have been made a little smaller so that 41 c[oul]d just have been filled.

§7

(p. 176)

"It is objected that, since, under diminishing returns, our argument makes the supply price of any quantity of output less than the marginal supply price, it implies that the marginal unit is continuously produced at a loss to the producer of it; and that this is impossible and absurd. This reasoning derives its plausibility from an implicit assumption that the *curve of marginal supply prices* employed here is equivalent to Dr. Marshall's *particular expenses curve*. That assumption, however, under conditions of simple competition is not correct".

Certainly the two seem to have nothing in common.

§8

(p. 176)

"When x units are being produced . . . the particular expenses to the representative producer of producing any one unit, *all costs, including the hire of the necessary land being reckoned in*, is equal to the particular expense of producing any other unit. That is to say, if p is the average full cost per unit of producing x units, the particular expenses curve, corresponding to the production of x units, is a horizontal line drawn parallel to the base line at a height representative of p."

No, my curve represents avowedly *no* actual conditions.

[1] The last two sentences in this passage are sidescored by Marshall and the words "lightly loaded" underscored.

§9

(p. 176)

"The general result is that, in industries of constant returns, the supply price and the marginal supply price of all quantities of output are equal; in industries of increasing returns the supply price is greater than the marginal supply price."

This, I think is better treated in my App[endix] H of Pr[inciples].

§10

(p. 176)

"In industries of diminishing returns the supply price is less than the marginal price . . ."

This seems invalid if rent be taken as a charge.

§11

(Top margin of p. 176)

Hobson, Work and Wealth, p. 174 says[1] that this page is "a virtual confession of the futility" of the doctrine of marginalism. Is it not the fact that the contrast between the supply price and marginal supply price is inconsistent with A. C. P[igou]'s own definition at top of §3 (p. 174);[2] and that the important facts on which he insists can be set out without suggesting any such contradiction [?].

§12

(p. 216)

Pigou argues against the proposition that the transport of copper and that of coal are joint products on the ground that "a very large fixed plant *for varied* purposes is essential to the operation of joint costs. . . . A sufficient answer . . . is to observe that the carriage of tons of different things from A to B *is*[3] a single homogeneous commodity, on precisely the same footing as plain cotton cloth."

No, it is not. The whole doctrine of costs of manufacturing in the higher technical, as well as academic developments, turns largely on the difficulty of assigning to different products their several shares of the common costs of such things as powerful shears, hand saws, turret lathes, etc.; which spend part of their time idly, but when at work perform almost identical operations for these various products. Like the supply of transport by the locomotive, the supply of every such machine of similar operations for different things is an instance of

[1] See p. 32, n. 6, above.
[2] Pigou's definition of the supply price of any quantity of output is: "the price which tends to call out the production of that quantity annually". The "marginal supply price" was defined by him as "the difference made to aggregate expenses of production of all producers, by an increase in production from x to $(x+\Delta x)$ units". "Producers' and Consumers' Surplus", *op. cit.* p. 363.
[3] This is underscored by Marshall as well.

common supply (not "joint" in the sense in which sirloin and shin of beef are joint, but joint in the ordinary use of the term). Similarly the cost of an expensive frontage for selling a hundred different products has to be shared out among them, and raises difficulties of joint supply of the same service to different things on all fours with the railway problem. This is not inconsistent with the position that monopoly plays an exceptionally large part in the vagaries of monopoly charges.

§13

(top margin of chapter on the Variability of Errors in Business Forecasts, p. 453)

This chapter puts many points in new settings; but on the whole it seems to repeat the old explanation of crises, without taking account of the new causes chiefly since 1857 (1866 was exceptional) which have checked the rise, mitigated the fall and blunted the sharpness of the apex.

§14

(p. 457, referring to Hull's *Industrial Depression*)

"Mr. Hull has rightly observed that the effect of forward buying, in expanding the range of variability of business expectations, would be mitigated, if the state were to publish monthly 'all pertinent information in relation to the existing volume of construction under contract for further months'."

But it is already done by trade journals better than it could be by government.

§15

(p. 464, footnote)

"It is, thus, a true saying which Mr. Burton quotes from John Mills: 'As a rule, panics do not destroy capital;* they merely reveal the extent to which it has been previously destroyed by its betrayal into hopelessly unproductive works . . .'."

* This use of "capital" is unsatisfactory. In effect it refers mainly to material capital, to the exclusion of business reputation, adjustment of means to ends. The collapse of a part of a printing press may destroy much capital invested in type tho' the lead can all be recovered.

§16

(p. 485, footnote, referring to the Minority Report in the Report of the Royal Commission on the Poor Laws, p. 1196.)

"The Minority's argument . . . is associated with the suggestion that an addition of £10,000,000 to the wage fund of the worst year would suffice to reduce unemployment in that year to the normal amount. This result, which is based upon statistical evidence by Mr. Bowley, assumes that the whole of the extra ten millions would go in employing

> new hands, and none of it in raising wages . . . To . . . equate the total wage fund of bad years to that of good would require a sum nearer to 100 millions than to 10 millions."

Both of these arithmetics seem hazardous. £m.10+ adjustment *might* do all. The question is w[oul]d adjustment improve much? If it did employment w[oul]d make employment.

II. Discussion

In his *Principles* Marshall suggested that a community's satisfaction could be increased by levying a tax on an industry subject to decreasing returns to finance a bounty to an industry in which the law of increasing returns "acts sharply". This "tentative" conclusion was arrived at by considering the effects, mainly on consumers' surplus, of a tax or a bounty. Marshall found the effects of a tax to be the least injurious to consumers when levied on an industry under decreasing returns, and that a bounty to an industry subject to increasing returns would add to the community's satisfaction.[1]

In *Wealth and Welfare*, Pigou, adopting the national dividend as a measure of a community's welfare, stipulated the equality of marginal net product of resources in all uses as the condition for maximum welfare. To show that, under certain conditions, the competitive output fails to satisfy this criterion, he introduced the notion of "the marginal supply price" of an industry, defined as "the difference made to aggregate expenses of production (in terms of money) of all producers by an increase in total production from x to $(x+\Delta x)$ units".[2] He argued that, while in the case of increasing returns, the marginal supply price curve lies *below* the supply curve, in the case of increasing returns it lies *above* it, so that the "ideal output", given by the intersection of the marginal supply price curve and the demand curve, exceeds competitive output under increasing returns and falls short of it under decreasing returns. Only under constant returns do the "ideal" and the competitive outputs coincide. These results led Pigou to advocate a tax on *every* industry subject to decreasing returns *and* a bounty to *every* industry subject to increasing returns.[3]

This unconventional result, that competition, in general, failed to achieve maximum satisfaction, provided the ground for Hobson to observe that Pigou's findings amounted to an admission of the futility of marginalism. And it was Hobson's remark which stimulated Marshall to criticize Pigou's method. Marshall's criticism is mainly directed against the notion of the "marginal supply price" which, he says, "has no reality" (§1). He objects to its use in the case of decreasing returns as well as that of increasing returns, but for different reasons. In the

[1] *Principles*, p. 462–76. Unless otherwise stated, all references are to the sixth edition, 1910 (see p. 34, n. 1, above); and those to Pigou are to his *Wealth and Welfare*.

[2] This notion was first defined by Pigou in his article, "Producers' and Consumers' Surplus", *op. cit.*, p. 363.

[3] *Wealth and Welfare*, p. 178–9.

former case, he finds the contrast between marginal supply price and the supply price to be inconsistent with Pigou's own definition of the supply price (§11). More important and interesting is the objection Marshall raises with regard to increasing returns: that, in applying the marginal method in a cut-and-dried fashion Pigou "overrates the possibilities of the statical method". Marshall had written in his *Principles* (already in the fourth edition of 1898): "The statical theory of equilibrium . . . is barely even an introduction to the study of the progress and development of industries which show a tendency to increasing return. Its limitations are so constantly overlooked, especially by those who approach it from an abstract point of view, that there is a danger in throwing it in definite form at all."

It may be noted at the outset that Pigou's use of the term marginal supply price is misleading, and indeed he himself appears initially to have been misled by it. In constructing the curve of marginal supply prices, Pigou appears to have assumed that the average cost curve of the industry is its supply curve under *both* decreasing and increasing returns. However, it is so only under increasing returns, and can hold for decreasing returns only if such returns are wholly due to external diseconomies. When decreasing returns are due to a fixed factor, as is generally supposed, the supply curve is itself the marginal cost curve, and the curve of marginal supply prices is then merely a derivative curve of this marginal cost curve.[1]

Marshall's comment that the marginal supply price has no reality can be understood, with regard to decreasing returns, from the preceding: a derivative curve of a marginal cost curve can be said to have no "real" significance. Marshall's §5 brings this out explicitly. He observes that "neglecting the influence of technical economies" the difference between the marginal supply price and the supply price "is not a real expense but an extra charge which landlords will be able to put on producers, in consequence of the increased value of land". It can be seen that the ordinate on the marginal supply curve at a given output measures the cost of producing the marginal unit which pays no rent (indicated on the supply curve) *plus* the additional rent payments on all the rest of the units, due to the marginal increase in output. These additional payments are not for the use of additional real resources but are increased costs of a fixed factor already in use. (This argument underlies §10 also.)

We may recall here that Allyn Young in his review of *Wealth and Welfare*[2] published in August 1913 had already pointed out that the

[1] In fact, Pigou himself wrote in his earlier article, "Producers' and Consumers' Surplus", *op. cit.*: "The supply curve for all values in respect of which it is inclined positively coincides with the curve of collective marginal supply prices and for all values in respect of which it is inclined negatively, with the curve of average full expenses of production." In *Wealth and Welfare*, however, he takes the supply curve to be *below* the curve of marginal supply prices for decreasing returns, while it continues to be *above* for increasing returns.

[2] *Quarterly Journal of Economics*, vol. XXVII (August 1913), p. 672–86.

difference between the marginal supply price and the supply price in the case of decreasing returns was to be interpreted as "transferences of purchasing power" to owners of the fixed factor rather than as additional cost in terms of real resources. Although this criticism of Young was thus before Marshall's (dated October 1914), there is nothing to suggest that Marshall was aware of it at the time of writing his own comment. Pigou, in response to Young's criticism, corrected this anomaly with regard to the case of decreasing returns in the second edition of *Economics of Welfare*, 1924. In the third edition of that book, 1928, he replaced the marginal supply price by "the supply price from the standpoint of the community" and defined it in such a way as to eliminate transfer elements (p. 222).

The more interesting comments of Marshall relate to the case of increasing returns.[1] He displays strong misgivings about Pigou's unqualified use of the statical method in relation to increasing returns. He himself had, in the *Principles*, appended cautionary remarks to the results arrived at in this case, drawing the readers' attention—as he does also in §§1 and 11—to Appendix H where he discussed at some length "the limitation of the statical method".

Before considering Marshall's own treatment of increasing returns in Appendix H, we adduce here an additional piece of evidence which helps one to formulate a little more pointedly Marshall's objection to Pigou's use of the long-period supply curve. This evidence is a pencilled comment by Marshall on Pigou's article "Producers' and Consumers' Surplus",[2] where Pigou gives the following definition: "Let the supply price, in any market, be defined as the price which is able, and any lesser price than which is not able, to evoke in the market the production of exactly $(x+\Delta x)$ units". Marshall adds to this: "in a given period of time"; and objects to Pigou's phraseology ("a price is *able* to evoke"): "Nor does the change of phrase obviate the necessity for the conditioning clause as to time. He excludes short periods but treats all long periods, say 10 to 50 years, as having the same effect. *That is, he commits, in silence, violence similar to and greater than that which I confess to in regard to consumption.*" (Italics added.) The implication of this

[1] Marshall raises here an objection against Pigou's use of the *aggregate expenses of the industry* (see §5). His objection that it lacks "specific motive force" could be interpreted to mean that, unlike the "supply price" which is defined in relation to producers' motivation (a price at which producers would be willing to supply the specified output), the marginal supply price in terms of *aggregate expenses of the industry* has no such motivational basis. It is somewhat puzzling, however, to find that Marshall rests a part of his objection on the ground that economies in one industry (say, shipbuilding) depend upon correlated economies in another (say, manufacture of plates). This recoils on the method of partial equilibrium itself since it challenges the notion that economies would be *internal to the industry* even if they are external to the firm, required to validate Pigou's partial equilibrium method. Moreover, Marshall's criticism strengthens further Pigou's argument that the welfare-maximizing output and the competitive output diverge under increasing returns.

[2] This copy of the *Economic Journal*, 1910, is in the Marshall Library, Cambridge.

becomes clear when we note that Marshall was greatly perturbed by the problem of ensuring the stability of demand and supply curves in the face of difficulties arising from what he called "the element of time". The comment reveals that, while he was more troubled over the hypothesis of the stability of the long-period supply curve, he was far from happy even about his long-period demand curve. Even the possibility that the conditions impounded in the *ceteris paribus* clause used in defining the demand curve would alter over time had led him to state that "our list of demand prices is highly conjectural except in the neighbourhood of the customary price".[1] However, Marshall relied upon the stability of the demand curve as, for example, in the present problem, when calculating changes in consumers' surplus. As for the supply curve, he appears to have had stronger doubts whether the theory coped satisfactorily with "the elements of time", especially in the presence of increasing returns. For he saw the difficulties as arising mainly from the irreversibility of changes in production conditions;[2] and it was to these that he mainly devoted Appendix H.[3]

In Appendix H Marshall focuses on the fact that increasing returns are due to "extensive improvements in organization, creation of skills" etc., which bring about changes through time that are not reversible: economies once created can scarcely be withdrawn. He also recognizes that irreversibilities violate the assumption, central to the equilibrium approach, that "if the normal production of a commodity increases and afterwards diminishes to its old amount the demand and supply price will return to their old positions" (p. 807). He argues that, if the supply is diminished, once having been expanded, "the supply price would not move back by the course by which it had come", and suggests that a method of handling irreversibilities would be to show the backward

[1] See *Principles*, pp. 109–13 and 129–35.

[2] It is of interest to find that in his early work, *Pure Theory of Foreign Trade and Domestic Value*, Marshall stressed the difficulties that custom and habits raised for the demand curve by introducing irreversibilities in consumption. He recognized that "consequently, every movement of the exchange index entails some alteration in the shape of the curves and therefore the forces which determine succeeding movements" (p. 32). In *Principles*, irreversibilities in consumption are not given the same importance, although they are alluded to in Appendix H.

[3] Marshall was so concerned about the difficulties created for his theory by irreversibilities that he appears to have devoted much thought as to where he should place their discussion in the text. The following manuscript note was found in the Marshall Papers, written by him on a sheet of paper in which were enclosed some printed pages taken from a copy of his *Pure Theory*:

> "General suggestions: 31: VIII: 96.
> Postpone case II altogether and treat it on different footing.
> Decide early what to do about elasticity.
> Make much shorter all attempts to bring the curves into reality."

Case II, in *Pure Theory*, it will be recalled, is that of the supply curve under increasing returns. It was as an attempt to bring the curves closer to reality that Marshall discussed irreversibilities at some length. Indeed, he treated irreversibilities on a different footing from the fourth edition of *Principles* (1898) onwards, when they were shifted from the central chapter to a "Note on Pure Theory of Stable and Unstable Equilibria"; and from the fifth edition onwards (1902) they were transferred to Appendix H, where irreversibilities were introduced in an argument against the possibility of multiple equilibrium positions under increasing returns.

movement by a separate curve. This treatment means, however, that there would be no uniquely defined "supply price" for a given output. This can be illustrated with the aid of Marshall's diagram (on p. 806). The supply price of the output OM could be MP, MP_1 or MP_2, depending upon whether output expands continuously to OM, or whether it decreases to OM after once having reached OM_1, or does so after having reached OM_2. In fact, since along SS there are economies operating continuously, there would be a separate curve for backward movement at each point and the supply price of OM would be indeterminate, in the sense that it would vary with every change in the *sequence* of output levels by which it is approached. Or, to put it differently, with every change in output, the supply curve needs to be redrawn. Such an ever-shifting supply curve cannot be used to determine equilibrium price and output, as it is essential for that purpose that the supply curve should remain stable for hypothetical movements along it. Here, *given a sequence of output levels*, we may depict the supply price at each output

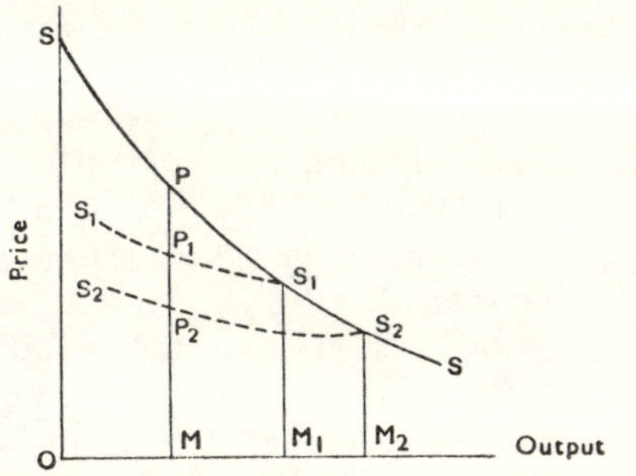

level in that sequence, taking into account irreversibilities. But such a curve would be in the nature of an "historical curve", and not the one required by the theory of equilibrium price.

In the same Appendix H, Marshall suggests a way of obtaining a "true long period normal supply curve" in the case of increasing returns, by treating "time" as a third dimension (pp. 809–10):

> "We might take a series of curves of which the first allowed for economics to be introduced as a result of each increase in the scale of production during one year; a second curve doing the same for two years . . . and so on . . . Cutting them out of cardboard and standing them up side by side we should obtain a *surface* of which the three dimensions represented amount, price and time respectively. If we had marked on each curve the point corresponding to that amount for which, so far as can be foreseen seems likely to be the normal amount for the year to which the curve related, then these points would form a curve on the surface and that curve would be a fairly true long period normal supply curve."

There are two points to be noted about this suggestion. First, the matter dealt with here is not one of irreversibilities but a different one, namely, that "a suitable time to allow for the introduction of economies appertaining to one increase in the scale of production is not long enough for another and larger increase"—which is a matter of the time lags in reaping economies of scale. However, the *long-period* supply curve is obtained under the hypothesis that sufficient time is allowed for forces to work out their full effects.[1] Second, the supply curve is needed to *determine*, in conjunction with the demand curve, the equilibrium price and output, whereas what is required here are the foreseeable "likely" normal outputs, in order to obtain the supply curve. There are any number of such curves, each corresponding to a sequence of likely outputs. Indeed, the exercise becomes meaningless for the theory of equilibrium price when we see that, since the forecasts are forecasts of equilibrium outputs, they could also be considered as forecasts of normal quantities demanded; and the curve connecting them could be said to represent the long-period normal demand curve. We are left then with only one blade of the well-known pair of scissors.

Marshall, while he was acutely aware of the difficulties posed by irreversibilities and "the element of time" in the case of increasing returns, nevertheless tried to present them only as "limitations" which qualified the results.[2] His criticism of Pigou is directed against Pigou's application of the statical method to the case of increasing returns without the qualifications that he himself had laid down. Pigou had thereby cast in a rigid form the results which he himself had put forward in tentative and flexible terms.

These differences in approach are reflected in policy implications as well. A tax on an industry subject to decreasing returns is favoured by Marshall only as the least harmful among the commodity taxes from the standpoint of the consumers. He showed that the tax receipts would exceed the loss of consumers' surplus if the supply curve were sufficiently steeply inclined relatively to the demand curve. However, the decrease in output would also bring about a loss of producers' surplus and the combined reductions of consumers' and producers' surplus would exceed the tax receipts.[3] Marshall's recommendation for a bounty to an increasing-returns industry rested on a positive argument—that it would increase the community's satisfaction. Here, too, he recom-

[1] On p. 497 Marshall explains that the long-period normal price relates to periods "... in which those economies that normally result from an increase in the scale of production ... have time to develop themselves".

[2] For example, in the context of the problem of *maximum satisfaction*, when discussing the shift of the supply curve following a tax, he warns us that the new supply curve in the case of increasing returns "ought properly not to have the same shape as the old one" (p. 469, n. 1). The argument he offers is that, even when the industry shrinks following the tax, it would at least in part preserve the economies already gained. This brings in the question of irreversibilities which jeopardizes the very notion of the supply curve and not only its shift as Marshall suggests.

[3] Marshall treated the effects on producers' surplus on a different footing and concerned himself mainly with those on consumers' surplus. He argues, for example, that the tax on an industry subject to decreasing returns is desirable as consumers would be discouraged thereby from incurring expenditure on a commodity which reduces the real purchasing power of income. No mention is made

mended the bounty only where increasing returns acted sharply. This qualification follows upon his treating the entire amount of the bounty as a cost to society which needed to be off-set by the gain in consumers' surplus arising from the bounty. However, the question whether the entire expense of the bounty is to be reckoned as a cost to society depends upon how the bounty is raised, and it cannot be answered without considering effects on the rest of the economy of raising the required revenue.

Pigou, as we have seen in *Wealth and Welfare*, treated decreasing returns and increasing returns symmetrically, the implication being that both are due to externalities. He favoured a tax on an industry subject to decreasing returns for the same reason as he favoured a bounty to an industry subject to increasing returns, namely, in order to correct deviations from "ideal output". Pigou appears to have treated the cost of the bounty as a transfer. This becomes explicit only in his *Economics of Welfare*, in which he added the following qualification for the grant of a bounty: "Provided that the funds for the bounty can be raised by a mere transfer that does not inflict any indirect injury on production" (4th ed., p. 224). The treatment of the amount of the bounty as a transfer had the consequence that *any* degree of increasing returns qualified the industry for the bounty.

Although Pigou continued to speak in terms of taxation, he had cast the net of tax policy very widely indeed, with a tax on *every* industry under decreasing returns *and* a bounty to *every* industry under increasing returns. Such complicated and comprehensive taxation would have brought the state into the economy on a grand scale. The boldness of this policy was in sharp contrast with Marshall's own position. Apart from the fact that his suggestions were limited in scope, he had further tempered them by the recognition of considerations "other than economic". He warned against the "administrative side of state interference" (pp. 712–13) and against evils such as the opportunities for the corruption of public officials opened up by a scheme of bounties; and he feared that bounties could "sap the springs of free initiative and strength of character" (p. 714).[1]

---

of increases in landlords' incomes (p. 474). Also, when discussing the effects of taxes and bounties in terms of diagrams (pp. 464–9), he is concerned with changes in consumers' surplus alone. Only in one case, where he discusses a tax on agricultural produce, does he take explicit account of producers' surplus (p. 473). But even here he adds that the question of the effects on landlords differs "so much as not to be fitly discussed here". Marshall realized that the concept of producers' surplus which had a clear interpretation in agriculture could not be extended to industry. He suggested a parallel in terms of the particular expenses curve in Appendix H, but realized that this curve is not a normal supply curve. (In §§7 and 8, Marshall disclaims any association between the particular expenses curve and the supply curve.) Producers' surplus calculated from such a curve cannot be treated conceptually as a counterpart of consumers' surplus calculated from a demand curve.

[1] Marshall's general reluctance to bring in the state is reflected in §§14 and 16, where he differs from Pigou on specific points of practical policies. In §14, Pigou having agreed that the variability of business expectations would be mitigated if

What appeared in Marshall as aberrations in the working of the competitive system were transformed by Pigou (in generalizing and extending Marshall's results) into the failure of the competitive system to achieve maximum welfare. When Hobson emphasized this failure of the system, Marshall was impelled to record—if only for posterity—his criticism of Pigou's conclusions. In the case of decreasing returns, he notices an error in the argument of Pigou. In the case of increasing returns, however, his criticism raises questions which are not confined to Pigou's application of the statical method to the problem of welfare, but relate more generally to the validity of the statical approach to the theory of equilibrium itself. Marshall, while bringing out the difficulties confronting that approach, nevertheless had characterized them as being no more than "limitations" of the method which qualified the results. They were locked up in that Pandora's box—Appendix H of Marshall's *Principles*.

Clare Hall, Cambridge.

the state published monthly statistics of the existing volume of construction, Marshall comments that the trade journals have done it already, better than it could be done by government. §16 relates to Pigou's questioning of the Minority's argument in the *Report on Poor Laws* that an addition of £10 mn. to the wage fund of the worst year would suffice to reduce unemployment in that year to its normal amount. Pigou argues that a sum nearer to £100 mn. would be required, since an allowance has to be made for a possible rise in wages. Marshall comments: "Both these arithmetics seem hazardous". He thinks a small adjustment should suffice, and that if it improves the situation, employment would then create further employment. In the *Principles* he had argued that the chief cause of unemployment was a want of confidence, and that "the greater part of it could be removed almost in an instant if confidence could return, touch all industries with her magic wand, and make them continue their production and their demand for the wares of others" (p. 711). While arguing that increased production itself creates increased demand, Marshall sees the way to the cumulative increases in employment through revival of confidence rather than large-scale public expenditure.

[8]

Pigou, Taxation and Public Goods [1,2]

A. B. ATKINSON
University of Essex

and

N. H. STERN
St Catherine's College, Oxford

I. INTRODUCTION

The results of Samuelson [5-7] in the theory of public goods have provided the basis for most subsequent discussion of the optimum provision of public goods. Samuelson showed that a necessary condition for Pareto Optimality (and hence for maximizing a social welfare function which responds positively to individual utilities) is that the sum of the marginal rates of substitution (Σ MRS) between a public good and a private good be equal to the marginal rate of transformation (MRT). The sole constraint is that production is in the aggregate production set. This optimum can be achieved as a competitive equilibrium with the government supplying the public good up to the point where $\Sigma \text{ MRS} = \text{MRT}$ and financing its production by lump-sum taxation. Lump-sum transfers may also be employed to achieve the appropriate income distribution.

The achievement of the " full " optimum described above depends on lump-sum taxes and transfers being feasible. If the taxation tools available exclude lump-sum taxation, then the optimization problem must be modified to include explicitly the means by which government revenue is raised. The importance of this point was clearly recognized by Pigou [3], who argued that the cost to consumers of the public good would be larger than just the necessary resources on account of the " indirect " damage caused by taxation:

> " Where there is indirect damage, it ought to be added to the direct loss of satisfaction involved in the withdrawal of the marginal unit of resources by taxation, before this is balanced against the satisfaction yielded by the marginal expenditure. It follows that, in general, expenditure ought not to be carried so far as to make the real yield of the last unit of resources expended by the government equal to the real yield of the last unit left in the hands of the representative citizen " ([3], p. 34).

This problem has recently received more formal attention from Diamond and Mirrlees [2] and Stiglitz and Dasgupta [8]. In particular, the latter authors have challenged Pigou's conclusion and have argued that in certain circumstances it may not be correct. The economics of their argument and the circumstances in which Pigou's reasoning breaks down was, however, obscure and they failed to distinguish between a number of different interpretations of Pigou's statement. The purpose of this paper is to clarify the meaning of the results obtained by Stiglitz and Dasgupta and to elucidate how Pigou's intuitively appealing (if informal) argument goes wrong.

1 *First version received July* 1972; *final version received April* 1973 (*Eds.*).
2 The authors are grateful to P. A. Diamond, A. K. Dixit, A. K. Klevorick, J. A. Mirrlees and A. Sandmo for their comments on earlier versions of this paper.

II. THE PROBLEM

In examining the effect of the means of finance on the optimum provision of public goods, it is important to distinguish two questions which have tended to be confused in the literature:

(i) the appropriate benefit measure for incremental output of the public good (e.g. for use in benefit-cost analysis),

(ii) the appropriate output level for public goods.

(i) *Benefit Measures and the Conventional Rule*

The first of these questions, which is the one to which we give most attention in this paper, may best be approached through consideration of the methods of benefit-cost analysis. This analysis proceeds by dividing the net effect of an increment in expenditure into costs and benefits. This division can in principle be carried out in many ways, but here we shall assume that the cost side is represented by the marginal rate of transformation and concentrate on the value to which this should be equated (or the *benefit measure*). The rationale for this procedure is that the cost-benefit analyst will usually work out the cost of producing a public good at some set of accounting prices and this will correspond to the marginal cost (or MRT). He will then want to know the benefit measure with which this cost should be compared. Traditional practice in cost-benefit analysis has been to use Σ MRS as the benefit measure (Prest and Turvey [4]): e.g. a road project where the benefits are measured by the sum of the value of possible savings to the users. In what follows the practice of using Σ MRS as a benefit measure will be referred to as the Conventional Rule.

The rationale for the Conventional Rule clearly derives from the first-order conditions for a full optimum, and where the expenditure has to be financed by distortionary taxation the benefit measure has to be modified.[1] The question with which we are concerned here is whether this modified benefit measure will be less than or greater than that indicated by the Conventional Rule. Pigou's intuition was that the Conventional Rule would overstate the true benefits because it ignored the " indirect damage " caused by raising revenue. Stiglitz and Dasgupta, on the other hand, argue that the condition for the Conventional Rule to over-state the benefits is that " the share of tax revenue from the *i*th commodity is . . . greater than the elasticity of tax revenue from an increase in the tax rate on the *i*th commodity: or equivalently, as the marginal revenue from raising the tax on the *i*th commodity by a unit is . . . less than C_i [consumption of good i] " ([8], p. 159). Unfortunately, no adequate interpretation of this result is given by Stiglitz-Dasgupta, and we have no means of telling from the above result whether the case where the Conventional Rule understates the benefits is a likely one or merely an abnormality. Moreover, Stiglitz and Dasgupta overlook the important consideration that their result depends on the choice of which goods are taxed. These questions are taken up in Section III.

(ii) *Output of Public Goods and Over- and Under-supply*

The second question concerns the level of output of public goods. The statements by Stiglitz and Dasgupta that the Conventional Rule would lead to an " under- or oversupply " (p. 159) suggest that they have thrown light on this question, but they do not in fact specify what they mean by under- and over-supply. There are a number of possible interpretations which could be given. It could mean that the solution to the problem where public goods are financed by distortionary taxation but where Σ MRS = MRT is imposed as a constraint leads to output levels which are larger or smaller than the output levels where the constraint is removed. Alternatively, it could mean that the optimum output levels where public goods are financed by distortionary taxation are larger or smaller than

[1] With the procedure followed here (which is that adopted by Diamond and Mirrlees), the costs of raising revenue are subtracted from the benefit side. The same results could equally well be described as adding the costs of raising revenue to the cost side—as is done by Pigou and Stiglitz-Dasgupta.

the levels in the full optimum (financed by lump sum taxation). The latter interpretation [1] is perhaps the more interesting and it is the one on which we focus—see Section IV. The approach adopted is to examine the changes in optimum output levels as the availability of lump-sum finance increases (from zero to the level of the full optimum). This raises slightly more general questions of the welfare effects of changes from commodity taxation to lump-sum taxation. These questions are discussed further in the Appendix.

III. BENEFIT MEASURES AND COMMODITY TAXATION

A wide range of taxes could be used to finance expenditure on public goods, but in this paper it is assumed that *ad valorem* commodity and factor taxes are employed. In this we are following Diamond-Mirrlees and Stiglitz-Dasgupta, and the model described below is based on their work (the notation is that of Diamond-Mirrlees).

Assumptions

Households. There are assumed to be h identical households [2] maximizing utility functions $U(x, e)$ subject to $q.x = 0$, where x denotes the net consumption of the n private goods by the household (factors supplied being treated as negative demands), q denotes the prices faced by consumers and e denotes the supply of public goods. The indirect utility function is denoted by $V(q, e)$. It is assumed that the utility function is such that x is a well-defined function of q and e.

Production. The production constraint is written as $G(X, e) = 0$, where $X = hx$ is the total net consumption and it is assumed that there are constant returns to scale. Private producers are price-takers and the first-order conditions for profit maximization mean that G_k is proportional to p_k where p_k is the producer price of the kth good.[3] The tax rate on the kth good is $t_k = q_k - p_k$.

Government. The government is assumed to maximize a social welfare function $hV(q, e)$ subject to the production constraint. (The requirement of market clearing ensures that the government budget is balanced.) The controls at the government's disposal are the tax rates t_k and the expenditure on the public good e (for simplicity attention is focused on the case where there is a single public good, but the analysis can readily be extended). It may also be noted that we may assume without loss of generality that one good is not taxed (given that there are no lump-sum transfers, net consumer expenditure is zero, so that a proportional tax on all commodities raises no revenue). It is assumed that the untaxed good is good one, and that this is taken as the numeraire ($p_1 = q_1 = 1$). If we further assume that G is defined such that $G_1 = 1$, this implies that $G_k = p_k$.

The government's maximization problem may be formulated in terms of the Lagrangean: $\mathscr{L} = hV(q, e) - \lambda G[X(q, e), e]$. The first-order condition [4] for e is given by (where $G_i = \partial G/\partial X_i$, $G_e = \partial G/\partial e$)

$$h\frac{\partial V}{\partial e} - \lambda\left[\sum_{i=1}^{n} G_i \frac{\partial X_i}{\partial e} + G_e\right] = 0, \qquad \text{...(1)}$$

which may be written as

$$h\frac{\partial V/\partial e}{\alpha q_k} = \frac{p_k}{q_k}\frac{\lambda}{\alpha}\frac{G_e}{G_k} + \frac{\lambda}{\alpha q_k}\sum_{i=1}^{n} p_i \frac{\partial X_i}{\partial e}, \qquad \text{...(2)}$$

where α denotes the individual marginal utility of income.

[1] The last sentence in the quotation from Pigou given above suggests that it was the comparison of output levels which he had in mind.

[2] This assumption is made for simplicity; for discussion of the case where consumers are not identical, see Diamond and Mirrlees [2].

[3] The production side is discussed further in Diamond and Mirrlees. If non-constant returns permit positive profits the results carry through, in the case of identical consumers, if 100% profits taxes are allowed (see e.g. [8])

[4] We assume in this paper that functions are differentiable to the relevant order.

The left-hand side of equation (2) is the sum of the marginal rates of substitution between the public good and the private good k. In order to proceed from this equation to discussion of the Conventional Rule (Σ MRS = MRT), we need to specify the good k used in the comparison. As usually presented (see, for example, Aaron and McGuire [1], p. 909) the Conventional Rule takes the marginal rate of substitution between the public good and the private good selected as numeraire, and in the present case this corresponds to the untaxed good ($k = 1$). Equation (2) may then be rewritten

$$\frac{G_e}{G_1} = \frac{\alpha}{\lambda} \frac{h \dfrac{\partial V}{\partial e}}{\alpha} - \sum_{i=1}^{n} (q_i - t_i) \frac{\partial X_i}{\partial e}$$

or ...(3)

$$\text{MRT} = \frac{\alpha}{\lambda} \Sigma \, \text{MRS} + \frac{\partial}{\partial e}\left[\sum_{i=1}^{n} t_i X_i\right],$$

where we have used the fact that $\sum_{i=1}^{n} q_i \partial X_i / \partial e = 0$ (from the budget constraint of the consumer).

Equation (3) allows us to see whether the benefit measure with commodity taxation is greater than or less than that with the Conventional Rule. Beginning with the second term on the right-hand side, we can see that this represents a factor overlooked by Pigou—the effect on tax revenue resulting from complementarity and substitutability between private and public goods. If increased government expenditure leads to a greater consumption of taxed private goods, this reduces the revenue which has to be raised and hence increases the benefit measure. An example of this would be if the provision of a further television channel increased demand for television sets and these were subject to an indirect tax. This point, which was brought out by Diamond and Mirrlees, is however a straightforward one and is not central to this paper, and in what follows it will be assumed that $\partial X_i / \partial e = 0$ for $i = 1, ..., n$.

If the second term vanishes, the right-hand side of equation (3) becomes $(\alpha/\lambda)\Sigma$ MRS and the departure of the benefit measure from the Conventional Rule depends simply on whether $\alpha \gtrless \lambda$. Since α is the marginal utility of income to the consumer and λ is the social marginal cost of raising revenue, Pigou's argument leads one to expect that where taxes are distortionary $\lambda > \alpha$ and hence that the true benefit is less than Σ MRS. In order to see where this breaks down, we need to look at the optimal tax structure. The first-order conditions are

$$h \frac{\partial V}{\partial q_k} = \lambda \left(\sum_{i=1}^{n} G_i \frac{\partial X_i}{\partial q_k} \right) = \lambda \frac{\partial}{\partial t_k} \left(\sum_{i=1}^{n} p_i X_i \right).$$

Since $V_k = -\alpha x_k$ and $\partial(\Sigma p_i X_i)/\partial t_k + \partial(\Sigma t_i X_i)/\partial t_k = 0$ (from differentiating the consumer budget constraint), we can write this as

$$\frac{\alpha}{\lambda} = \frac{\dfrac{\partial}{\partial t_k}\left(\sum_{i=1}^{n} t_i X_i\right)}{X_k} \qquad \text{...(4)}$$

on which the Stiglitz-Dasgupta condition is based (see p. 120). However, this condition is not framed in terms of readily recognizable parameters (neither of the demand functions nor of the utility function) and does not provide much insight into whether or not it is in fact likely that $\alpha > \lambda$.

Using the Slutsky relationship, equation (4) may be rewritten as

$$\frac{\alpha}{\lambda} = 1 - \sum_{i=1}^{n} t_i \frac{\partial X_i}{\partial I} + \sum_{i=1}^{n} t_i (S_{ik}/X_k), \qquad \text{...(5)}$$

where S_{ik} denotes the Slutsky term and $\partial X_i/\partial I$ denotes the income term

$$\text{(i.e. } \partial X_i/\partial q_k = S_{ik} - X_k(\partial X_i/\partial I)).$$

From this we can see that whether $\alpha \gtrless \lambda$ depends on two factors.

(i) *A " distortionary effect "*, represented by the third term on the right-hand side. If we multiply by $t_k X_k$ and sum, we obtain

$$\left(\frac{\alpha}{\lambda} - 1 + \sum_{i=1}^{n} t_i \frac{\partial X_i}{\partial I}\right) = \left(\sum_{i=1}^{n} \sum_{k=1}^{n} t_i S_{ik} t_k\right) \Big/ R, \qquad \ldots(6)$$

where $R = \sum_{k=1}^{n} t_k X_k$, from which it can be deduced (following Diamond and Mirrlees) that where the revenue is positive (as it will be for positive government expenditure) then

$$\sum_{i=1}^{n} t_i (S_{ik}/X_k) \leq 0 \qquad \ldots(7)$$

using the negative semi-definiteness of the Slutsky matrix. This term works in the direction of $\alpha < \lambda$, and may be interpreted as representing the distortionary effect with which Pigou was concerned—the excess burden (at the margin of tax revenue) associated with commodity as opposed to lump-sum taxation. (This may be demonstrated by examining the effect of allowing the government to use lump-sum taxation up to an amount T—see the Appendix.) To this extent Pigou's excess burden argument is, therefore, correct; however, he overlooked the second term in equation (5).

(ii) *A " revenue " effect*, represented by the second term on the right-hand side of (5) or the marginal rate of tax as income I increases. If this were always positive, then it would be guaranteed that $\alpha < \lambda$ and hence (where $\partial X_i/\partial e = 0$) that the benefit measure is less than Σ MRS. However, this condition cannot be guaranteed and the term may well be negative. Moreover, the sign of the term depends on the choice of which goods are taxed. This may be illustrated by the case where there is one private consumption good, and one factor supplied by the household. If public expenditure is positive, revenue must be positive, so that if the factor is untaxed the consumption good must be taxed at a positive rate. The marginal tax rate will then be positive where the consumption good is a normal good, which is clearly a rather weak requirement. If, on the other hand, the consumption good is untaxed, we have to subsidise leisure (a negative tax rate on leisure raising a positive revenue) and the marginal tax rate will only be positive where leisure is an inferior good.[1] The reason for the dependence of the sign on the choice of the taxed good is fairly clear: the " income " effect of taxation *reduces* the revenue from a consumption tax given normality but *increases* the revenue from a factor tax given normality of leisure.

In their paper, Stiglitz and Dasgupta give the impression that Pigou's intuitive argument was quite wrong. From the more detailed analysis given in this section it appears that —if interpreted carefully—the excess burden argument has some relevance; however, Pigou overlooked the other aspects of distortionary taxation described under (ii) which may reverse his conclusion that the Conventional Rule over-estimates the benefits.

IV. OUTPUT LEVELS AND DISTORTIONARY TAXATION—AN EXAMPLE

The second question outlined above—the relationship between the optimum level of public good output under distortionary taxation and that in the full optimum—may be approached by supposing that the government levies a lump sum tax T per household, with the balance of the revenue required to finance public expenditure being raised by

[1] In this case, the condition for $\alpha > \lambda$ (combining (i) and (ii)) is that the supply curve of labour be backward-bending, which is not implausible. This result is given by Stiglitz and Dasgupta (p. 159), but they do not appear to appreciate its dependence on the choice of untaxed good.

commodity taxation. We may then examine the relationship between T and the output of public goods, and in particular compare e_{CT} with e_{LS} where the subscript CT denotes the commodity tax optimum (where $T = 0$) and LS the lump-sum optimum (where $t = 0$). To keep things simple, we consider the special case where there is one private good and one factor, and where producer prices are taken as constant (at unity). It may be noted that the comparison of e_{CT} with e_{LS} is not affected by the choice of untaxed good, since the physical quantities in the two optima do not depend on the normalization. We assume for the details of our analysis that the factor (L) is taxed at rate t (so that the wage faced is $(1-t)$) and the commodity (X) is taken as the untaxed good. We also assume that the utility function is separable in public and private goods: $U(X, L)+H(e)$.

The government's maximization problem may be written in terms of the Lagrangean

$$hV(t, T, e)+\lambda[hT+thL-e]$$

and the first-order conditions are

$$V_t+\lambda\left[L+t\frac{\partial L}{\partial t}\right]=0 \qquad \text{...(8)}$$

$$hV_e-\lambda = 0 \qquad \text{...(9)}$$

$$hT+htL-e = 0. \qquad \text{...(10)}$$

In the maximization described above, T is taken as a parameter; we are interested in the way in which t and e change as T is allowed to vary. Differentiating the first-order conditions with respect to T,[1]

$$\begin{bmatrix} V_{tt}+\lambda\left(2\frac{\partial L}{\partial t}+t\frac{\partial^2 L}{\partial t^2}\right) & 0 & L+t\frac{\partial L}{\partial t} \\ 0 & hV_{ee} & -1 \\ h\left(L+t\frac{\partial L}{\partial t}\right) & -1 & 0 \end{bmatrix}\begin{bmatrix} \frac{dt}{dT} \\ \frac{de}{dT} \\ \frac{d\lambda}{dT} \end{bmatrix} = -\begin{bmatrix} V_{tT}+\lambda\left(\frac{\partial L}{\partial T}+t\frac{\partial^2 L}{\partial t\partial T}\right) \\ 0 \\ h\left(1+t\frac{\partial L}{\partial T}\right) \end{bmatrix}. \qquad (11)$$

Evaluating at the full optimum ($t = 0$, $\alpha = \lambda$), and denoting the matrix of coefficients by A, we obtain

$$\frac{1}{h}|A|\frac{de}{dT} = \left(V_{tT}+\alpha\frac{\partial L}{\partial T}\right)L-V_{tt}-2\frac{\alpha\partial L}{\partial t}.$$

Since

$$V_{tT} = -\alpha_t,\ V_{tt} = -\alpha_t L-\alpha\frac{\partial L}{\partial t}$$

this gives

$$\frac{1}{h}|A|\frac{de}{dT} = \alpha L\frac{\partial L}{\partial T}-\alpha\frac{\partial L}{\partial t} = \alpha S,$$

where S denotes the compensated change in L in response to a rise in the wage rate. The second-order conditions require $|A| \geqq 0$, and since $S>0$, it follows that a small reduction in the possibilities for lump-sum taxation from the full optimum would lead to a fall in the optimum quantity of the public good.

The establishment of global results is more difficult, but the points at issue are brought out in Figure 1. From equation (9) we can draw the " demand " schedule for public goods

[1] It should be noted that the assumption of constant producer prices is important at this point.

$\lambda = hV_e$; and we can use equations (8) and (10) to define a social " supply " curve for the commodity tax optimum. From (8), and using the fact that $V_t = -\alpha L$,

$$\lambda = \alpha \Big/ \left(1 + \frac{t}{L}\frac{\partial L}{\partial t}\right), \qquad \text{...(12)}$$

where t is a function of e from (10). Similarly, we may derive a " supply " curve $\lambda = \alpha$ for the case where the revenue is raised solely by lump-sum taxation. It should be noted

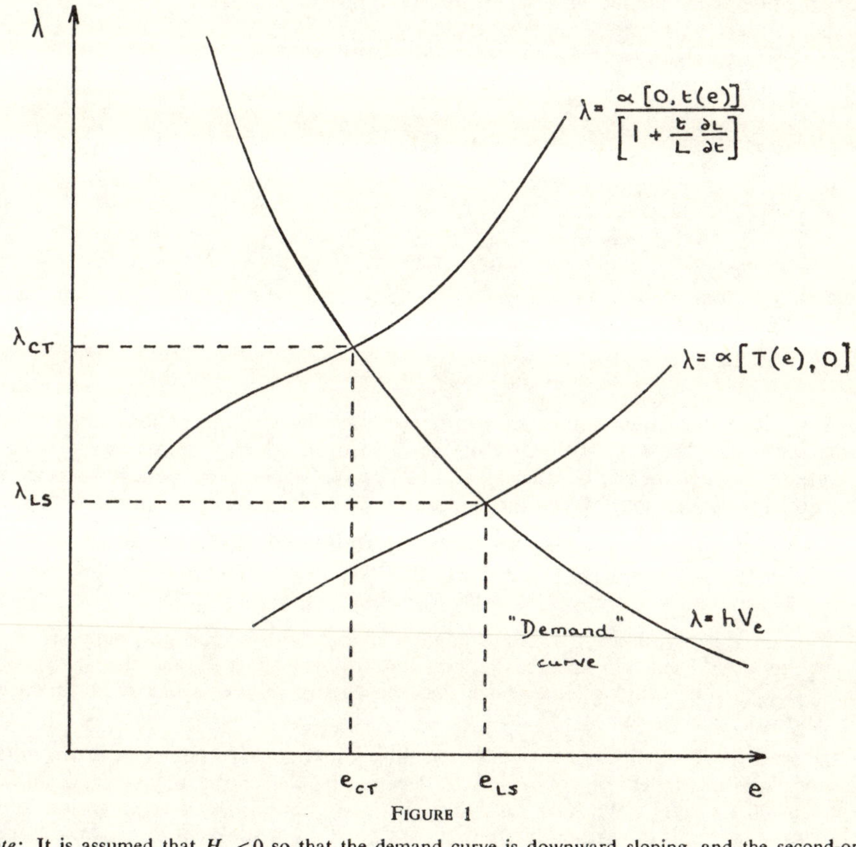

FIGURE 1

Note: It is assumed that $H_{ee} < 0$ so that the demand curve is downward sloping, and the second-order conditions ensure that the supply curve cuts the demand curve from below.

that α is a function of T and t, so that in the first case we may write $\alpha[0, t(e)]$ and in the second $\alpha[T(e), 0]$. For $e_{CT} < e_{LS}$ (as shown in the diagram), we require

$$\lambda_{CT} > \lambda_{LS} (= \alpha_{LS}).$$

The condition given by Stiglitz-Dasgupta (in this case that the supply curve of labour be upward sloping) ensures that

$$\lambda_{CT} > \alpha_{CT},$$

but it is clear that this condition is not by itself sufficient for $e_{CT} < e_{LS}$. It has still to be demonstrated that $\alpha_{CT} > \alpha_{LS}$.

The case of the Cobb-Douglas utility function

$$U(X, L, e) = a \log x + (1-a) \log (1-L) + H(e)$$

(where $0 < a < 1$) illustrates the inadequacy of the Stiglitz-Dasgupta condition since the condition is exactly satisfied at the commodity tax optimum,[1] and according to their analysis we should expect the Conventional Rule to give the right answer. However, it is clear (see Figure 1) that

$$e_{CT} \gtrless e_{LS} \text{ as } \alpha_{CT} \lesseqgtr \alpha_{LS}.$$

From the first-order conditions and the individual budget constraint,

$$1/\alpha = (1-t) - T.$$

From the government budget constraint

$$hT + ht\left(a + \frac{(1-a)T}{1-t}\right) = e$$

so that

$$1/\alpha_{CT} = (1 - e_{CT}/ah)$$

$$1/\alpha_{LS} = 1 - e_{LS}/ah$$

Since $e_{CT} > e_{LS}$ and $\alpha_{CT} < \alpha_{LS}$ is inconsistent with this pair of equations, it follows that the level of public good provision is lower in the commodity tax optimum than in the lump-sum optimum.

V. CONCLUSIONS

The analysis of this paper supports the criticism made by Stiglitz and Dasgupta of Pigou in the sense that the Conventional Rule as defined above may be an over- or under-estimate of the incremental benefits of a public good. The correct benefit measure with distortionary taxation may exceed the sum of the marginal rates of substitution:

(*a*) where the public good is complementary with taxed private goods,

(*b*) where a rise in exogenous income would lead to a fall in the net tax paid

$$\partial(\Sigma t_i X_i)/\partial I < 0).$$

This is likely to occur where taxed goods are inferior or normally supplied factors are subsidised. In such cases, substitution away from the taxed good is not as large as it would otherwise be, and the change in taxation needed to raise an extra £1 is smaller.

On the other hand, Stiglitz and Dasgupta failed to point out that whether the Conventional Rule provides an under- or over-estimate depends on the choice of taxed goods (as is clear from (*b*) above). We have also seen that the question of the appropriate output level for public goods is a rather different one—a point not made clear by Stiglitz-Dasgupta —and that their analysis throws no light on whether output levels in the full optimum are greater or less than the optimum output levels when expenditure is financed by distortionary taxation.

APPENDIX

In the text (p. 123) it was asserted that the term $\sum_{i=1}^{n} t_i(S_{ik}/X_k)$ corresponded to the excess burden associated with the use of (optimum) commodity taxes as opposed to lump-sum taxes. This may be demonstrated by examining the effect of allowing the government to use lump-sum taxation at level T. The government's maximization problem may then be formulated in terms of the Lagrangean (where $h = 1$)

$$\mathscr{L} = V(q, e, T) - \lambda G[X(q, e, T), e] \quad \text{...}(A.1)$$

[1] The supply curve of labour is given by $L = a + T(1-a)/(1-t)$, so that $\partial L/\partial t = 0$ at $T = 0$.

giving the same first-order conditions for the choice of t_k as before (equation (5))

$$\sum_{i=1}^{n} t_i(S_{ik}/X_k) = \alpha/\lambda - 1 + \sum_{i=1}^{n} t_i \frac{\partial X_i}{\partial I}. \qquad \text{...}(A.2)$$

Let us examine the effect of allowing the government to make a small increase dT in the lump-sum tax (moving away from the optimum described above), where adjustments are made in the commodity tax rates to hold e constant and ensure that the production constraint holds. Since $\partial\mathscr{L}/\partial t = 0$ it follows that $d\mathscr{L}/dt = \partial\mathscr{L}/\partial T$. Moreover, given that the production constraint continues to hold $d\mathscr{L} = dV$, which is the change in welfare brought about by the adjustment.[1] From (*A.1*),

$$\frac{\partial\mathscr{L}}{\partial T} = -\alpha - \lambda \sum_{i=1}^{n} G_i \frac{\partial X_i}{\partial T} = -\alpha - \lambda \sum_{i=1}^{n} (q_i - t_i) \frac{\partial X_i}{\partial T}$$

(since $V_T = -\alpha$). From the consumer budget constraint we may note that

$$\sum_{i=1}^{n} q_i \frac{\partial X_i}{\partial T} = -1.$$

Moreover, $\partial X_i/\partial T = -\partial X_i/\partial I$, so that

$$\frac{\partial\mathscr{L}}{\partial T} = -\alpha + \lambda\left(1 - \sum_{i=1}^{n} t_i \frac{\partial X_i}{\partial I}\right)$$

which from (*A.2*)

$$= -\lambda \sum_{i=1}^{n} t_i(S_{ik}/X_k). \qquad \text{...}(A.3)$$

In the text it has been shown that the right-hand side of this expression is positive, so that there is a welfare gain to the increased use of lump-sum taxes. It should, however, be emphasized that this result only holds where *optimum* commodity taxes are employed. In the case where the tax rates are selected arbitrarily, there is no guarantee that a switch to lump-sum taxation will raise the level of welfare.

A similar argument shows that there is a " route " from the commodity tax optimum to the lump-sum optimum such that welfare increases all the way. For each level of T choose the optimum $e(T)$ and $t(T)$, so that along the path $\partial\mathscr{L}/\partial e = \partial\mathscr{L}/\partial t = 0$. Then at each point on the path we have $dV/dT = d\mathscr{L}/dT = \partial\mathscr{L}/\partial T > 0$.

REFERENCES

[1] Aaron, H. and McGuire, M. C. " Public Goods and Income Distribution ", *Econometrica* (1970).

[2] Diamond, P. A. and Mirrlees, J. A. " Optimal Taxation and Public Production ", *American Economic Review* (March and June 1971).

[3] Pigou, A. C. *A Study in Public Finance,* Third edition (Macmillan, 1947).

[4] Prest, A. R. and Turvey, R. " Cost-Benefit Analysis—A Survey ", *Economic Journal* (December 1965).

[5] Samuelson, P. A. " The Pure Theory of Public Expenditure ", *Review of Economics and Statistics,* **36** (1954).

[1] An identical change in welfare would be brought about by increasing lump-sum taxation by dT and spending all the revenue on the public good (keeping commodity taxation unchanged).

[6] Samuelson, P. A. " Diagrammatic Exposition of a Theory of Public Expenditure ", *Review of Economics and Statistics*, **37** (1955).

[7] Samuelson, P. A. " Aspects of Public Expenditure Theories ", *Review of Economics and Statistics*, **40** (1958).

[8] Stiglitz, J. E. and Dasgupta, P. " Differential Taxation, Public Goods and Economic Efficiency ", *Review of Economic Studies*, **38** (April 1971).

[9]

THE APPOINTMENT OF PIGOU AS MARSHALL'S SUCCESSOR: THE OTHER SIDE OF THE COIN

TREVOR W. JONES
University of Edinburgh

Two previous contributors to this journal have discussed the events surrounding the election, in 1908, of A. C. Pigou to the Cambridge chair of economics. Professor Coase's contribution came as a comment on an earlier piece by A. W. Coats about the 1903 Tariff Reform Controversy.[1] There Coats had suggested that Marshall's differences with H. S. Foxwell over the issue of free trade versus protection had been instrumental in the forging of Marshall's attitude to the other man's subsequent candidature for the Cambridge chair. For it is undeniable that Marshall's support of one of Foxwell's rivals for that appointment—A. C. Pigou—was both open and active.

Professor Coase sought to modify this view, adducing evidence in support of his assertion that Marshall's differences with Foxwell were long-standing, the implication being that the events of 1903 ought not to be seen as crucial to the outcome of the later election.[2] Professor Coats[3] then brought forward counter-evidence which indicated that, over the longer period, Marshall's attitude to Foxwell had been less unambiguous than Coase had alleged—reinforcing the suggestion that the public debate of 1903 over free trade *had* been vital to the deterioration of relations between the two. As Coats admits, however, "the matter still remains in doubt, and there is no point in prolonging these speculations."[4] With that comment I agree; there is, however, another side to the election. This concerns the lengths to which Marshall felt able to go in his support of Pigou and, in particular, the manner in which this impinged on one of the electors in 1908, J. N. Keynes.

Clearly, one of the main problems we meet in judging, in a historical setting, such a familiar event as a professorial election is that we may

[1] A. W. Coats, Political Economy and the Tariff Reform Campaign of 1903, 11 J. Law & Econ. 181 (1968).

[2] Ronald H. Coase, The Appointment of Pigou as Marshall's Successor, 15 J. Law & Econ. 473 (1972).

[3] A. W. Coats, The Appointment of Pigou as Marshall's Successor: Comment, 15 J. Law & Econ. 487 (1972).

[4] *Id.* at 495.

wrongly interpret actions in the light of standards current today. Thus it may be assumed—as did Professor Coase—that, at least by our standards, Pigou would have been the natural choice, with his impressive publication record counterbalancing his relative youth at the time of the election. We should, however, bear in mind Professor Coats's warning, when he argues that

> In the early years of this century publications carried less weight in the ancient English universities than they do today, and in assessing Foxwell's long and loyal service to the university we should not necessarily join Marshall in shuddering when Foxwell protested that the electors had "set aside the claims of friendship." For it has been said of the greatest Cambridge economist of this century, that "Throughout his life the claims of friendship came first with Maynard." Some of the electors, most of whom had known Foxwell for many years, may have felt the same. *Indeed, this largely explains why J. N. Keynes found the matter so distasteful.*[5]

At the time, Foxwell seems to have been sure that Keynes voted for him, and Coats reckons it to be "not wholly unlikely" that this was indeed the case. And, though it may not in fact be true that—as Foxwell suggested—a single vote separated him and Pigou on the day,[6] it is of some interest to examine the pressures felt by Neville Keynes in his conflicting roles of philosopher-economist, elector, friend to Foxwell, and—crucially—of father. For we must remember that the brilliant career of his son Maynard was at this time only at its beginning. We should, to be sure, adopt an historically sensitive stance towards the importance of the "claims of friendship" in that election, and this is especially true when we examine, as I go on to do here, the part played by Neville Keynes in it. He was torn, I believe, by a set of conflicting loyalties which explains rather better than Professor Coats's remark why it was that he found the "whole matter so distasteful."

The elements of the story can be pieced together using well-known published sources, in conjunction with a somewhat fuller account than was given by Professor Coase[7] of the material contained in J. N. Keynes's diary. Maynard Keynes was Twelfth Wrangler in 1905 and decided to extend his stay in Cambridge for a fourth year, to be spent in preparation for the Civil Service examination.[8] During that year, he attended Marshall's lectures and was guided in his economic reading by both Marshall and Pigou. The former, in fact, encouraged him to enter for part II of the new economics

[5] *Id.* at 495 (emphasis added).

[6] *Id.* at 493.

[7] Ronald H. Coase, *supra* note 2, at 478-80.

[8] The sources of the biographical details which follow are: 15 Collected Writings of John Maynard Keynes (Elisabeth Johnson ed. 1971); and Roy F. Harrod, The Life of John Maynard Keynes (1951).

tripos, which was being offered for the first time in 1906,[9] but his interests at that time—perhaps as a natural extension of his mathematical studies—leaned more towards logic and philosophy.[10] Thus it was that Maynard kept to his plan of joining the Civil Service, and he subsequently began work in the India Office in October 1906, having come second out of 104 candidates in that summer's Civil Service examination.

By this time he was already working on the dissertation which he was to present for a prize fellowship at King's College in the spring of 1908; this work continued throughout 1907, and in October of that year he moved into King's for a fortnight's energetic labour at it. The work came to completion shortly afterwards, in December. The fellowship election took place in March 1908 and was, from all accounts, keenly contested. Maynard was unsuccessful, though he was told by Pigou that it had been a close thing. In a letter to G. L. Strachey, Maynard suggests that a block of fellows had voted against him from the beginning on the grounds purely of seniority and that he had been damaged by the report of Alfred Whitehead, one of the two assessors appointed by the college to comment on his dissertation.[11] Even so, it appears that Cambridge friends spoke encouragingly to him, "with rosy hopes of success in the following year."[12]

To understand the significance of this event, and to fit it into its proper place in the sequence, a number of considerations have to be taken into account. Firstly, as Harrod notes,[13] success in the fellowship examination would not, in principle, have meant Keynes's giving up his Civil Service position. The fellowship did not carry a large stipend (£120) and it could have primarily been seen as honorific—as, indeed, many such Cambridge offices were at the time. On the other hand, the kudos attaching to it might well have persuaded its holder—if he were so inclined—that he was of suitable calibre to pursue an academic career. Such a course of action did, in fact, seem to be in Maynard's mind, for his father's diary carries the following note on March 1, 1908.

Maynard wishes to throw up the India Office if he gets a Fellowship at King's. I have

[9] We find, for example, that Marshall wrote on one of Keynes's essays at this time: "This is a very powerful answer. I trust your future career may be one in which you will not cease to be an economist. I should be glad if it could be that of an economist." See John Maynard Keynes, *supra* note 8, at 1.

[10] Indeed, in the winter of 1907-08, Maynard indicated to Pigou that if he returned to Cambridge he would want to extend his involvement in the fields of logic and statistical theory. See Roy F. Harrod, *supra* note 8, at 126.

[11] Letter from John Maynard Keynes to G. L. Strachey, March 23, 1908. But see Roy F. Harrod, *supra* note 8, at 127-28; Harrod suggests that Keynes was probably being unfair to Whitehead in these comments.

[12] Roy F. Harrod, *supra* note 8, at 128.

[13] *Id.* at 127.

argued with him in vain. I think he would give up the idea if I had said definitely that I desired him to do so. But I do not think that I ought to take such a decided position as that. He will be throwing up a certainty and taking risks. That fits in with his scheme of life, not with mine.[14]

The element of risk entered the equation because, had Keynes returned to Cambridge with only his fellowship secure, he would have had to rely for supplementary income on fees paid to him by the colleges of students attending any lectures that he gave. His only other certain income would have been the allowance of £100 annually made to him by his father. Events, however, began to overtake Maynard in the weeks following his initial disappointment at King's. It was on these developments that his father's discomfiture came to turn; developments which had essentially begun when Marshall tendered his resignation to the Vice-Chancellor in a letter dated October 4, 1907.

Though this letter, as would be expected, was largely formal, its fourth paragraph contains a hint as to what Marshall's subsequent attitude to Foxwell's candidature for the vacant chair might be. It reads:

But, not to lay stress on the fact that *I have already passed the age at which it is generally expedient to make room for younger men,* I must be able to give the remainder of my energies to attempting to finish however inadequately the task which I undertook long ago.[15] (emphasis added)

Foxwell, of course, was only Marshall's junior by seven years, a fact contrasting sharply with Pigou's relative youthfulness.

The forthcoming professorial contest was, therefore, already in the air at the time of the King's fellowship election to which reference has been made above. It is Marshall's letter to Maynard, dated April 3, 1908 which makes the connection between the two. Its importance to my account makes it worth quoting in full:[16]

My dear Keynes,

Quite recently, since your father left E[ng]land, I have heard in a round-about way, that it is just possible you might be willing to return to Cambridge, if you had work to do here. I have also heard that your chance of an election to a Fellowship at King's next year is good.

Under these circumstances, and taking account of the fact that [D. H.] Macgregor is going to Leeds, my course would have been clear if I had not been about to vacate the professorship. I should then have asked you to allow me to propose you to the Economics Board as a lecturer on general economics probably for the first year, but

[14] John Neville Keynes, Diaries, March 1, 1908, in Cambridge Univ. Library [hereinafter cited without cross-reference as Diaries].

[15] Letter from Alfred Marshall to the Vice-Chancellor, Oct. 4, 1907, in Cambridge Univ. Archives, Cambridge Univ. Library.

[16] John Maynard Keynes, *supra* note 8, at 13.

possibly for the second; and I should have said I would gladly pay you the £100 which I have paid in similar cases.

But I shall cease to be a member of the Economics Board on April 21st: and at its last meeting I said that I should do nothing to hamper the freedom of the reconstituted Board which will meet (probably on June 3rd) to make up its lecture list.

It has however been suggested to me by the same person, to whom the notion of your coming to Cambridge to teach economics is due, that there may be an advantage to calling your attention to the situation. I am in a position to state two things. First (subject to some reserve in the case of one possible election to the Professorship in May) if you approve, a suggestion will be made by a member of the Board on (probably) June 3rd, that you be asked to lecture. Secondly, if the Board concur—and I have no doubt that (subject to the above mentioned reserve) they will concur gladly—the sum of £100 will be forthcoming to you, just to make you feel that you really are a lecturer. I do not think that the £100 will be paid by me: but I can guarantee that it will be paid either from some other source or by me.

There is a certain air of mystery in this letter, and I dislike mystery. But later on you will understand that it was inevitable.

Answer at your convenience. There is no hurry.

Yours very sincerely
Alfred Marshall

Maynard received this letter while his parents were holidaying in France, and it seems that he was excited by Marshall's offer. The salary paid by Marshall to his lecturers, while not an unusual practice, was entirely unofficial; but it would obviously have made Maynard's return to Cambridge more secure, financially speaking. His father's diary, resumed on his return to Cambridge, notes

Maynard writes that he has had from Marshall an offer—subject to proviso and reserve—of a lectureship in economics with a salary of £100. He would like to accept this and give up the India Office without waiting for the Fellowship election at King's.[17]

The same day Neville wrote to his son, counselling caution:[18]

My dear Maynard,

I am glad we shall see you Saturday. We shall then be able to talk over Marshall's proposal. I may as well, however, at once mention two points that occur to me.

(1) If you have to prepare a course of lectures on Economics it does not seem to me that you will have more time, or even as much, for your dissertation than if you remain at the India Office.

(2) Any stipend that Macgregor has received is a matter of purely private ar-

[17] Diaries, April 23, 1908.

[18] John Maynard Keynes, *supra* note 8, at 14.

> rangement. Becoming his successor would not I think give you any University status beyond what you would have as a recognised lecturer and this position you could no doubt get at any time.

Is not Marshall's letter in some respects very vague? I am glad you have not in any way committed yourself at present.

Ever your loving father
J. N. Keynes

Exactly a week later, his diary contains the following item, to which Professor Coase has also drawn attention:

> Interview with Marshall on the subject of the Election to the Political Economy Professorship. He speaks in the highest possible terms of Pigou and is clearly most anxious that he should be elected. He very distinctly does not want Foxwell to be elected. *I very much wish that I were not an elector.*[19]

His father's advice did not seem to weaken Maynard's resolve regarding the desirability of a return to Cambridge; Neville notes in his diary that "Maynard . . . . is still keen to give up the India Office."[20] What apparently convinced him, however, was the receipt of another letter from Cambridge about this time. Curiously, this fact is missing from the accounts of both Harrod and Johnson of these events. His father records:

> Letter from Maynard,—"I have heard from Dickinson. His first letter was one of hesitation, but has now written again in the opposite sense as follows: 'I spoke to Macaulay about the position, and he was most unusually positive as to your chances of a fellowship. Said he thought it was the "softest" thing he had ever known, and that your coming up now would make it almost certain. I had not realised that there is no serious rival of yours starting, & two certain vacancies.' "[21]

The election of Marshall's successor took place a week later, on May 30th, by which time Neville Keynes had had a further interview with Marshall on the subject (on May 27th), although what passed between them is not recorded. In his note on May 30th about the election, he says that "the whole thing has worried me very much." The likelihood that it was not simply the rejection of Foxwell which had caused this worry now seems well established. Cambridge society being what it was, and with Pigou being one of Maynard's sources of information about events there, it seems hardly credible that Keynes father and son could have failed to realise that it was Pigou's preparedness to offer Maynard a lectureship which lay behind Marshall's superficially cryptic April letter. At the same time, the foreknowledge of his

[19] Diaries, April 30, 1908 (emphasis added).

[20] *Id.*, May 17.

[21] *Id.*, May 23.

chances in the next King's fellowship election must have cemented Maynard's hopes of a return to Cambridge. Though his father had advised caution from the outset, he too could hardly have failed to see things in a different light once both these pieces of information were at hand. And in any case, the tone of both his correspondence and his diary indicates that, in the final reckoning, he would be willing to support Maynard in his choice of future—withholding his undoubted paternal right, by the standards of his class and time, to be listened to seriously by his son had he advised contrarily.

Thus, when the day came to appoint Marshall's successor, Keynes was forced to weigh the claims of the main competitors knowing that if Pigou were preferred, that fact would have profound and favourable significance for his eldest son. It is not unreasonable to suppose that it was the tension induced by this situation, as well as the actual outcome in which the older man was overlooked, which led to his later characterisation of the election as a "black cloud throwing its shadow over the whole of the term."[22]

Immediately after Pigou was chosen, Marshall resigned from the chairmanship of the Special Board for Economics and Politics, which had overseen the affairs of the new tripos since its inception in 1903. The meeting of that board on June 3, 1908 chose a somewhat reluctant Neville Keynes to succeed Marshall in this role. For that meeting, however, the chair was taken by Professor James Ward, who conducted business having the following background. Firstly, Marshall had made it known that he wished to cease his lecturing duties; secondly, a letter was read from Foxwell in which he stated bluntly that he too would lecture no more. Thirdly, Pigou had written offering to pay £200 from his own pocket for two lectureships. Not unexpectedly, one of these was offered to Maynard, an offer he found easy to accept; his resignation from the India Office was dated June 5, 1908, which was, coincidentally, his twenty-fifth birthday.[23] The sequence was completed in March 1909, when he was elected as fellow of King's College, a position he occupied until his death.

What are we to make of all this? At first blush, Marshall's part in the matter appears to have been a somewhat clumsy and obvious attempt on his part to influence the course of the election, which interpretation is made all the stronger by our knowledge of his vigorous support of Pigou's candidature. Here, too, however, we have to make sure that we are not applying inapplicable contemporary standards to Marshall's behaviour: what might invoke censure today may have been beyond reproach in the past. Oddly enough, it is Marshall himself who is our best guide in this respect. In his

[22] *Id.*, June 14.

[23] John Maynard Keynes, *supra* note 8, at 15.

letter of congratulation to the new lecturer, dated June 10, 1908, he says the following:

> I am delighted that you are indeed to join our economic staff. I think it is a brilliant, compact group of earnest men, full of the highest promise for the future. But you are wrong in supposing that I had anything to do with your coming back, any more than the postman had. It did not enter my head that you might do so till Pigou spoke to me of it. As your father is an 'elector' he could not approach you: so I put his message on paper and the postman delivered it: the postman and I are factors of the second order of smalls and may be neglected.[24]

Marshall admits, then, that for Pigou to have approached Maynard directly would have been considered an impropriety. Looking back, it is difficult to see how Marshall—given the various parties' states of knowledge—could have made the same offer without similarly construing it as an infraction of the rules of play.

What we may never know is how much Pigou knew at the time of Marshall's activities. Could he have merely mentioned casually that, if elected, he would like to see Maynard lecturing under him? Did Marshall seize on this to make his rather unfortunate intervention? Certainly, in terms of the objective, that is, getting Keynes back to Cambridge to teach under the new professor, the timing of the offer to him was hardly crucial: he had expressed a willingness to return and would have thus been virtually certain to have taken the opportunity, even had it not been opened to him until *after* Pigou's election. It is arguable that Marshall's intervention, then, was at best ill-conceived and rather sadly mistimed. It is possible that it was made without malicious intent; but in any case it certainly fits in with what we are able to glean about his political sense. Neville Keynes himself makes several unfavourable references in his diary to Marshall's ineptitude in such matters, as the following selection shows:

> May 3rd, 1897: M.Sc. Board—Marshall was not there, and in a little over an hour we got through as much as we generally manage in two long meetings.

> September 21st, 1900: Marshall and Ward are getting very much angry with one another over the question as to who shall be Sidgwick's successor as Chairman of the Moral Sciences Board. Marshall wants to put me in, but has managed very much to irritate Ward by the manner in which he has suggested it.

> September 22nd, 1900: I called on Ward in the after$^{\underline{n}}$ and tried to pour oil on the troubled waters. Marshall has shewn extraordinary want of tact, and Ward shows undue sensitiveness. My own view is that Ward should be Chairman.

> January 31st, 1902: Marshall is starting an agitation for the establishment of an

[24] *Id.* at 14-15.

Economics and Politics Tripos, & he has written a paper on the subject with which I am in considerable disagreement. We are having a correspondence that bothers me and I am sure worries him considerably. I want to nip it in the bud if possible.

May 29th, 1902: First meeting of the Economics Syndicate. Marshall said a good many silly things, and I am afraid he had in consequence a rather bad time. Even Maitland appeared to be hostile to him.

October 15th, 1902: Economics Syndicate. We are to meet every week. Marshall was as ridiculous as usual.

February 1st, 1905: Economics Board. I really have not the time to be on a Board of which Marshall is a member.

Certainly, these comments are the personal views of one man, and cannot be considered a complete discussion of Marshall's political temperament. Nevertheless, it does seem that his management of men left a lot to be desired; in his famous memorial essay on Marshall, Maynard Keynes notes that he "might sometimes seem tiresome and obstinate . . . to his colleagues."[25]

We cannot tell what effects Marshall's actions had on the voting in that election of May 1908, though the reexamination offered here of the period leading up to it enables us to see more clearly why one of the electors, at least, should have been so exercised by his responsibilities. If all the evidence presented here could have been pieced together in the same way at the time, a contemporary commentator might have been more severe on Marshall than perhaps we are inclined to be now. If we employ some version of the "all's well that ends well" approach, then we can note that Pigou did, at any event, have a strong claim on the chair, and few now would regret the resultant appointment of Maynard Keynes to a position in Cambridge, an appointment that was to bear so much intellectual fruit. At the time, though, Pigou could have been doing a little more than making an admittedly informed guess at Keynes' powers as an economist; some may think, furthermore, that Marshall's undiplomatic intercession cast an additional and unnecessary shadow over Foxwell's misery. A concluding extract from Neville Keynes' diary provides a fittingly ironic ending to this essay:

Nicholson tells me he hears on all sides that Maynard is the rising economist at Cambridge. Two of his informants appear to have been Foxwell and Fay.[26]

[25] 10 Collected Writings of John Maynard Keynes 223 (1972); the order in which I have used the phrases is reversed from the original, though the sense is maintained.

[26] Diaries, April 10, 1910.

[10]

History of Political Economy 11:4

Pigou: an extension of Sidgwickian thought

Margaret G. O'Donnell,
University of North Carolina, Asheville

I. *Introduction*

Basic concepts of early welfare theory were attributed to the work of A. C. Pigou. As Marshall's successor in the chair of Political Economy at Cambridge in 1908, Pigou was in a position to have his ideas promulgated by many. However innovative Pigou may have been in other respects, many of his major theoretical contributions to welfare analysis were actually based upon pre-Marshallian theoretical concepts and were dressed in the analytical apparatus conceived by Marshall. Furthermore, a major element in this pre-Marshallian thought was the work of Henry Sidgwick.

Of the writers prior to Marshall, Mill is usually considered the main channel through which the direction of classical economic thought concerning laissez-faire was altered. However, Sidgwick's comprehensive approach to the issue of market failure was more fundamental than Mill's observational approach. Sidgwick did use Mill's analysis as a point of departure, examining and expanding Mill's cases of digression from a perfectly functioning market in order to direct his ethical concepts for use in practical applications. He took the ideas that Mill proposed and subjected them to detailed analysis; he sought the logical justification for Mill's suggestions about government interference.

Pigou, as a disciple of Marshall, was trained in the analytics of the market process. Marshall viewed himself as a part of the continuing line of the defenders of laissez-faire, a defense based upon Ricardian theories. However, his emphasis on discussion of pure analytics and disregard of innovative approaches to policy making was a side step in the progression of economic thought which stressed ways to maximize total welfare. Therefore, when Pigou sought to proceed with the problems of external effects and government solutions, he had to circumvent the newly founded Marshallian tradition at Cambridge and return to the Sidgwick-Mill approach. The result was Sidgwickian philosophy couched in Marshallian methodology.

Sidgwick's work in political economy has not gone unnoticed, although many historians of thought regard Sidgwick as merely an expositor of Mill.[1] Hutchison, however, introduces Sidgwick as "the last major English moral philosopher who made a noteworthy contribution to political economy," and looks briefly at Sidgwick's analysis of laissez-faire deficiencies and distribution in relation to the functions of the state.[2] Generally, authors of treatises on the theory of welfare economics have been more willing to give Sidgwick credit for his efforts than historians of thought. Hla Myint observes Sidgwick's influence in the construction of the foundations of modern welfare economics, and Baumol refers to Sidgwick's welfare analysis as "penetrating," while noting the Pigovian connection.[3]

The purpose of this article is to provide a comparative analysis of the welfare contributions of Sidgwick and Pigou. The study will bring to light the similarities and differences between Pigou's work and the earlier work of Sidgwick and show how Pigou modernized Sidgwick's thoughts by imposing Marshallian analytics on them.

II. *The Measurement of Welfare*

Despite semantical differences, the similarities between the basic welfare considerations of Pigou and Sidgwick are obvious. Sidgwick and Pigou both sought to maximize the same general welfare criterion based on utilitarian ethics. In the *Economics of Welfare*[4] Pigou popularized the word "welfare" as the embodiment of the utilitarian goals of happiness and well-being, and he concluded that increases in total welfare were the same as increases in economic welfare, but economic welfare had the advantage of being measured by the "measuring rod of money."

Sidgwick used more traditional utilitarian phrases to describe the

1. See E. Whittaker, *A History of Economic Ideas* (New York, 1940), pp. 163, 226, and 349; M. Blaug, *Economic Theory in Retrospect* (Homewood, Ill., 1968) pp. 80, 280, and 604; and J. Schumpeter, *History of Economic Analysis* (New York, 1954), pp. 408, 433, 540, 671, and 805–6.

2. T. W. Hutchison, *A Review of Economic Doctrines: 1870–1929* (Oxford, 1966), p. 50.

3. U. Hla Myint, *Theories of Welfare Economics* (Cambridge, Mass., 1948), p. 125, and W. Baumol, *Welfare Economics and the Theory of the State* (New York, 1952), p. 130.

4. An extension of *Wealth and Welfare*, published in 1912, the *Economics of Welfare* (1920) was a revision and explanation of key points. The following abbreviations will be employed in making reference to the main works of Pigou cited here:

EW:	*Economics of Welfare* (4th ed., London 1932).
SAL:	"State Action and Laissez-faire," in *Economics in Practice* (London, 1939); p. 112–28.
SAWE:	"Some Aspects of Welfare Economics," *American Economic Review* 41 (June 1951): 287–302.

social optimum—"some desirable result not for an individual but for a political community or aggregate of such communities."[5] He sought the greatest (community) utility or satisfaction from some action. Furthermore, Sidgwick examined the possibility of adopting some money measure of well-being, but concluded that owing to the difficulties in measuring wealth and value, "the real exactness of economic . . . estimates is generally overrated" (p. 397). The concept and the problems of welfare measurement were not ignored by Sidgwick, but were couched in more traditional terms.

However, in "Some Aspects of Welfare Economics" (1951; SAWE 287–302) Pigou's approach to the concept of welfare parallels Sidgwick's in terminology as well as in thought. Pigou wrote:

> Welfare economics is concerned to investigate the dominant influence through which the economic welfare of the world, or of a particular country, is likely to be increased. The hope of those who pursue it is to suggest lines of action—or non-action—on the part of the State or of private persons that might foster such influences [SAWE 287].

Pigou continued with the comment that money measures are not accurate, and that satisfaction must be compared "in principle." And finally, in examining the meaning of "satisfaction," he concluded that satisfaction is synonymous with utility, and therefore man's welfare is made up of his utilities. This is no more than a repetition of the basic logic behind Marshall's system, but the point is clear. Pigou's concept of "welfare" is not clearly a progression over utilitarian concepts, *and*, since in the last resort Pigou reverted to the use of "utility" to connote his ideas, he himself may have doubted the clarity of his advance.

The *Economics of Welfare* is built around the concept of welfare as defined and related to the size and distribution of the *national dividend*. Although Pigou's analysis of the problem of improving social welfare has as one of its starting points Marshall's doctrine of maximum satisfaction, as his thoughts proceeded he sought a general framework for investigation. He eschewed Marshall's partial equilibrium consumers' surplus approach, leaving Marshall's analysis for use in solving specific cases.

To examine a movement toward higher social satisfaction Pigou set up dual criteria: first, an increase in the national dividend without

5. H. Sidgwick, *The Principles of Political Economy* (3d ed., London 1924). Compare this with Oser's implication that Pigou is to be credited with the emphasis on the fact that the welfare of each need not imply the welfare of all; see J. Oser, *The Evolution of Economic Thought* (New York, 1970), p. 379.

any increase in the supply factors, and second, a transfer of wealth from the rich to the poor:

> (1) Generally speaking economic causes act upon the economic welfare of any country, not directly, but through the making and using of that objective counterpart of economic welfare which economists call the national dividend or national income [EW 31].
>
> (2) Any cause which increases the absolute share of real income in the hands of the poor, provided that it does not lead to a contraction in the size of the national dividend from any point of view, will, in general, increase economic welfare [EW 91].

In regard to the first criterion, Pigou's thought can be interpreted as meaning that where there are insurmountable difficulties in measuring the national dividend as a total figure, an increase in its total value—brought about either by increasing some good without diminishing others or by transferring factors to activities in which their social value is higher—is deemed an improvement in welfare, provided that the share of the poor is not thereby reduced. As for the second criterion, Pigou asserts that any reorganization of the economy which increases the share of the poor without diminishing the national dividend is accepted as a gain in social welfare.[6]

Like Pigou, Sidgwick specified the signs which would indicate an increase in welfare. In the Art of Political Economy, Book II of his *Principles*, Sidgwick examined the criteria to be used in determining an increase in community happiness: (1) to make "the proportion of produce to population a maximum, taking generally as a measure the ordinary exchange value, so far as it can be applied," and (2) to "rightly" distribute "produce among members of the community, whether on any principle of equity or justice, or on the economic principle of making the whole product as useful as possible" (p. 397). It can be seen that Sidgwick's first proposition states that the maximization of the national dividend is one goal in establishing the highest level of social well-being, and the second proposition seeks a redistribution of income consistent with some (undefined) sense of justice or consistent with the maximization of total social utility. The similarities between Sidgwick's propositions and Pigou's are evident.

6. Between 1912 and 1924 Pigou included a third main proposition to advancing economic welfare (in *Wealth and Welfare* and the first edition of the *Economics of Welfare*, but withdrawn in subsequent editions): "any cause which diminishes the variability of the national dividend, provided that it neither diminishes its volume nor injures its distribution, will, in general, increase economic welfare." This case for macroeconomic stability was later dropped as a welfare consideration. See T. W. Hutchison, *Positive Economics and Policy Objectives* (Cambridge, 1964), pp. 144f.

The first proposition espoused by each offers no problem. Increases in the value of the national dividend as an indication of increases in the welfare of the community are usually accepted without question. But the second proposition does create a difficulty. Marshall had observed that one of the major criticisms of his doctrine of maximum satisfaction was that it assumed that the marginal utility of income was the same for all. He said that the negation of this fact in reality made his doctrine limited in practical applications. Pigou used his second proposition—that transfers of money from the rich to the poor increased total satisfactions—*based* on the assumption of diminishing marginal utility of income. In defense of this position he wrote:

> This reasoning will not appeal to anyone who believes that people [who] are now rich are different from people now poor, having in their fundamental nature greater capacities for enjoyment. . . . I see no reason for believing anything of the sort. If we agree that representative members of the two groups are probably by and large pretty much alike, the argument from the law of diminishing marginal utility holds [SAWE 300].

Although Sidgwick doesn't specifically mention the assumption of diminishing marginal utility of income in his proposition, it is implicit in his concept of an "equitable" or "just" distribution.[7] This is especially true in the light of his qualifying phrase regarding maximizing *total* utility; his specification of "making the whole produce as useful as possible" should be considered an extension of his thought "that any given quantum of wealth is generally likely to be less useful to its owner, the greater the total of private wealth of which it forms a part" (*Principles*, p. 160).

Therefore, in identifying welfare and in the general qualifications for a welfare criterion, Pigou is not original. He used Marshall's doctrine of maximum satisfaction as a starting point, but using it alone would not have yielded any positive results for a full analysis of welfare. Therefore, Pigou looked at Sidgwick's pre-Marshallian analysis—and here he was able to find a clear meaning for "welfare." Not only was the terminology consistent with Pigou's need for the examination of how to maximize the total well-being of the community, but also in Sidgwick's work, the extension of Pigou's basic criteria can be found.

7. Sidgwick noted the relativity of justice. Each country and age decides its own code: "Actual human beings will not permanently acquiesce in a social order that common moral opinion deems unjust." In the context of the "justice" of socialism Sidgwick expressed a Millian idea: "I object to socialism not because it would divide the products of industry badly, but because it would have so much less to divide." See *Principles*, pp. 499, 516.

Pigou sought an organized analysis of the whole question of economic welfare. With this goal in mind, he presented his two propositions. Sidgwick had analyzed these propositions more than a half-century before.

III. *Marginal Social Net Product Versus Marginal Private Net Product*

To explain the divergences from the welfare maximum, Pigou introduced the terms marginal social net product and marginal private net product. In this, his work was genuinely innovative. He clarified and identified the general case of divergence and could apply it to specific instances. Sidgwick, also, had a generalized concept of divergences from the welfare maximum. However, it was less concise than Pigou's. This section will examine the similarities of these general concepts.

After having defined welfare and specified how changes in it could occur, Pigou remarked that many imperfections and many obstacles to the most efficient use of social resources remain, "although the free play of self-interest, so far as it is not hampered by ignorance, tends, in the absence of costs of movement, so to distribute resources among different uses and places as to render rates of return everywhere equal" (EW 144). In order to discuss optimal production in cases where the price system proved inefficient, Pigou introduced the terms marginal social net product and marginal private net product. These he defined and explained:

> (1) marginal social net product is the total net product of physical things or objective services due to the marginal increment of resources in any given use or place, no matter to whom any part of this product may accrue. It might happen . . . that costs are thrown upon people not directly concerned, through, say, uncompensated damage done to surrounding woods by sparks from railway engines. All such effects must be included—some of them will be positive, others negative elements—in reckoning up the social net product of the marginal increment of any volume of resources turned into any use or place, and
>
> (2) marginal private net product is that part of the total net product of physical things or objective services due to the marginal increment of resources in any given use or place which accrues in the first instance, i.e., prior to sale—to the person responsible for investing resources there [EW 134].

Pigou thought that only when marginal private and marginal social net product were identical would the free action of the price system result in the maximization of the national dividend and, hence, the maximization of social welfare.

Sidgwick saw variations in public and private *utilities* which are quite similar to Pigou's concept of "net product." Some examples of Sidgwick's variations in welfare due to variations in net product or utility are (1) in the case of land:

> the theoretical question is simply whether the whole amount of utility obtainable when the land is allotted to the exclusive use of individuals is clearly greater or less than the whole amount of utility that may be expected to result from leaving it common.[8]

And (2) in the case of railroads:

> where private enterprise may be socially uneconomical because the undertaker is able to appropriate not less but more than the whole net gain to the community of his enterprise; for he may be able to appropriate the main part of the gain of a change causing both gain and loss, while the concomitant loss falls entirely on others.[9]

And (3) in the case of natural resources:

> where it is the duty of the Government as representing the community to prevent the bounties of nature from being wasted by the unrestricted use for private interest.[10]

The divergence between private and social benefits is clearly expressed by Sidgwick in all these circumstances. However, marginal considerations were not part of Sidgwick's analysis. The search for a social optimum based on changes in total utility—either greater or less utility due to social or private ownership or control of a resource—was his main concern.[11]

Furthermore, Pigou specified external effects in production as

8. H. Sidgwick, *The Elements of Politics*, 2d ed. (London, 1897), p. 76.

9. *Principles*, p. 408; Pigou (EW 188–90) referred to this specific line of reasoning as a "somewhat specious fallacy." "Marginal social net product is not different from marginal private net product in this case for whatever loss the old producers suffer through a reduction in the price of their products is balanced by the gain which the reduction confers upon the purchases of these products." Sidgwick was concerned with the over-investment of resources in capital intensive increasing returns industries, as an indication of the loss of total utility to the community; Pigou's balancing on the margin does not account for this.

10. *Elements*, p. 147.

11. It should be noted it is precisely this point—that "total conditions of the Optimum are more important than the Marginal Conditions"—which is the main criticism against Pigou's analysis; see E. J. Mishan, "A Survey of Welfare Economics 1939–59," *Economic Journal* 70 (June 1960): 197–266.

examples of a positive element in "reckoning up the social net product":

> Again an increase in the quantity of resources employed by one firm in an industry may give rise to external economies in the industry as a whole and so lessen the real costs involved in the production by other firms of a given output [EW 134].

He also specified external effects in consumption:

> For some purposes it is desirable to count in also indirect effects induced in people's tastes and in the capacity to derive satisfaction from their purchases and possessions [EW 135].

But the continuation of the discussion is most important; Pigou concluded with this:

> Our principle objective, however, is the national dividend and changes in it. . . . Therefore, psychical consequences are excluded, and the marginal social net product of any given volume of resources is taken, except when special notice to the contrary is given to consist of physical elements and objective services also [EW 135].

It is apparent that Pigou was attempting to refine Marshall's consumers' and producers' surplus analysis and to incorporate it into the concept of total welfare maximization by suggesting the balancing of advantages and disadvantages of different producers.[12] But Pigou limits his discussion to "physical elements and objective services," which suggests his stress on production externalities rather than consumption externalities.[13]

Sidgwick's work on the other hand, was more involved with consumption externalities. Although his measurement of welfare changes

12. Pigou varies from Marshall here mainly in method. He uses the marginal apparatus to deal with small changes in economic welfare, while Marshall uses surplus analysis to analyze larger units of economic welfare.

13. Pigou underplayed consumption external effects because they were less determinate, less able to give analysis that would "bear fruit," not just "shed light," than externalities in production; but even so, his analysis "cannot be made rigorous" and "is frankly normative and geared to practical application." See M. Blaug, *Economic Theory in Retrospect* (Homewood, Ill., 1968). Hutchison in his *A Review* (p. 233) remarks that by 1939 "the bottom seems to have fallen out of the 'fruit' market." Pigou, "Presidential Address (Reminiscences of Changes in the Economics Profession)," *Economic Journal* 49 (June 1939): 220–221, wrote, "the hope that an advance in economic knowledge will appreciably affect actual happenings, I fear, is a slender one. It is not likely that there will be a market for our produce. Nonetheless, by sort of reflex activity, we cultivate our garden. For we also follow, not thought, but an impulse to inquire—which, futile though it may prove, it is at least not ignoble."

was the same as Pigou's he stressed changes in consumer satisfaction as a means to alter social well-being (*Elements*, p. 12). This can be observed in two fundamental ways to promote happiness through law (they both are expressed in terms of individual happiness): (1) the government may aim at making each of the individuals to whom its commands are addressed promote his own happiness better than he would without interference, and (2) the government may make each individual's conduct more conducive to the happiness of others (ibid.). The first class of laws, were admittedly "paternal," and Sidgwick accepted their justification with some reservation. The second class of laws, however, led him to the consideration of externalities—specifically in consumption.

Therefore, through an analysis of the reasons for general divergences from a welfare optimum, both Pigou and Sidgwick are led to examine cases of external effects. Pigou followed Marshall's direction and concentrated on production externalities, with the object of pursuing tax-bounty analysis (as we shall see in a later section). Sidgwick concentrated on external effects in consumption. However, the fundamental thoughts on general divergences from a welfare maximum are essentially the same.

IV. *Divergences*

Pigou analyzed three principal groups of specific "divergences" where marginal social net product did not equal marginal private net product. The divergence in each group arose out of the fact that under pure competition "in some occupations, a part of the product of a unit of resources consists of something, which, instead of being sold by the investor, is transferred, without gain or loss to him, for the benefit or damage of other people" (EW 175). The three cases were tenancy and ownership, neighborhood effects, and increasing returns industries. In contrasting these cases with Sidgwick's thoughts on the same topics, Pigou's reliance on Sidgwick's ideas is clearly demonstrated.

1. *Tenancy and ownership*

The first type of divergence which Pigou discusses arises in connection with those wasteful forms of tenancy of land or of other durable instruments of production, the repairs and improvements of which the tenant may have undertaken during his tenure. Pigou notes that the tenant will provide as little as possible in terms of maintenance or improvements (EW 175). Similar waste occurs when private companies are permitted to supply a town with gas or electricity or water on the condition that the plants of these companies pass into the hands of the municipality after a certain time without compensation (EW 176). The excessive rate of use of the resources involved results from the loose forms of tenancy which fail to impose "economic rent."

The main trouble here is the failure to introduce the competitive pricing process in these parts of the economic system. What is needed is not a correction of the private product to yield true social product, but actually a more accurate calculation of the private product from the standpoint of the resource owners.[14] Pigou seemed to recognize this as he noted that the solution lay in the provision of "legal security of tenure coupled with the legal prohibition of renting tenant's improvements" (EW 181). This would, therefore, specify the receiver of the economic rewards accruing to the improvements.

Sidgwick also realized the problems which occurred due to ill-defined property rights and the failure to define the recipient of economic rent.[15] He examined the case of ownership and tenancy in detail in his chapter on Rent (*Principles*, pp. 293–96). The similarity of Pigou's treatment of this problem with that of Sidgwick is striking; Pigou seems to have added little but historical examples of Sidgwick's original ideas. Sidgwick thought that the

> possibility of improvement and deterioration rendered it a matter of some difficulty to frame a rent-contract which shall give the farmer adequate inducement to treat the land in a manner most economical on the whole [p. 294].

His solution, similar to Pigou's, recognized the question of dubious property rights, but he added:

> each improvement [should] be made the subject of special agreement between the farmer and landlord—which practically requires the latter, or his agent, to take a certain share in the management of the farm [pp. 294–95].

It is especially noteworthy that Sidgwick had included in his analysis an important concept which Pigou had overlooked—a "mutual contracting" solution between the parties involved.[16] Sidgwick relied on this solution frequently throughout his work.

14. F. H. Knight, "Some Fallacies in the Interpretation of Social Cost," *Quarterly Journal of Economics* 38 (Aug. 1924): 582–606.

15. Sidgwick's views on the lighthouse as an example of a spillover benefit are well documented. However, he also examined the fisheries question and the problems involved with reforestation (see: *Principles*, p. 406).

16. Coase took the Pigovian tradition to task over Pigou's narrow and inapplicable solutions to internalizing externalities in R. Coase, "The Problem of Social Cost," *Journal of Law and Economics* 3 (Oct. 1960): 1–44. Coase's main argument is precisely for mutual recontracting solutions.

2. *Neighborhood effects—the problem*

The second type of divergence which Pigou examined was one in which the production of a commodity gives rise to incidental uncharged services or uncompensated disservices to a third party who is neither its producer nor consumer but who merely happens to be near the site of production. Pigou noted several cases which illustrate this point. The first is the lighthouse whose benefits are "enjoyed by ships on which no toll could be conveniently levied." He used two other "Sidgwick cases" —afforestation and scientific research—to show external effects for which free exchange does not provide adequate remuneration.[17] Pigou regarded the services of the lighthouse or research worker as a "new commodity" for which latent consumers' demand exists and which can, therefore, generate a great deal of consumers' surplus. However, it is not produced, because the producers' surplus is negative or zero. Consequently, a genuine divergence between marginal social net product and marginal private net product exists.

Pigou added a list of social economies and diseconomies which result from urbanization and industrialization: (1) private parks which, even though public admittance is prohibited, improve the air of the neighborhood, (2) roads and tramways, which increase the value of adjoining land, (3) lamps erected at the doors of private houses which necessarily throw light on the streets, and (4) smoke from factory chimneys which injures buildings and vegetables, dirties clothes and rooms, and makes artificial light a necessity.[18] In all these cases, as in the case of the lighthouse, there are obvious divergences between private and social product.

Although the main thrust of his analysis concerned changes in production to alleviate divergences between marginal social net product and marginal private net product, Pigou did mention several cases of consumption externalities which lead to divergence also. First, he saw the external effects in the offense to public taste by the production and sale of intoxicants. He also noted the injurious effects on the health of children and women caused by allowing women to work in factories, "particularly during the periods immediately preceding and succeeding confinement" (SAWE 187). He viewed this latter example as "the crowning illustration of this order of excess of private over social net product" (ibid.).

17. In relation to scientific research, Pigou (EW 185) noted (as Sidgwick, *Principles*, p. 443, did before him) that "patent laws aim, in effect, at bringing marginal private net product and marginal social net product more closely together."

18. It is interesting that Pigou's "disservice connected with the running of motor cars" was that they wear out the surface of the roads; see SAWE 186.

Sidgwick's discussion of external effects can be compared with Pigou's on two points—one major point which Pigou made, the lighthouse case, and the second, which Pigou considered a minor point, the sale of intoxicants and the health of working women and children. In relation to the lighthouse case, there is hardly anything more to be said than that Pigou repeated an example of externalities in production that Sidgwick had taken from Mill.[19] In relation to the paternalistic cases, Sidgwick, in keeping with his desire to search deeply into cases of external effects related to individuals, examined these in detail.

The question of the welfare of women and children was in keeping with the basic duties of government—to provide protection from force and fraud. Sidgwick remarked that the protection of children from mischief caused actively or through the neglect of their parents was an inherent duty of any government. To him the question of individual rights versus social rights was not legitimate here. He extended this analysis to include women during child-bearing and child-rearing years "as an indirect protection to the physical well being of children" (*Elements*, p. 140). For Sidgwick, then, this case was not under consideration as a possible instance for government interference, but fell within the essential *duties* of any established government.[20]

The same reasoning which applied to the restriction on the sale of intoxicants was applicable to the passing of legislation requiring sanitary housing conditions, Sidgwick thought. Since his analysis of housing conditions was more "economic" and free from "moral" implications, it will be used as the relevant example in this discussion. It should be noticed once again that in Sidgwick's analysis there is no concept of marginal conditions; the total welfare of society was his main concern, as he wrote:

> When a man is forced to cooperate with his fellow citizens in a common system of drainage and water supply, when he is prevented from using a house unfit for habitation, or from overcrowding any part of a house, it may be said that concern is applied to him in his own interest; and no doubt it is designed that he should derive benefit from the coercion; still its main justifica-

19. J. S. Mill, *Principles of Political Economy*, W. Ashley, ed. (New York, 1964), p. 975.

20. Sidgwick included among the basic *rights* of the individual, the right to smoke-free air and minimally congested neighborhoods: "The owner of a house is not merely protected against forcible entry of a stranger, but for the loss of utility caused by the pollution of the surrounding atmosphere." It is important to note that in *The Elements of Political Economy*, p. 69, Sidgwick does *not* suggest a mutual-contracting solution.

> tion lies in the need of protecting his children and neighbors who might suffer if his house became a focus of disease [*Elements*, p. 133].

The welfare of all would decline if the individual were free to comply with health measures or not as he wished, but the individual's welfare would also suffer if he did not cooperate. Therefore, partially, on the basis of the greatest good for the individual, Sidgwick justified legislation for the benefit of society; but more importantly, he justified it on the basis of the total welfare of the community.

3. *Neighborhood effects—the solution*

The variation found in Sidgwick's and Pigou's approaches to solving the divergence between social net product and private net product is consistent with the analysis presented by each. First, Sidgwick sought a total welfare solution in the light of undetermined property rights; his cases were generally external economies and diseconomies in consumption, and his solution was given in this prescription:

> how far such protection of A from indirect interference should be given, where it involves a material restriction on the freedom of action of other persons, can only be settled in any particular case by a careful balance of conflicting inconveniences [*Elements*, p. 69].

And regarding many questions of social versus private welfare, he remarked that "in any concrete case, the balance of utilities may be difficult to ascertain" (p. 66), and that the best way to solve each specific case is through "the aid of special experience on a balance of conflicting considerations" (pp. 75–76).

Pigou's solution to external effects was as determinate as Sidgwick's was indeterminate. He saw the mitigation of divergences between marginal and social net product and marginal private net product as infeasible on a person-to-person basis. True to his extension of Marshallian analysis, he believed that the state (if it so chooses) could remove the divergence in any field by "extraordinary restraints":

> a tax should be placed upon the production of goods where the private net product of any unit of investment is unduly large relative to the social net product, for example, alcoholic drinks, petrol duty, and motor-car license tax, [and] if the private net product of any unit of investment is unduly small in an industry, a

bounty should be provided by government, such as town planning and police administration [EW 193].[21]

The welfare effect of taxes on the consumption of products where the private net product was greater than the social net product was not overlooked by Sidgwick:

> taxes that reduce the consumption of commodities liable to be abused, such as alcoholic stimulants, tend to benefit consumers thus prevented from injuring themselves, and indirectly increase production by diminishing the loss of efficiency caused by such production [*Principles*, p. 578].

Sidgwick noted that the tax on the sale of opium and tobacco was an attempt to lower the quantity of the good demanded, for the welfare of society. He also noted that bounties could be an incentive for the provision of goods when the private net product was lower than the social net product as

> for the sake of some general utility which the competitive system cannot be trusted to provide; . . . if the price [that the government charges] be reduced below a certain point, a special bounty is conferred on the purchases at the expense of the rest of the community [*Principles*, pp. 554-55].

But even though it is clear that Sidgwick knew of the tax-bounty solution for internalizing external effects, he did not suggest it as a major policy measure to correct the problems of the free market to the extent that Pigou did. Sidgwick's main concentration was a balancing of rights—to maximize social justice as well as social welfare. He realized the existence of many techniques, but maintained that there remained no perfect solution to fit all the problems which were considered.

4. *Divergences from optimal social output due to industrial organization*

The third type of case which Pigou discussed concerned less than optimal output due to the industry's structure. The first case he dis-

21. The tax-bounty solution is the main aspect of the Pigovian tradition. W. J. Baumol, *Welfare Economics and the Theory of the State* (New York, 1952) suggests that, at best, the solution narrowly assumes that a few taxes and bounties will correct all the divergences of a free market system and therefore achieve some social welfare ideal. Much recent literature has been devoted to prove that Pigou's solution doesn't work. See: U. Hla Myint, *Theories of Welfare Economics* (Cambridge, Mass., 1948); J. Buchanan and W. Stubblebine, "Externality," *Economica*, n.s. 29 (Nov. 1962): 371-84; and W. J. Baumol, "On Taxation and Control of Externalities," *American Economic Review* 34 (June 1962): 127–51.

cussed under this heading involved the instance where the marginal social net product of the resources employed in an industry with "Decreasing Supply Price" is greater than their marginal private product. This is similar to Marshall's suggestion that subsidies should be given to increasing-returns industries.[22] Pigou took into consideration the opposite effect which occurs in industries of increasing cost and presented the general solution of "State bounties to industries in which condition of Decreasing Supply Price *simpliciter* are operating and State taxes upon industries in which conditions of Increasing Supply Price from the standpoint of the community are operating" (SAWE 224).

The second case Pigou discussed involved the fact that increasing-returns industries tended toward monopoly. This particular case of divergence from optimal output was well exemplified by the railway industry:[23]

> One of the notable instances of this is afforded by the industry of railway transportation along any assigned route. In view of the great cost of preparing a suitable way, it will, obviously, be much less expensive to have one or, at most, a few railways providing the whole of transport service between any two assigned points than to have this service undertaken by a great number of railways each performing an insignificant proportion of the whole service [SAWE 251].

In general, Pigou stated, "where the gain from unification exceeds the cost and trouble involved, unification will occur" (SAWE 264). The solution proposed was a government commission to regulate price.[24]

The final divergence between private and social net product was exemplified in the case of monopolistic competition—specifically, in relation to advertising outlays. Pigou noted that advertising expenditures of competitive firms not only involve considerable expense but frequently neutralize one another or, at best, lead to substitution between similar goods. Since investment in advertising is likely to yield a social net product less than the private net product, he suggested either no-advertisement agreements (like barristers and doctors) or tax-

22. For a detailed explanation of the problems involved with Pigou's analysis, see U. Hla Myint, *Theories of Welfare Economics*.

23. He noted that the same holds true for water, gas, electricity, or tramway service.

24. The problem of establishing price in these industries was examined by Pigou in his analysis of discriminating monopoly pricing. His main point was that "while no uniform price can be found which will cover the expense of producing any quantity of output, a system of discriminating prices is practical that will make some output profitable" (see SAWE 308).

ation and prohibition of certain types of advertising by the state. Once again, Pigou sought to optimize output by taxing away negative external effects.

Sidgwick discussed the detrimental effects of a monopoly market structure—"the important class of cases in which the individuals have an adequate motive for rendering *some* service to society, but not for rendering as much service as it is in their power to render" (*Principles*, p. 149). But he recognized that these monopolistic cases occur because "a decided economic gain [is] to be obtained by that organization of a whole department of production under a single management . . . from the saving of labor and capital it renders possible" (ibid.). In the case of decreasing-cost industries, such as the provision of water and electricity to towns, a "practical monopoly (is) manifestly the most economic arrangement" (*Principles*, p. 445).[25] Sidgwick's solution was to allow government intervention, either ownership or control. Although he did not recognize pricing problems which differed because of differing elasticities of demand, he did not extend the analysis into the area of public utilities (*Principles*, pp. 343-47).

Sidgwick was concerned with the "waste incident to the individualistic organization of industry"—specifically, advertising costs in monopolistically competitive industries. He noted the case where there exist many producers who have difficulty in finding customers and who rely on "forming and maintaining the habits" of customers they get. The expenditure incurred for the sole purpose of "finding purchasers" is a social waste and "a large part of the cost of advertisements, of agents and 'travellers,' of attractive shop-fronts, etc., comes under this head" (*Principles*, p. 47). He did not suggest government action here, however, but merely remarked upon the deficiency of the system.

Therefore, in relation to the divergences between private net product and social net product, Pigou's and Sidgwick's analyses are in more respects similar than dissimilar. On tenancy and ownership, the analysis keyed around the recognition of the fact that property rights are inadequately defined. The divergence which results due to externalities is sufficiently covered by Sidgwick as well as Pigou. It should be noted that Pigou's attempt to use Marshallian market analysis to discuss total welfare led to some basic problems of transition. Finally, in relation to problems involving industry market structure, Pigou relies heavily on Marshall's ideas and terminology for decreasing-cost

25. This also applies to public utilities construction and the maintenance of roads, bridges, canals, railways, harbors, and lighthouses.

industries, but Sidgwick has written enough to indicate his thorough understanding of the problem also. Consequently, an analysis of these divergences has shown that although Marshall's influence on the direction of Pigou's thought is obvious, Sidgwick's ideas undoubtedly formed a good part of his basic analysis.

V. *Pigou's Ideas on the Limits to Government Intervention*

The analysis of Pigou's relation to Sidgwick's work has shown that he leaned heavily on the ideas of the new concept of government action which Sidgwick had so thoroughly analyzed. His analysis was constructed to help an economy structured on capitalistic ideas to better promote social well-being. Large measures of government intervention were not part of his system. Pigou, like Mill and Sidgwick, suggested tinkering with the laissez-faire system to achieve the desired social output.

Pigou was wary of government intervention and government operation of industry, and he freely admitted that "under any form of State control over private monopoly . . . a considerable gap between the ideal and the actual is likely to remain" (SAWE 379). Consequently, Pigou sought the solution to the problem of "natural monopolies" in regulatory agencies. His description of the industries which could best be run by government has a very Marshallian ring: "those industries [which] have been reduced more or less to routine and in which there is comparatively little scope for daring adventure" (SAWE 405). Throughout most of his work Pigou used Marshall's thoughts to yield determinate answers to policy questions. He would propose some specific solution and present it as a rule for real decision making.

However, a later work of Pigou's gives the reader a somewhat different impression. In 1939 he reexamined the conflicting concepts of state action and laissez-faire. He reiterated the major point he had made in defense of state action in the *Economics of Welfare* and presented specific cases to demonstrate these. But a notable change is evident in the conclusion to his article. Pigou's works suggest an *attitude* change—away from the exactness of a follower of Marshall towards a philosophy with a definite Sidgwick-type reasoning:

> The moral is plain. The issue about which popular writers argue—the principle of laissez-faire versus the principle of state action—is not an issue at all. There is no principle involved on either side. Each particular case must be considered on its own merits in all details of its concrete circumstances. . . . Accumula-

tion of evidence, the balancing of probabilities, judgment of men, by these alone practical problems in this region can be successfully attacked [SAL 217-18].

Therefore, Pigou's return to Sidgwick's school of thought was now not only implied but also admitted. He admitted that to maintain that within a competitive system market failure is unimportant is as foolish as claiming that government action can solve all problems. Pigou's final selection of "the balancing of conflicting circumstances" approach completes his confirmation as a disciple of Sidgwick's philosophy.

VI. *Concluding Remarks*

Pigou's contribution to welfare economics is undeniable. As Marshall's successor he had a tailor-made audience. The ideas he supported became part of the mainstream of economic thought.

Pigou began his investigation of welfare with Marshallian analytical concepts, but returned to Sidgwick not only for a philosophical foundation but also for practical applications of and solutions to welfare problems. Furthermore, it must be noted that the main point upon which Pigou's analysis was subsequently criticized was not the philosophical thought of Sidgwick, but rather, Pigou's unsuccessful attempt to impose Marshallian ideas on top of them.

Although Sidgwick's work has not been recognized as pivotal in welfare theory, the comparison between Pigou and Sidgwick clearly demonstrates the fact that it does contain the components essential to the theoretic welfare base. Like Sidgwick, Pigou clarified welfare in terms of "utility"; he set out criteria for increasing welfare in terms of Sidgwick's two propositions; and he analyzed the divergences from optimum output with ideas that can be found scattered throughout Sidgwick's writings.

There is no doubt that Pigou gave welfare economics a name and defined categories for organization and discussion, but there should also be little doubt that many of the basic ideas that Pigou used were not original with him, but were the work of Sidgwick. Pigou reinstated Sidgwick's ideas into the prevailing current of economic thought; however, their penultimate source should be appreciated.

[11]

The Economic Journal, **93**, (*June* 1983), 411–414
Printed in Great Britain

PIGOU ON EXPECTATIONS AND THE CYCLE

David A. Collard

This note draws attention to Pigou's treatment of rational expectations and the 'surprise' supply function. In modern terminology he argued that:

1. equilibrium and rationality implied the absence of systematic forecasting errors,
2. monetary factors could independently affect output only by means of unanticipated inflation (deflation).

But that:

3. asymmetrical errors due to 'psychological causes' could be a separate source of fluctuations and, what is more, could be set up in response to the monetary factors in 2.

In order to establish these points it will be necessary to quote from Pigou's more substantial works on macro-economics; *Industrial Fluctuations* (IF), *The Theory of Unemployment* (TU) and *Employment and Equilibrium* (EE). His treatment of expectations was by no means incidental for,

> 'the varying expectations of business men...and not anything else, constitute the immediate and direct causes or antecedents of industrial fluctuations' (IF, pp. 33–4; EE, p. 214).

These expectations could concern real factors (harvests, innovations, discoveries, disputes, tastes) but could also, in principle, be an independent source of fluctuations (see IF, pp. 83–90). Having distinguished between the Classical Stationary State, in which net investment was zero, and short-period flow equilibrium, Pigou insisted that expectations must be fulfilled as a condition even of the latter;

> over any period for which short-period flow equilibrium rules, expected prices...must be equal to actual prices (EE, p. 36).

But

> future prices (are)...expected to be different from actual prices. So long as any expectation of this kind is present the system is not in short period flow equilibrium (EE, p. 244).

A more explicit 'rational expectations' point had earlier been made in *Industrial Fluctuations*

> in a stationary state, or, more accurately a state of steady self-regulating movement, real causes of varying expectations could not, by definition, exist. Neither, as a matter of fact, though not of logic, could psychological causes exist, because, with everything repeating itself regularly, *rational beings would be bound to realise that this was happening, and so could not fall into error. In a non-stationary state peopled exclusively by perfectly intelligent persons*

> *psychological causes, as defined above, could not exist since they imply error*: but there would be nothing to prevent real causes from existing (IF, pp. 30–1), (italics added).

In spite of the above remarks Pigou evidently believed that 'psychological causes' could persist so that the system would fail to get into equilibrium. Thus expectations might be formed extrapolatively due to,

> our general tendency to expect processes that we observe in action now to continue in action at all events for some time to come (TU, p. 235).

And they might have to encompass genuine uncertainties, not merely routine risks, in which case,

> there is no secure basis of past experience to act as a guide (IF, p. 76).

Pigou believed that the methods of modern business made forecasting more important than it had previously been and that generalisation of errors was promoted by psychological interdependence among business men. He also believed that forecasting errors had a multiplicative rather than a mere additive effect so that in the system as a whole large net forecasting errors were possible. Though it is almost impossible to quantify these complex factors Pigou characteristically had a stab at doing so, asserting (IF, p. 199) that elimination of errors of optimism or pessimism would reduce industrial fluctuations by about half.

It was clear to Pigou that anticipated inflation could have no *independent* effect on output and that,

> if somehow errors of optimism and pessimism could be rendered impossible, little advantage would result from stabilising prices (IF, p. 189).

But unanticipated inflation could have an effect:

> if the trend of demand for money over a given period shows an annual increase of 3 per cent – and if the conditions governing the supply of money between any two years *change* in such a way as to cause the supply to grow by more or less than 3 per cent, there is a *monetary* cause making for industrial fluctuations (IF, pp. 192–3), (italics added).

Unanticipated inflations lead to real transfers in favour of debtors (principally business men)

> it is not the fact that changes in the price level occur, but that they occur without being perfectly foreseen that is responsible for realised losses and gains between creditors and debtors.
> transfers favourable to business men may be expected to induce in the actual world, some slight expansion in the real demand function for labour (TU, pp. 234, 235).

So much for realised gains and losses. Could there be *any* output effects arising from anticipated inflation? Pigou argued that there could be, if expectations were asymmetric:

> an expectation of upward price movements more marked among business men than among lenders must stimulate a real demand for labour (TU, p. 242).

The asymmetry or heterogeneity of expectations had been clearly set out in IF:

> Suppose that prices are really going to rise 10 per cent. If both borrowers and lenders think that they are going to rise 0 per cent or to fall 20 per cent or to rise 100 per cent, both will agree to adjust the money rate of interest (and of wages) to the expected change, and business men will not expect either to reap benefit or to suffer loss from monetary movements. If, however, borrowers and lenders think different things, the fact of their difference – the inequality between their forecasts – gives ground for altered expectations of profit (IF, pp. 163–4).

The effect is somewhat marred in an erroneous footnote but the point remains. Compounding this error of business optimism:

> though the typical business man will often expect that the general level of prices is going to rise, he will often also expect that the price of his own particular commodity is going to rise *relatively* to other commodities (IF, p. 190).

Pigou stated, but did not acquiesce in, the New Classical Macroeconomics conclusion about cycle policy:

> the old doctrine of the economic harmonies...taught that, in general, the pursuit by individuals of their private self-interest will make the sum of economic satisfactions a maximum, subject to the fact that the surrounding facts are what they are...whatever causes and conditions of industrial fluctuations may be in play, such reactions to them as are worth their cost will already have taken place, as it were automatically, and, therefore, there is no room for anything further (IF, p. 225).

Indeed he advocated various policy measures though he did not consider the statistical Phillips' curve type of relationship, described in IF (charts facing pp. 150, 194), to represent an available policy trade-off. Modest attempts to even out booms and slumps were permissible but deliberate resort to deficit finance was only to be contemplated at a time of 'national catastrophe' (IF, p. 93). Indeed Pigou came to adopt an accelerationist position (Collard, 1981) but that discussion is beyond the scope of this note.

Pigou's reflections are much more thorough than those of Marshall and would repay deeper study. At the very least they show his criticism of Keynes' *General Theory* (Pigou, 1950) for its lack of a properly worked out theory of expectations to have been no idle grumble.

University of Bath

Date of receipt of final typescript: *November* 1982

REFERENCES

Pigou, A. C. (1927). *Industrial Fluctuations*. Macmillan.
—— (1933). *The Theory of Unemployment*. Macmillan.
—— (1941). *Employment and Equilibrium*. Macmillan.
—— (1950). *Keynes' 'General Theory': A Retrospective View*. Macmillan.
Collard, D. A. (1981). 'A C Pigou'. In *Pioneers of Modern Economics in Britain* (ed. D. P. O'Brien and J. R. Presley). Macmillan.

[12]

Journal of Economic Literature
Vol. XXII (June 1984), pp. 507–530

Were the Ordinalists Wrong About Welfare Economics?

By

ROBERT COOTER
University of California, Berkeley

and

PETER RAPPOPORT
New York University

Useful comments on earlier drafts were provided by Sean Flaherty, Marcia Marley, Tim Scanlon, Andrew Schotter, Mark Schankerman, Lloyd Ulman and two anonymous referees. We are grateful to the National Science Foundation and the C. V. Starr Center at New York University for financial support. Responsibility for accuracy rests with the authors.

THE DEVELOPMENT of utility theory has experienced two definitive episodes: the "marginalist revolution" of the 1870s and the "Hicksian" or "ordinalist revolution" of the 1930s. While the first event established a central place for utility theory in economics, the second restricted the concept of utility acceptable to economics. The term "ordinalist revolution" refers to the rejection of cardinal notions of utility and to the general acceptance of the position that utility was not comparable across individuals. The purpose of this paper is to analyze the events comprising the ordinalist revolution with a view to determining whether they achieved the advances in economic science usually claimed for them.

The developments of the 1930s are often regarded as unambiguous progress in economics.[1] The intuitive idea of scientific progress is that new theories are discovered that explain more than old theories. We shall contend that the ordinalist revolution was not scientific progress in this sense. For example, the older school was concerned with economic policies to bring about income redistribution and alleviate poverty, and the ordinalists did not offer a more general theory for solving these problems. Instead, the trick that carried the day for the ordinalists was to argue that the questions asked by the older school, and the answers which they gave,

[1] For example, Kenneth Arrow, referring to the earlier school, wrote:

> . . . the proponents of measurable utility have been unable to produce any proposition of economic behavior which could be explained by their hypothesis and not by those of the indifference-curve theorists [1963, p. 9].

were meaningless.[2] We shall argue that ordinalists offered different questions, not better answers. Thus, the ordinalist revolution represented a change, not progress in economics.

In order to understand why the questions asked by the older school seemed meaningless to the ordinalists, it is necessary to understand the dramatic change in the *conceptual framework* of economics. Important elements of a conceptual framework are a definition of the subject matter to be studied, a method of investigation and proof, and some substantive empirical claims. The older framework defined economics as the science of "material welfare"[3] and employed an empiricist methodology. In addition, its practitioners held that their conception of utility was comparable across people. The newer framework adopted a scarcity definition of economics, and employed a positivist methodology. The salient feature of utility was held to be its ordinal nature.

The elements of the newer framework—the scarcity definition, positivist methodology, and ordinal utility—are familiar to contemporary economists. In contrast, the elements of the older framework—the material welfare definition, empiricist methodology, and interpersonal utility—are now viewed through the distorting lens of the ordinalist framework.

This essay aims to help the reader to recover a clear view of the older framework and to understand why it was rejected by the ordinalists.

In order to avoid misunderstanding, we shall offer a brief explanation in contemporary economic language of the material welfare conception of interpersonal utility. Economists of the older school are often characterized as having relied extensively on the belief that utility is cardinally measurable (unique up to a positive affine transformation), a belief that cannot be validated by examination of consumer behavior, and one that is unnecessary for deriving results in the theory of consumer demand. We do not consider in detail whether economists at the turn of the century believed individual utility to be cardinally measurable, since this issue is tangential to the question of interpersonal comparisons. Instead, we concentrate on the special assumptions concerning utility that justified the interpersonal comparisons made by these economists.

The different roles of assumptions about measurability and comparability of utility can be elucidated by borrowing from the modern approach to social welfare theory (for example, Amartya Sen 1977). Let each individual $i = 1, 2$ be represented by a set, L_i, of utility functions. Each utility function is defined over the set of social states, and, for the present purpose, is best regarded simply as a list of numbers, one for each state. Measurability assumptions restrict L_i to particular classes of functions or, equivalently, particular lists of numbers. For example, if utility is cardinally (ordinally) measurable, then each L_i will contain functions or sets of numbers that are related to each other by positive linear (monotone) transformations.

In this framework, we may view the problem of making interpersonal comparisons of utility as that of selecting a utility function from each L_i. This determines the magnitude of the number that will

[2] The following is a partial list of questions that material welfare economists claimed to answer and ordinalists claimed were unanswerable by economics: Is a dollar more valuable to the average poor person than to the average rich person? Should economists give different weight to additional income for the rich and poor when doing cost-benefit analysis? Does a hungry person need food more than a bored person needs theater tickets? If income is redistributed to the poor, with no change in total income, does national welfare go up or down? Is there an economic justification for progressive income tax schemes?

[3] In his *Essays on the Nature and Significance of Economic Science* Lionel Robbins stated that this was "(t)he definition of Economics which would probably command most adherents, at any rate in Anglo-Saxon countries" (1937 [1932], p. 4).

represent each person's utility in comparisons. For reasons explained below, we will call such a choice a "comparability convention." In general, there will be comparability conventions from which it will follow that person 1 derives more utility than 2 in a particular state, and conventions that entail the reverse.[4] In particular, even if individual utility is cardinally measurable, it can be seen that the L_i have not been restricted sufficiently to make the outcome of a comparison independent of the comparability convention adopted. For example, one can find a pair of utility functions for which the state that yields 1 lowest utility has a higher number attached to it than 2's highest utility state, and a pair for which the reverse occurs. A fortiori, we are not prevented from employing conventions that yield these results when utility is ordinally measurable.

It is apparent from the above that the "arbitrariness" involved in making interpersonal comparisons arises from the difficulty of discriminating among comparability conventions. Restricting the L_i by appeal to the standard measurability conditions does not materially limit the number of possible comparability conventions.

As we shall see, the material welfare school did opt for a particular comparability convention, and evaluated social welfare on the basis of it. This choice could be defended in the context of the interpretation of utility employed by the material welfare school. Utility rankings were not seen as coextensive with preference orderings, nor were they derived from them. Essentially, goods were seen as having utility if they contributed to a person's physical well-being, which was conceived as nearly equivalent to productive capacity. Physical well-being is objective, like the condition of a person's health, not subjective, like a person's enjoyment of a good meal. Furthermore, productive capacity of people is closely related to economic efficiency, which is also objective.

When ordinalist writers criticized this comparability convention, they attributed to the material welfare school their own conception of utility rankings, derived from individuals' preference orderings. If utility is related to preference in this way, then interpersonal comparisons inevitably seem arbitrary, as if the writer were imposing his or her preferences on society. However, the material welfare school did not equate utility with preference.

The body of this paper examines the conceptual frameworks of the two schools. The substantial difference between them is offered as evidence against the view that the ordinalist revolution may be explained as part of the progress of economic science. The first section summarizes general developments in utility theory up to the early twentieth century. The next section describes the conceptual framework of the material welfare school. Following this, a comparison is made with the ordinalist school, which reveals that the two schools were using the common elements in their vocabularies to refer to different things. The final sections of the paper summarize the argument, and suggest lines along which to explain the success of the ordinalist view.

The aim of this paper is to demonstrate that the arguments developed some fifty years ago to criticize the material welfare school do not in fact address the claims of that school, whose scientific integrity remains intact. This suggests that it may be fruitful to draw on the material welfare perspective in the analysis of present-day

[4] This is so, even though, to be accurate, a comparability convention defines an equivalence class in L, the Cartesian product of L_1 L_2, in the sense that elements of this class will return the same results for interpersonal comparisons of utility. The class will contain elements of L that are related by positive monotone transformations. By this it is meant that the *same* positive monotone transformation is applied to every individual's utility function in the element selected by the comparability convention. This invariance condition is called "ordinal level comparability" by Sen (1977, p. 1542).

welfare problems, and perhaps warrants a comparison of the older view with the achievements of modern welfare economics. However, we stress that these issues are not pursued in the current research, which limits itself to recounting the development of doctrine. Consequently, we have concentrated only on the welfare problems stressed by the material welfare school, and contrast its work only with early ordinalist welfare economics.

I. *Utility Before the 1920s: Thumbnail History*

Contemporary economics offers a separate account of consumer and producer theory, then combines them together in an analysis of markets. The classical economic theories of Adam Smith, David Ricardo, and John Stuart Mill lacked a systematic account of consumer theory. Mill wrote:

> Political Economy . . . has nothing to do with the consumption of wealth, further than as the consideration of it is inseparable from that of production, or from that of distribution. We do not know of any laws of the consumption of wealth as the subject of a distinct science: they can be no other than the laws of human enjoyment [1844, p. 318].

Mill did not develop "laws of human enjoyment" to explain how consumers allocate expenditures among different commodities. He was a utilitarian who did not make utility maximization by consumers into an important element of economic theory.

One reason why utility theory was not of great significance to economics in the first three-quarters of the nineteenth century is explained by the "paradox of value." Since water had a high use-value but a low price, and the reverse held for diamonds, utility apparently was not the cause of price. With this dismissal, English economists concentrated on cost of production as the explanation of price.[5]

In England this situation persisted until W. Stanley Jevons (1871) demonstrated that the paradox of value could be resolved by associating price with the "final degree of utility," or marginal utility, rather than total utility. Using techniques of calculus, Jevons showed that equilibrium in exchange requires everyone to consume commodities in quantities such that the ratio of marginal utilities equals the price ratio for each pair of commodities.

This demonstration that mathematics could be used to fuse the theory of markets and the theory of utility convinced Jevons that it was wrong to separate them. He spoke out boldly on this matter: "Utility is plainly the subject-matter of economics from beginning to end" because "the object of Economics is to maximize happiness by purchasing pleasure, as it were, at the lowest cost of pain" (1905, p. 6 and 1911 [1871], p. 23). Jevons' contemporaries did not share his opinion of the significance of his discoveries, and although he did not die in obscurity, he did not receive the recognition that later generations have accorded him.[6] Nevertheless, research did continue in the same vein as Jevons', and by the turn of the century much progress had been made in the theory of price by economists of a mathematical bent, although few of them were in England.[7]

Vilfredo Pareto (1896, 1906) articulated a theory of markets based upon constrained optimization, and successfully integrated production into the marginal framework. This approach gave consumer demand equal standing relative to producer costs in determining prices, which conflicted with the older tradition of economic thinking. For example, the margin-

[5] Standard references are Mark Blaug (1978) and Joseph Schumpeter (1954).

[6] Jevons' disappointment at his lack of acclaim is displayed in a paper entitled "The Noxious Influence of Authority" (1871), and in Hutchison (1953, Ch. 2).

[7] Some details of the works of continental writers are given in Emil Kauder (1965).

alist theory denies that prices are proportional to the labor time needed for production, except in very restrictive circumstances. The cost-of-production theory of value was replaced by a theory of simultaneous determination of prices by consumers and producers.

The marginalists accomplished more than injecting consumer theory into the core of economics. From the standpoint of the history of ideas, they brought Newton's mathematics and Bentham's utilitarianism into intimate association with economic theory. The assimilation of Newtonian mechanics, which began in the 1870s and was completed in the 1940s, was decisive in establishing the mathematical character of economics. The assimilation of utilitarianism was decisive in policy science, because utilitarianism suggests ways to evaluate economic policies according to how efficiently they satisfy the wants and needs of individuals.

Measurability and Comparability of Utility

A question faced by the marginalists was whether their conception of utility was really the same as the concept that Jeremy Bentham (1948 [1776]) had made prominent in political philosophy and ethics. According to Bentham, under ideal conditions, utility can be treated as an observable quantity of pleasure with the same measurable properties as weight.[8] The utility of one person could be observed and added to another's if it were necessary to arrive at the total utility for society.

Among nineteenth century economists, opinion varied on the measurability of utility. Francis Y. Edgeworth proposed to measure utility in terms of the "just-noticeable differences" in pleasure experienced by an individual confronted with a series of choices (1961 [1881], p. 7–9, 60). By equating the just-noticeable difference in utility across people, Edgeworth proposed to carry out the utilitarian calculus.[9] In contrast, Jevons wondered whether it was possible to observe and compare individual utilities:

> The reader will find, again, that there is never in any single instance, an attempt made to compare the amount of feeling in one mind with that in another. I see no means by which such comparison can be accomplished. The susceptibility of one mind may, for what we know, be a thousand times greater than that of another. But, provided that the susceptibility was different in a like ratio in all directions, we should never be able to discover the difference. Every mind is thus inscrutable to every other mind, and no common denominator of feelings seem to be possible [1911 (1871) p. 14].[10]

When Jevons derived the conditions for equilibrium in exchange, he recognized that it was not necessary to add together the utilities of different people. Pareto and Fisher (1892) developed Jevons' observation mathematically by analyzing how much must be known about utility functions in order to compute a market equilibrium. Fisher summed up this information:

> Thus if we seek only the causation of the *objective facts of prices and commodity distribution* four attributes of utility as a quantity are entirely unessential, (1) that one man's utility can be compared to another's, (2) that for the same individual the marginal utilities at one consumption-combination can be compared with

[8] When Bentham takes up the issue of measurement (1948 [1776], Ch. IV) he describes the addition of the utilities of different people, which assumes that the utilities have the same properties as weight. However, he stresses that this exact process can be followed in ideal cases, but not in every case.

[9] For a discussion of Edgeworth's work, see Menahem Yaari (1981).

[10] Elsewhere, Jevons appears to have expressed a different opinion, indicating that records of transactions kept by commercial enterprises would afford the necessary data for measuring "pleasures and pains" (1911 [1871], pp. 10–11). Irving Fisher (1927, p. 158) offers this passage as evidence in favor of the view that Jevons considered utility to be measurable. It has also been pointed out by George J. Stigler (1950, p. 320) that Jevons implicitly employed interpersonal comparisons of utility in his reference to "trading bodies."

> those at another, or at one time with another, (3) even if they could, total utility and gain might not be integratable, (4) even if they were there would be no need of determining the constants of integration [1965 (1892), p. 89].

By 1900, therefore, there was no reason for anybody who was numerate to suppose that anything more than ordinal utility was required for price theory.[11]

Insights such as Fisher's are cited as reasons why concepts such as marginal utility were expelled from scientific economics. However, the ordinalist revolution occurred some forty years after publication of Fisher's book in 1892. Fisher and other pioneers of utility theory persisted in using utility concepts that went beyond ordinality in their published work. In the late 1920s Fisher was still trying to measure marginal utility.[12]

Why was the ordinalist revolution delayed so long after all the necessary discoveries were made? The answer lies in recognizing that price theory was not so central to economics until after the ordinalist revolution. Although concepts such as measurability and comparability of individuals' utility functions were known to be superfluous to price theory, they were not at the time superfluous to economics.[13] Economists retained a keen interest in the problems of producing and distributing necessities to alleviate want, which was principally the condition of physical deficiency that arose from poverty. For these purposes, it was desirable to have a conception of utility that was comparable among people.

II. *The Material Welfare School*

There were several schools of thought among economists, but by the 1920s the material welfare approach was followed by prominent academics constituting the mainstream of English economics.[14] This section will document this claim and at the same time extract from the classic texts the characteristics which define the material welfare school.

The conceptual framework offered by the material welfare school can be contrasted with contemporary ordinalism in terms of three central elements: the definition of economics, the conception of economic method, and substantive empirical claims about utility. The older definition of the subject focused upon material welfare, whereas the contemporary approach emphasizes scarcity. The older conception of method was called empiricism, whereas the contemporary method is positivism. Finally, the two approaches differ on the nature of the utility concept

[11] A reading of the appendices of Arthur C. Pigou (1920) and Alfred Marshall (1920 [1890]) will convince the reader that these economists' use of cardinal concepts did not result from limited mathematical vision.

[12] Cf. Fisher (1927). Ragnar Frisch's *New Methods of Measuring Marginal Utility* (1932) is dedicated: "To Irving Fisher, the pioneer of utility measurements."

[13] In his inaugural lecture at Cambridge, Marshall noted that a "task [that] most properly belongs to the economic organon" was the computation of benefits of industrial or social change, "taking account of the fact that the same sum of money measures a greater pleasure for the poor than for the rich" (1885, p. 31).

[14] The term "material welfare school" is our own, although, as we have mentioned above, Robbins (1937 [1932]) stated that material welfare was the subject matter of economics at the time. He ascribed the material welfare view to Edwin Cannan, Marshall, Pigou and John Bates Clark (1937 [1932], p. 11). Other writers use different categories. Schumpeter, for example, talks of a Marshallian school of thought, "the membership of which thought in terms of a well-defined scientific organon," but fails to elucidate its defining characteristics (1954, p. 833). Tibor Scitovsky (1951) talks of the "Cambridge School," and characterizes this as a group of practical men, with little patience for the gathering storm of theoretical problems attending their inferences, which finally swept them away with the publication of Robbins', *Essay* in 1932. Hla Myint identifies the "neoclassical school" of which Marshall, Cannan and Pigou are members (1948, p. 124). He also includes Joseph S. Nicholson, Henry Sidgwick, Frank W. Taussig and Allyn Young. This school is seen as straddling the classical "man against nature" and modern "subjective" views of economics. Myint is unclear as to the relationship of his neoclassical school with the scarcity school, as well as to the origins of the latter.

relevant for the analysis of economic behavior. We shall analyze each of these elements in turn.

Material Welfare Definition of Economics

The exposition of the conceptual framework of the material welfare school will refer mainly to Marshall, Cannan, and Pigou. In the 1920s Pigou's *Economics of Welfare* was used in teaching at Cambridge and Cannan's *Wealth* was the principal text for the "Elements of Economics" course taught at the London School of Economics (cf. London School of Economics, 1920–1940). Marshall's *Principles of Economics* had entered the intellectual culture as a classic and was still widely read.

As represented in these texts, economics confined itself to a part of the well-being of the community, to which Cannan referred as "material welfare" (1928 [1914], Ch. I), and Pigou as "economic welfare" (1932 [1920], Ch. I). The material welfare school made a distinction among the *types* of satisfactions that could be derived from goods. Indeed, goods, the motives for acquiring them and the satisfactions yielded by their consumption were arranged in a hierarchy that proceeded from the "purely economic" or "material" at one end to the purely noneconomic or nonmaterial at the other. It was stressed that there was no hard-and-fast line separating the economic part of the scale from the noneconomic, although the extremes were clearly distinguishable.[15] The material end of the hierarchy was concerned with survival and health. The goods that fell most securely within the purview of material welfare economics were food, "clothing, house-room and firing," followed by rest. These were dubbed "necessaries" by Marshall. As one proceeded further along the hierarchy, one came to "comforts" and "luxuries," whose material content was less certain (Marshall, 1920 [1890], p. 6).

According to Pigou, a reason for confining attention to the material or economic end of the scale was that it permitted exploitation of the form of measurement that was available to economists, the "measuring rod of money." Given the information that a person's income was a certain money value, under certain conditions, it could be inferred that they would enjoy material welfare of a level that could be purchased by that income.[16] However, it was far more difficult to establish a connection between increases in income and the other parts of welfare. Pigou cited several authors who testified to the deleterious spiritual effects of advances that had brought greater productivity and material wealth (1932 [1920], pp. 12–14). After considering these arguments, Pigou concluded it was likely that material and total welfare would be positively related (p. 20).

To make statements about the effects of policies on material welfare, at the aggregate level, a measure was required. Pigou proposed a partial ordering based upon the size and distribution of the "national dividend" or national product.[17] On the assumption that the rich spend so as to satisfy all their material wants, a redistribution in favor of the poor would permit more material wants to be satisfied. Thus, material welfare was said to increase if the distribution of the dividend shifted in favor of the poor, without decreasing

[15] Thus, Cannan maintained that, "Although everyone is agreed that the satisfaction of hunger is economic and the satisfaction that a Tibetan fanatic feels when he has himself immured for life in the dark is non-economic," it is possible to "proceed from the undoubtedly economic at one end of the scale to the undoubtedly non-economic at the other end without finding anywhere a fence to climb or a ditch to cross" (1928 [1914], p. 4).

[16] These conditions relate to the concept of rationality in the work of the material welfare school. See below, p. 516.

[17] This was the way in which Pigou planned to employ the "measuring rod of money" in the analysis of welfare (1932 [1920], p. 31).

its total (1932 [1920], p. 89). In addition, an increase in the dividend increased material welfare if the absolute share accruing to the poor did not fall. This measure is only partial because nothing can be inferred from an increase in the dividend accompanied by a decrease in the poor's share, or from a decrease in the dividend accompanied by an increase in the poor's share.

Evidently, increases in material welfare brought about by redistribution would occur at the expense of the nonmaterial welfare or of less urgent elements of the material welfare of the expropriated. However, consideration of long-term effects somewhat mitigated this difficulty; it was held that many types of redistribution would actually increase the dividend in the long run. This result followed from the direct relationship between the extent to which an individual's material needs had been satisfied, and his or her productive efficiency. Thus, in modern terminology, there were redistribution measures for which there was no "equity-efficiency trade-off;" instead, the two were viewed as complementary. Pigou argued that the poverty of a significant proportion of the population, especially children, indicated an untapped resource, investment in which would pay more in terms of increases in the dividend than further investment in machines. The investments expected to yield the highest return were those in school meals, health care, and industrial training (1932 [1920], Pt. IV, Ch. XII). Substantive predictions of this kind constituted the central policy conclusions of the material welfare school.

Discussion of policies was carried out by considering the effects on incentives, as it was possible that, if the work effort of rich or poor were impaired, the eventual effect on the dividend would be negative. Material welfare economists were thus most confident when defending egalitarian policies on grounds of efficiency. A more tentative approach was required when policies involved an equity-efficiency tradeoff. Pigou rejected rationing and wage subsidies as impairing incentives to work. Payments in kind showed much more promise, as they were considered less likely to have an adverse effect on effort than money transfers. As far as revenue is concerned, death duties were favored by Pigou over income taxes, in order to avoid adverse effects upon savings (Pt. IV, Ch. IX).

While the proximate reason for relieving poverty was its detrimental effect on industrial efficiency, the recommendations of the material welfare school were reinforced by a more grandiose master plan. The goal was to liberate the race from the wants of "the brute and the savage,"[18] in order to permit people to develop their "higher faculties."[19] These were of a more spiritual nature than material wants. Marshall argued firmly against religious views that insisted these virtues could be cultivated even in the presence of material privation (1920 [1890], p. 2).

In summary, this school of thought was concerned with deriving economic conditions that would bring about improve-

[18] Pigou gave careful consideration to the findings of eugenicists. In a chapter entitled "The National Dividend and the Quality of the People" (Part I, Ch. X) he faced the argument that economic policies would be devoid of long-run effect, since the problem they were designed to cure was hereditary. He proposed that improvements in the quality of education and sanitation would cause improvements in environment, particularly in the area of child-rearing, that would be transmitted to future generations.

[19] Marshall was quite explicit in his discussion of the role of economics in the development of the human race. Thus, while the proximate reason for the development of policies to alleviate poverty came from its deleterious effects on industrial efficiency, a more profound reason was that it stultified the development of man's "higher nature." This aspect of Marshall's thought is discussed in detail by Talcott Parsons (1931), who lists the facets of higher nature envisaged by Marshall as: energy, initiative, enterprise, rationality, frugality, industry and honorable dealing (1931, p. 107).

ments in material welfare. Economists could discuss necessaries with assurance but encountered increasing difficulties in the consideration of comforts and luxuries. The difficulties did not arise in the explanation of prices—for the material welfare school, the price of bread had the same explanation as the price of opera tickets. The problems arose in the attempt to establish firm conclusions about the practical effects of policy. It was more defensible to argue that free school lunches and industrial training would increase the dividend significantly than to argue that subsidized opera would have that effect.

The Material Welfare Conception of Utility

(a) *Utility and Ophelimity*

Economists of the material welfare school tended to use the concept of material welfare for analysis at the aggregate or "national" level. The term "utility" was reserved for discussion at the level of the individual. If one substitutes "utility" for "welfare" in the above discussion, it appears that an interpersonal comparison is present in one of Pigou's criteria for the establishment of increases in material welfare. This is the condition that material welfare can increase if there is a shift in the distribution of the national dividend, but no decrease in its size. The grounds for this comparison seem arbitrary, and this would lead one to believe that the work of the material welfare school was normative. Indeed, it is in this manner that they have been represented by modern historians of thought and ordinalist writers. However, this view comes from thinking in terms of the subjective notion of utility that is current today. In fact, at the turn of the century the definition of utility was not so clear-cut, and there coexisted two distinct ideas. This was recognized implicitly by many ordinalist pioneers, and was explicitly treated by Pareto.[20]

In his *Cours d'Economie Politique* (1896), Pareto noted that economists had traditionally understood "utility" in the everyday sense of "usefulness." Thus, to economists, something had utility if it was "conducive to the development and prosperity of an individual, a people, or the human race" (Pareto, 1896, p. 3). In his discussion of equilibrium, Jevons had employed the term in a different sense, which Pareto understood as the capacity to satisfy the desires of an individual, "whether legitimate or not," (1896, p. 3). Pareto coined the term "ophelimity" to refer to this type of utility, which he regarded as "subjective" (1896; 1971 [1906], *passim*). *The difference between utility and ophelimity is thus the difference between "socially useful" and "desired."* At the level of the individual "socially useful" is construed as being conducive to physical health. To illustrate the contrast, Pareto suggested that bad-tasting medicine has utility for sick children, but not ophelimity.[21]

In Pareto's view, the science of ophelimity had proceeded to an advanced state. In contrast, the study of utility was problematic. The usefulness of things was a sticky issue: Pareto listed air, water, light and wheat as among the things that were undoubtedly useful, but he was ambiva-

[20] The distinction to be discussed is merely to be regarded as a useful terminological device. It is not intended to suggest that Pareto is to be counted among the ranks of material welfare economists, or to imply that material welfare views were prominent on the continent. (A hierarchy of wants is discussed in Carl Menger, 1976 [1871], Ch. 3, however.)

[21] The idea that interpersonal comparisons might have an objective rather than a subjective basis is a theme of current philosophical inquiry. For example, in the *Theory of Justice*, John Rawls compares the material well-being of different people by an index of "primary social goods," rather than subjective satisfactions. Rawls' approach can be viewed as extending the idea of material well-being into a setting of moderate scarcity, where everyone's basic needs are satisfied.

lent about potatoes, as excessive reliance on them had caused great problems in Ireland. Difficult as these questions were, Pareto believed that the progress of the social sciences depended on their resolution. Furthermore, unequivocal answers to questions of usefulness could be given if a criterion for "economic utility" were adopted, and Pareto proposed to take this as "material well-being."[22]

When economists of the material school thought about interpersonal comparisons of utility, they thought in terms of comparing the material well-being of people. Physical objects were considered useful in so far as they could satisfy material needs, and the power of commodities to satisfy material needs was called utility. They believed that the *needs* of individuals, and, therefore, the power of given quantities of useful objects to satisfy them, could be compared. The comparison of needs, not the comparison of subjective desires, was what they usually meant by comparing utilities of different people. Thus their conception of utility was similar to the old idea of use-value and dissimilar to ophelimity.[23]

It is worthwhile to dwell on the difference between focusing on needs and focusing on desires, since this underlines the crucial differences, for our purposes, between utility and ophelimity. The noun "need" is synonymous with "deficiency," as measured against a norm of "completeness." For the material welfare school, this norm was the condition of the physically fit individual. The significance of such a norm is that the important deviations from it (those relating to "industrial efficiency") are physical in nature, and hence *observable*. One can thus dispute meaningfully with someone as to whether they or others have a need: Departures from industrial efficiency may be documented by pointing to inadequacy of diets, frequency of illness, high mortality rates and so on.[24] Thus, an important implication of confining utility to the material end of the hierarchy of goods or satisfactions, is that it made the production of utility observable and verifiable. On the other hand, the generation of ophelimity for a particular individual is not answerable to any standard of verification external to that individual because each person is the best judge of his or her own preferences.

(b) *Maximization of utility vs. maximization of ophelimity*

For the material welfare school, the coincidence or divergence of the pursuits of ophelimity and utility assumed great importance for policymaking.[25] The issue arose in the debate about whether money transfers would yield the same results as payments in kind. If the poor desire what is useful, then they will spend extra money to increase utility, i.e., transfers will be spent on food, clothing, industrial training and the like. If the poor do not desire what is useful, then instead of being spent so as to maximize utility, money transfers would be squandered, i.e., spent to maximize ophelimity.

[22] *"Le bien-être matériel."* He did not attempt to justify this choice explicitly, but seems to have had in mind some Spencerian ideas of evolutionary fitness. Evolution is seen here as improvement rather than adaptation.

[23] Pareto asserted that a rational person would view the two as identical. Thus, in contemporary usage, rationality was viewed as "doing what is good for you."

[24] There are some difficulties with this approach, in particular that the norm may not be easy to establish, and may vary considerably among tasks, cultures and even individuals of different physical size or construction. However, these do not vitiate the claim that deviations from the norm are measureable *in principle*. For a discussion of these matters, see Sen (1981, pp. 11–14).

[25] The greatest divergence between calculations of ophelimity and utility was believed to be present where the planning of expenditures for the future was involved. This was held to have a deleterious effect on material welfare, as a result of the lower rate of capital formation it engendered (Pigou 1932 [1920], pp. 24–30).

This problem caused some consternation for the material welfare school. On the one hand, Pigou maintained that "to charge the whole body of the poorer classes with ignorance and lack of capacity for management would, indeed, be to utter a gross libel" (1932 [1920], p. 754). On the other hand, he bemoaned the limitations of the wisdom of the typical household in its purchases and use of goods, likening it to technologically primitive cottage production of textiles (1932 [1920], p. 754).[26] Considerable care had to be exercised in the practice of doling out subsidies to people who had been at or below the margin of subsistence:

> For, if anybody accustomed to a given standard of living suddenly finds his income enlarged, he is apt to dissipate the extra income in forms of exciting pleasure, which, when their indirect, as well as their direct, effects are taken into account, may even lead to a positive loss of satisfaction [1932 (1920), p. 91].

In view of this, Pigou advocated that any redistribution of income be carried out gradually and imperceptibly.

Despite such caveats, Pigou and Marshall believed that the poor would tend to use additional money in the most useful ways. This outcome could be expected because the desire to spend on necessities is prompted by the want of them:

> For we may fairly expect that most material commodities, and especially those of wide consumption, that are required, as articles of food and clothing are, for direct personal use, will be wanted as means to pleasure, and will consequently be desired with varying intensity in proportion to the pleasure they are expected to yield [Pigou 1903, p. 68].

It could therefore be assumed, in discussions of the disparities of material welfare, that the effect of transfers of money would be quite similar to the effect of transfers in kind.

If people typically desire what they need, and if needs are more urgent when people are poor, it follows that additional income is more useful to the poor than the rich. The marginal utility of income declines because additional income is devoted to needs whose urgency diminishes as a person's income increases. For example, Pigou wrote:

> It is evident that any transference of income from a relatively rich man to a relatively poor man of similar temperament, since it enables more intense wants to be satisfied at the expense of less intense wants, must increase the aggregate sum of satisfaction. The old "law of diminishing utility" thus leads securely to the proposition: Any cause which increases the absolute share of real income in the hands of the poor, provided that it does not lead to a contraction in the size of the national dividend from any point of view, will in general, increase economic welfare [1932 (1920), p. 89].[27]

Given the material welfare conception of utility, it is possible to understand Pigou's welfare criterion in terms of the condition that money be allocated so that its marginal utility is equal between people. This scheme will produce the greatest ma-

[26] It was the argument of John A. Hobson and the "humanist school" that even if someone desired possession of an object that was capable of satisfying their wants it did not follow at all that these wants would be satisfied by endowing the person with the good in question: "the amount of utility or welfare to be got out of any goods depends upon the character, the natural or acquired capacity of the particular consumers or classes of consumers into whose hands they fall" (Hobson 1914, p. 37). Extracting utility from goods was a skill which had to be learned in the same way as one learned productive skills. William Robson (1925, Ch. 2) presented a more detailed study in this vein, in which he demonstrated that variations in family income around a low level were uncorrelated with occurrence of rickets in the children concerned. He took these and other findings on the lack of relationship between health and income as evidence that the principal needs of the time were for education in the best use of income to satisfy wants and that increases in income or payments in kind alone would not help.

[27] This quote is characteristic of the language of the material welfare school. The term "want" is often used to mean the objective fulfillment of a need and the corresponding subjective pleasure. In retrospect the material welfare school could have avoided confusion by observing Pareto's distinction more rigorously; however, their mode of expression is not inconsistent with ordinary speech.

terial welfare (and the greatest improvement in productive efficiency), given the available resources. It will lead to an equal distribution of wealth only if the relationship between individual wealth and the production of utility is the same for each individual. The fact that utility was confined to the material end of the hierarchy of wants thus suggests the possibility of an egalitarian bias.[28] However, this was tempered in Pigou's writing by consideration of the deleterious effects on incentive and thus ultimately on the dividend, that an egalitarian policy might create (1932 [1920], Pt. IV, Chs. VIII–X, XII).[29]

(c) *The Use of Interpersonal Averages*

Material welfare economists were most comfortable in making comparisons of utility, not between specific persons, but between broad classes of people who differ widely in their unmet needs—e.g., the rich and the poor. The terms "the rich" and "the poor" were used to describe averages, not individuals, much as modern economists talk about "the consumer." Comparisons between two *named* individuals were declared impossible or infeasible. However, this was not considered to be of particular importance for policy. Thus, Marshall argued:

> It would therefore not be safe to say that any two men with the same income derive equal benefit from its use; or that they would suffer equal pain from the same diminution of it . . . Nevertheless, if we take averages sufficiently broad to cause the personal peculiarities of individuals to counterbalance one another, the money which people of equal incomes will give to obtain a benefit or avoid an injury is a good measure of the benefit or injury. If there are a thousand persons living in Sheffield, and another thousand in Leeds, each with about £100 a-year, and a tax of £1 is levied on all of them, we may be sure that the loss of pleasure or other injury which the tax will cause in Sheffield is of about equal importance with that which it will cause in Leeds [1920 (1890), pp. 18–19].

Indeed, it was scarcely to be expected that one would be able to make any sense of individual comparisons. In his attempts to measure the marginal utility of money, Fisher resorted to the device of the average family. His justification in modern usage, was that individual data contains "too much noise" (1927, p. 181). The claim that poor people have more urgent needs than rich people was thus made with similar caveats as the claim that the consumer allocates a smaller share of his or her budget to housing as income rises. Both propositions smooth out the statistical outliers.

That material welfare economists, as we have described them above, had no difficulty with this use of averaging is scarcely surprising.[30] Their view that utility sprang from conditions associated with physical survival and development led them natu-

[28] Sen (1973, p. 16) observes that utilitarianism is, in general, "supremely unconcerned with the interpersonal distribution" of total utility, and points out that maximizing the sum of total utility will lead to an egalitarian outcome only in the special case in which everybody has the same utility function. The assumption of identical utility functions was attacked by Robbins and others, which "gave utilitarianism a reputation for being equality-conscious." From the above, it is clear that the "special case" arises from the particular conception of utility held by the material welfare school, and, indeed, any assignment of utility indices that varied dramatically among persons would be considered inadmissible. Only when "utility" is interpreted in terms of ophelimity does the egalitarian version of utilitarianism become a special case, placed on an equal footing with all other possible assignments of utility functions to individuals.

[29] This particular solution to the allocation problem is reminiscent of Edgeworth's formulation of the problem of the "Utilitarian Calculus" (1951 [1881], p. 56). The difference between two approaches is that Edgeworth believed that the pleasures derived by all people from all commodities may be compared, whereas the material welfare school confined itself to a more modest list of commodities. Edgeworth's approach is discussed in Yaari (1981).

[30] What is remarkable is that the process of averaging was advocated by economists who have gained a reputation for being the forerunners of the more modern sort of economics, in which "interpersonal comparisons" are vigorously eschewed. Phillip H. Wicksteed, whom Blaug (1978 [1962], p. 514) cites as a precursor of Robbins' conception of the scope of economics, argued that there could be no doubt that the pain experienced by torturing one hundred

rally to believe that people were fundamentally alike except for an insignificant personal component, rather than that the personal component swamped the shared one.

The ability to make interpersonal comparisons of utility is already implicit in the hierarchical conception of human needs. The significance of the hierarchy is that it arranges needs in the order in which they unfold as income increases. This order is the same for different people, in particular it is shared by the average rich person and the average poor person. In order to compare the welfare of two different people it is necessary to locate their positions on the hierarchy. The person higher on the hierarchy enjoys a greater level of welfare. For example, a person deprived of food has a more urgent need than a person deprived of entertainment. Giving food to the hungry increases material welfare more than giving theater tickets to the bored. However, material welfare economists did not claim any jurisdiction over the "higher faculties," as Marshall called them. They did not pretend to know whether one person was more capable of enjoying the theater than another. All they said about these commodities was that, in comparison to food, their contribution to material welfare was less significant.

The "Scope and Method" of Material Welfare Economics

Material welfare economists held that social reform is an important motive for studying economics.[31] However, they were particularly conscious of the distinction between positive and normative economics, and of the necessity of abstaining from prescription based on normative judgments. Thus, Pigou contended that economics "will not . . . be an art, or directly enunciate precepts of government. It is a positive science of what is and what tends to be, not a normative science of what ought to be" (1932 [1920], p. 5). According to Schumpeter and Denis H. Robertson, the methodological bible of the time was John Neville Keynes' *Scope and Method of Political Economy.*[32] Here, three aspects of political economy were distinguished: The studies of "economic uniformities, economic ideals and economic precepts." The first were seen as the subject of positive inquiry, the second as the concern of a "normative science" and the last as the province of an "art," "a system of rules for the attainment of a given end" (p. 35). Keynes insisted that it was both possible and desirable to restrict economics to the positive study of economic uniformities (1917 [1890], Ch. 2, p. iii). Similar views are advanced in Marshall's Inaugural Lecture at Cambridge (1885, p. 38). The pronouncements of the material welfare school on the scope of economics are thus in keeping with

men was greater than that experienced by another hundred men each subject to a gnat bite. "There might in one odd case be extraordinary sensitivity, and in another extraordinary anaesthesia, but they would not be typical" (1932, p. 149). Similarly, Pareto, whom John R. Hicks and Roy G. D. Allen (1934, pp. 52–54) name as the father of ordinal utility theory, argued that comparison of utilities (as opposed to ophelimities) of two people was legitimate as long as they did not depart too much from the average (Pareto 1896, Vol. II, pp. 48–49).

[31] Pigou saw this motivation as emanating not from the desire for "knowledge for its own sake," but from "the social enthusiasm which results from the sordidness of mean streets and the joylessness of withered lives" (1932 [1920], p. 5). Marshall believed that the possibility of banishing poverty depended on the outcome of economic investigations, and imparted to them "their chief and their highest interest" (1920 [1890], p. 4).

[32] From what one can judge, this book was, for many years, the main source of information on methodology, to the extent that such information was sought. Schumpeter refers to the "excellent performance of J. N. Keynes that settled most . . . methodological issues . . . to the satisfaction of the profession. For two decades this book held a well-deserved position of authority" (1954, p. 824). D. H. Robertson affirms its importance, but is more reserved about the interest it excited (1952, p. 14).

those at the base of modern economics.

The material welfare economists saw themselves in a long tradition of empiricism. British empiricism was characterized in theory by the claim that knowledge comes from experience, rather than reason and, in practice, by meticulous attention to detail and the collection of facts. The material welfare economists, like other empiricists, took pride in being sober scientists whose theories were grounded in facts. They took pains to collect and analyze data on wealth and welfare,[33] and they were pioneers in mathematical economics and statistics. They aspired to the same high standards of proof as present-day economists, but had a different idea of what to do when that standard was hard to reach.

If quantitative evidence was insufficient to decide an issue then the material welfare school accepted common sense and introspection as legitimate evidence. Thus, Marshall observed that "as human nature is constituted, man rapidly degenerates unless he has some hard work to do" (1920 [1890], p. 136). Similarly, Frank Taussig, in his discussion of the law of diminishing marginal utility, appealed to the fact that "all human enjoyments tend to pall rapidly when repeated" (1946 [1911], Ch. 9). Such passages are relics of the prose style of 19th century British classics, which modern economists can find embarrassing, like a photograph from adolescence.

In fact the appeal to common sense was part of a carefully considered method formulated by J. S. Mill (1844). According to Mill, all knowledge is obtained inductively from experience, and the scientific ideal involves performing an exact experiment whose outcome is decisive among rival theories. However, in economics it is rarely possible to perform the *experimentum crucis*, e.g., the Bank of England will not alter its policies merely to test economic theories. The absence of experimental data can be overcome in part by statistical methods, but in the end Mill thought it was necessary to draw upon ordinary experience and common sense. According to Mill, abstract economic theory proceeded by deduction from common sense generalizations.

From our argument in Part II it is clear that the elements of the conceptual framework of the material welfare school were closely bound together. The material welfare definition of economics committed the subject to the analysis of economic needs. The arrangement of needs in a hierarchy was motivated by common sense, as well as by scientific evidence. The methodology of empiricism admitted common sense into social science. These foundations supported the conception of utility as an objective, public phenomenon, comparable across individuals. Critics of this conceptual framework were more likely to succeed if they could offer a complete alternative, which is exactly what Lionel Robbins did.

III. *The Critique of the Material Welfare School*

The tradition exemplified by Cannan, Pigou, and Marshall was attacked by Robbins in his *Essay on the Nature and Significance of Economic Science*, first published in 1932. The parts of this critique that generated the most controversy were the first and last chapters, which dealt with "The Subject Matter of Economics" and "The Significance of Economic Science," respectively. Our development of the arguments of these chapters will correspond to the discussion above of the material welfare school, dealing with Robbins' definition of economics, and his conceptions of method and utility.

[33] The findings of the Royal Commission on the Poor Law are cited frequently by Pigou and Marshall.

Scarcity Definition

In the first chapter Robbins criticized the material welfare definition of economics on the grounds that it did not comprehend the full range of topics that economists study. For example, wheat is more material than opera, but the demand for opera tickets is as fit for study by economists as the demand for wheat. He proposed an alternative definiton:

> Economics is the science which studies human behavior as a relationship between ends and scarce means which have alternative uses [1937 (1932), p. 16].

Only this definition possessed the "capacity to describe exactly the ultimate subject-matter of the main generalizations of the science," (pp. 4–5) according to Robbins. He called this definition "analytical," rather than merely "classificatory," because it "focuses attention on a particular aspect of behavior, the form imposed by the influence of scarcity" (p. 17).[34]

The crucial feature of Robbins' definition is that it expands the list of goods that are equally legitimate concerns of the economist. Under the material welfare definition, economics was particularly but not exclusively concerned with goods that people need for the sake of physical and mental well-being. Under Robbins' definition, one good is as appropriate for study by economists as another so long as someone does not have as much of it as he or she desires. Bread and opera are on an equal footing in scarcity economics, whereas they occupy different positions in the hierarchy of needs.

Robbins stated that "what is rejected is but a definition," and not "the body of knowledge which it was intended to describe" (p. 22). However, it is important to realize that change of definition was instrumental in uprooting the existing body of knowledge. For, if the "unity of the subject of Economic Science" were to come from "the forms assumed by human behavior in disposing of scarce means" (1937 [1932], p. 15), then the natural primitive concept for studying economic welfare would be *ophelimity* rather than *utility*. Robbins did not make this distinction, and continued to use the term "utility" in his analysis of the work of the material welfare school.

As we have noted, ophelimity cannot be observed, and there is no way to know that it will be the same for two "average" individuals confronted with the same objective circumstances. Therefore, Robbins would find that his conception of utility offered no scientific support for statements about the effects on welfare of redistributive measures. This argument was couched in terms of Robbins' conception of science, as we shall now explain.

Positivism

During the 1930s, economists at the London School of Economics, where Robbins taught, were exposed to the philosophy of logical positivism,[35] which was imported into England from Vienna (William H. Beveridge 1960, Ch. 4). Positivism had a dramatic impact upon Anglo-American philosophy and social science.

Positivism shared many of the predilections of empiricism, e.g., both held that knowledge comes from experience rather than reason, both advocated testing theo-

[34] Much of Robbins' argument was anticipated by Frederic Benham (1930), who condemned "economic welfare" as a loose concept, vulnerable to misinterpretation, and the "law of diminishing marginal utility" as the result of "an amateur incursion into the domain of psychology" (p. 184). However, Benham was more skeptical about the scarcity conception of economics that Robbins was to introduce. The scarcity definition was not unknown to the earlier generation of economists. J. N. Keynes explicitly rejected the notion that political economy is concerned with scarcity or the "specially reasonable adaptation of means to ends" (1917 [1890], p. 35).

[35] There were two positivisms in the history of philosophy, logical positivism being the twentieth century version (Paul Edwards 1967: "Positivism" and "Logical Positivism").

ries by quantitative methods, and both held that prescriptions and policy judgments are outside of science. However, these traditional tenets of empiricism were given a much narrower interpretation by the positivists. This change in tone had a large effect upon the practice of social science.

At this stage, we can focus upon one aspect of positivism, namely its strictures against mental and moral concepts. A basic claim of positivism is that science can be demarcated from nonscience according to whether or not the propositions in question predict observable events.[36] Positivists tended to interpret "observable events" in a very restrictive sense. Concepts with an ethical tinge (duties, obligations, values, norms, etc.) were deemed "unobservable." For example, it is said that the existence of a duty to tell the truth cannot be confirmed by observation and is therefore regarded as metaphysical, and outside the pale of science. Those concepts with a subjective tinge (intentions, wishes, purposes, pleasures, happiness, etc.) were suspect. For example, another person's pleasure cannot be observed so directly as chairs or horses. Some positivists went so far as declaring all subjective and mentalistic concepts to be unobservable, and became behaviorists in their approach to science.

Robbins went a long way in the positivist direction of excluding ethical and mental concepts from science. The material welfare school had long recognized that neither cardinal utility, nor interpersonal comparability of utility is necessary to explain *market* behavior. Robbins claimed that no *observable* behavior could be explained by placing such structure on utility. Since observability is the demarcation criterion for science, he concluded that interpersonal comparisons of utility are outside science. In order to understand this claim we must appreciate Robbins' conception of utility.

Ordinal Utility

The claim that interpersonal comparisons of utility are outside of science may seem bizarre in light of the careful research by the material welfare school into the consequences of material deprivation. Hunger is plainly observable, open sewers assault the senses, the relationship between infant mortality and prenatal care is documented, etc. For the material welfare school, "utility" referred to the extent to which material needs were satisfied, which is observable. What did Robbins mean by claiming that utility is unobservable?

We noted that the material welfare school adopted an objective definition of utility (socially useful), whereas the ordinalists adopted a subjective definition (satisfaction of desire). As noted, Jevons used the subjective definition and remarked that there is no compelling way to compare the pleasures of different people. Robbins merely embedded this familiar claim in positivist philosophy. Specifically, he regarded utility as relating to preferences (i.e., ophelimity) and he stressed that alleged comparisons of utility among persons cannot meet the criterion of observability which demarcates science from nonscience (Robbins 1937 [1932], pp. 136–42).

Robbins' commitment to the positivist line is exemplified by his treatment of the law of diminishing marginal utility in the last chapter of his *Essay*. Here he offered a discussion of the assumptions underlying the "theory of public finance," especially progressive income taxation. The defense of progressive taxation by Robbins' opponents proceeds from the assumption that the marginal utility of income declines to

[36] This claim takes a somewhat different form in different writing: Karl Popper (1972 [1934]); the collection of writings in Alfred Ayer (1959).

the conclusion that total utility will be increased by the transfer of a pound of income from the rich to the poor.

Robbins condemned this argument as "merely specious," representing "an extension of the conception of diminishing marginal utility into a field in which it is entirely illegitimate." The unextended, legitimate law refers only to the income and utility of one individual; to extend it "begs the great metaphysical question of the scientific comparability of different individual experiences" (1937 [1932], p. 137; also, Benham 1930).

Two sources of evidence are recognized in Robbins' *Essay:* introspection and observation. He reported that he could find no introspective evidence in favor of the extended law of diminishing marginal utility of income. He also asserted that observation had no bearing on this extension, because no one can observe the satisfaction enjoyed by other people. We may, by chance, agree on which satisfaction is greater, but if we disagree, then there would be no way to resolve the dispute. He concluded that the extended law of diminishing marginal utility

> . . . cannot be justified by appeal to any kind of positive science. It involves an element of conventional valuation. Hence it is essentially normative [1937 (1932), p. 139].

Economists were thus presented with a dilemma: either they adopted a convention that made interpersonal comparisons possible, or they abandoned comparisons altogether. If they took the former course, then, according to Robbins, they would have to eschew the pursuit of positive science. On the other hand, were they to dedicate themselves to positive science, there would need to be a "substantial curtailment of much of what [now] assumes the status of scientific generalization in [current] discussions of applied economics" (1937 [1932], p. 141).

As noted, the material welfare school thought that propositions about needs and their satisfaction concern observable facts, not ethical judgments. Of course, "needs" has an ethical tinge and "satisfaction" sounds mental, which arouses the suspicion of positivists. Robbins proposed to purge utility of its ethical tinge, but he did not propose to eliminate its subjective tinge. In his day there was a tendency to describe utility as a psychological impulse or mental spring to action. He did not object to such descriptions, but he insisted that subjective impulses were not measurable or comparable among persons. The possibility of a strictly behaviorist interpretation of utility was not part of the vision of his *Essay*.

In 1934, John Hicks and R. G. D. Allen offered "A Reconsideration of the Theory of Value," which supplied the technical basis for a behaviorist account of consumer theory. Their article reconstructed consumer theory by isolating and developing those parts that did not rely on cardinality. Two notable casualties were the concepts of the marginal utility of a good, and complementarity between two goods, which were replaced respectively with the concepts of the marginal rate of substitution between two goods, and a revised conception of complementarity that required the presence of three goods. These changes did not alter any of the standard results about consumer equilibrium, but the implications for the meaning of utility were substantial: A concept that described mental impulses (marginal utility) was replaced by a behaviorist concept (marginal rate of substitution).

In conclusion, we note that Robbins assembled the elements of a new conceptual framework by joining together the scarcity definition of economics, the positivist conception of method, and the ordinalist view of utility. The only piece missing from the modern view was a behaviorist interpretation of ordinal utility, and that was supplied by others.

IV. *Debate Between the Schools*

We have described two internally consistent but mutually incompatible conceptual frameworks. The ordinalist framework eventually came to dominate the exposition of economic theory, but tracing this movement is difficult.[37] The ordinalists did not convert the members of the material welfare school, but students were won over. The material welfare school died out gradually as it failed to reproduce itself. In this section of the paper we recount these developments as reflected in the leading journals and books.

Replies to Robbins

The initial responses to Robbins' *Essay* were unfavorable, although muted. In the same year as it was published, the *Economic Journal* offered two critical reviews. The first, by Cannan, was directed primarily at Robbins' definition, the apparent virtues of which failed to attract him. It appeared to Cannan that Robbins had broadened the definition of economics to the point where it encompassed most of life. For example, Robbins saw the tradeoff between pursuit of pleasure and fulfillment of duty as an economic decision, whereas Cannan viewed it as "one of the problems of life" (cf., George M. Janes 1933).

In a second review, entitled "How Do We Want Economists to Behave?," Lindley Fraser (1932) pointed out that the scarcity definition had not been distilled from the actual practice of economists. Economists had long concerned themselves with comparing the well-being of different segments of the population, yet Robbins defined this practice out of economics. Robbins had proceeded by laying down a definition of economics and deducing the activities which economists could legitimately pursue.

Later (1937), Fraser characterized two methods of definition as themselves either "positive" or "normative." He reasoned that the material welfare definition is positive because it describes the actual practice of economics, whereas the scarcity definition is normative because it prescribes the appropriate practice for economics. Robbins was portrayed by Fraser as defining economics normatively while advocating the exclusion of norms from economics.

Fraser also criticized Robbins' application of scientific method.[38] He claimed that it was not the rigor of scientific method that Robbins had imposed on the practice of making interpersonal comparisons of utility, but rather a variant of the skeptical method. According to Fraser, people agreed that there was "no ground for supposing that poor men are *in general* less capable of enjoying a given amount of wealth than rich men" (p. 562). From this, it followed that egalitarian policies were *likely* to increase welfare, even though "the metaphysical doubt remains." Thus, while one could never rule out the possibility that redistributive policies would decrease welfare there was no reason for acting on the basis of this unlikely state of affairs, instead of the one that people considered more likely.

[37] Fraser (1938), in a review of Barbara Wootton's *Lament for Economics* (1938), indicated that the views of "Robbins and his colleagues are utterly unrepresentative of economists as a whole" (p. 196). By contrast, Roy Harrod (1938, p. 388), in the article referred to below, remarked that in recent years the history of thought had been discussed far more from the standpoint of the theory of exchange than from the standpoint of improving material welfare.

[38] Fraser's identification of ordinal utility theory with the skeptical method, rather than the scientific method, anticipated seminal criticisms made years later by C. West Churchman (1966). A full account of Fraser's concept of economic method is found in *Economic Thought and Language* (1937). This admirable and much-neglected work discussed economic theory from the viewpoint of the philosophy of language. The philosophy of language has had profound influence on the other social sciences; Fraser is unique in trying to work out some of its implications for economics.

Little more was written about these issues until Harrod raised them again in his essay entitled "Scope and Method of Economics" (1938). He, too, was critical of the practice of writers who stipulated methods and definitions instead of discussing those actually employed by economists. The suggestion that economists limit themselves to developing causal laws, and leave it up to policymakers to decide which course of action would be pursued, was illegitimate as it was "in manifest contradiction with the actual practice of economists" (p. 388). Robbins' proscriptions were seen to entail the principle that economists offer no advice whatsoever, as a result of which the interest in their causal laws would diminish markedly.

The advisory role assumed by economists also formed the basis for Harrod's dissent on the matter of interpersonal comparisons of utility. Economists could not afford to reject the common sense view of such comparisons. The objection that they were unscientific

> . . . would be very weighty if economics itself were a mature and exact science. Yet in fact its achievements outside a limited field are so beset on every side by matters which only admit of conjecture that it is possibly rather ridiculous for an economist to take such a high line . . . [p. 396].

While it was necessary to assume equality of ability for satisfaction in order to make comparisons, this assumption, when used with care, need not lead to problems.

Robbins' response to Harrod, which appeared in the *Economic Journal* a few months later, merely reiterated his earlier positions (1938b). In this and another article written at the same time, he insisted that the question of the scope of economics was dead (1938a, p. 344).

One cannot but come away from this discussion between Robbins and his critics with a sense of dissatisfaction. They argue past each other, instead of defining the issue clearly. Neither side seems to appreciate that the other is using the same words to mean different things. Consider for example the fate of the term "utility." We mentioned that Pareto distinguished utility (usefulness) from ophelimity (satisfaction of desire). Robbins used one name, utility, to refer to both concepts. Pareto had shown that *ophelimity* was not comparable, but Robbins discussed the incomparability of *utility*. In Robbins' *Essay* the meaning of "utility" to the material welfare school is ignored.

Another source of confusion arose from the examples used to illuminate the debate about the interpersonal comparisons. The material welfare school compared the rich to the poor, speaking in terms of abstract individuals widely separated on the scale of material well-being. Robbins made comparisons in terms of named individuals who were not so far apart in terms of income. This shift in examples affects the plausibility of the assertions that levels of welfare can be compared.

Ordinalist Welfare Economics

It appears unlikely that the work of Robbins and Hicks and Allen could, in isolation, precipitate the dramatic changes in the practices of economists that occurred. However, the development of the literature on compensation criteria may offer a clue to the victory of Robbins' framework.

Harrod had noted that Robbins' scientific ideal would not have allowed economists to endorse repeal of the Corn Laws which almost all British economists had endorsed (1938, p. 388). Nicholas Kaldor (1939) suggested that the repeal of the tariff was justifiable because the increase in wealth brought about by this reform, if redistributed appropriately, was more than sufficient to put everybody at the same level of utility as previously. Thus, repeal of the Corn Laws made a Pareto improvement possible by appropriate wealth redistribution. This procedure promised to rank a state of the world by comparing the *hypothetical* redistributions it permitted to other actual states of the world, using the Pareto criterion. According to Kaldor, using hypothetical rather than actual redistributions permitted economists to make policy recommendations without making value judgments (Kaldor 1939, p. 550). Use of the Pareto criterion made interpersonal comparisons of utility unnecessary. Thus, it appeared that some of the conclusions of the material welfare school might remain intact, even when Robbins' strictures were obeyed.

The recommendations that flow from Kaldor's principle are sometimes different from the recommendations of the material welfare school. Suppose we are considering the desirability of a redistribution policy that raises marginal tax rates at low incomes and lowers marginal tax rates at high incomes. This policy is expected to raise the national income, the increase accruing to the rich. Suppose further that their eventual gain in income exceeds the loss in the income of the poor. Using Kaldor's criterion, we would say that the policy results in an economic gain, even if the rich do not compensate the poor. However Pigou's criterion yields no definite result in this case. (Although it would agree with Kaldor's criterion if compensation were paid.) Alternatively, if the eventual money gain to the rich were exactly equal to the loss of the poor, Kaldor's criterion would evaluate the two situations equally, whereas the original situation would dominate under Pigou's rules. The difference in conclusions occurs because Kaldor's approach requires the economist to proceed as if a dollar were equally valuable to everyone, whereas Pigou's requires the economist to proceed as if a dollar were more valuable to the poor than to the rich. Thus, Kaldor made a *different* conventional judgment from Pigou, rather than no judgment. However most subsequent discussion of compensation criteria did not consider this point.[39] This suggests that a generation of economists was trained to believe that science treats a dollar as equally valuable to everyone, whereas a nonscientific approach treats a dollar as more valuable to the poor than to the rich.

Nevertheless, compensation criteria did offer some degree of rapproachement between the two schools. In the Introduction to his textbook on the new welfare economics, Melvin Reder precedes his development of compensation criteria with this statement:

> . . . if our welfare criterions were applicable only to the few policies that harm none, welfare economics would be quite sterile. Fortunately, this is not the case [1947, p. 18].

Subsequently, the technical difficulties with compensation criteria were exposed by Paul Samuelson (1950) and William M. Gorman (1955). One may wonder whether the new welfare economics would have been so readily adopted in the late 1930s had its "sterility" been evident at that time.

V. *Evaluating and Explaining the Ordinalist Revolution*

The body of this paper has reconstructed the conceptual frameworks of the two schools of thought involved in the debate on the possibility and relevance to economics of interpersonal comparisons of utility. A comparison of these frameworks leads to the conclusion that phrases such as "the comparability of utility across persons" meant different things to each school. The observation that the earlier conceptual framework was not generalized by the later motivates a reconsideration of the question of whether scientific progress occurred. To this we now turn.

[39] An exception is William Baumol (1965 [1952], pp. 161–70).

Received history of economic thought accounts for the difference between the two schools in terms of rival views of the scope and method of economics. Thus, material welfare economics is seen as normative and the banishment of interpersonal comparisons of utility as the consequence of the attempt to make economics a positive science (Blaug 1978 [1962], pp. 636–37). This view is in keeping with Robbins' recollections:

> All that I had done was to assert, in regard to discussion of economic affairs, the distinction between propositions involving existence and obligation, well recognized elsewhere since Hume pointed out the distinction between "ought" and "is" [1971, p. 148].

Yet, as we have argued above, in our discussions of scope and method, material welfare economists were well aware of this distinction. They did not consider normative statements to be part of the economics they practiced. Further, they affirmed "Hume's guillotine" in much the same breath as they made statements that were later criticized for ignoring it.

In his discussion of the development of utility theory from 1790 to 1915, Stigler pointed to the method of empirical investigation by appeal to "casual knowledge" used by economists practicing during this period. He went on to suggest:

> Had specific tests been made of the implications of theories, the unfruitfulness of the ruling utility theory as a source of hypotheses in demand would soon have become apparent . . . That such able economists were delayed and distracted by the lack of a criterion of refutable implications of theories should be a finding as useful to us as any of the fine theoretical advances they made [1950, p. 396].

It is true that the material welfare economists appealed to everyday experience for evidence, which resulted from their use of an empiricist rather than a positivist methodology. However, this does not explain why they retained their version of utility theory.[40] Instead, the explanation resides in the fact that, cumbersome as their conception of utility was for price theory, it was well adapted to the examination of propositions about material welfare, which were the major preoccupation of the school.[41] Moreover, their conception of admissible scientific evidence was congruent with their view of utility. The belief that a utility structure was common to people made introspection an appropriate empirical tool. The fact that the production of utility was linked to the material end of the hierarchy of needs made the incidence of utility readily observable, and so offered a place for observations based on everyday experience.

The theses that economics developed as it did in the early decades of this century because it confused normative and positive concepts, or because of inadequate scientific method, must be rejected. They attribute to apparent differences in scope and method the effects of differences in research agenda. An account of the doctrinal changes of the 1930s must concentrate on differences in research agenda which influenced the two rival schools' definitions of "economics," and the denotation they gave to the term "utility."

Each school was guided by a separate definition of economics, which mandated that they focus their attention on different phenomena. Considerations of scarcity directed economists to study the production and exchange of all commodities, for which the appropriate concept of human behavior is preference, or ordinal utility. Considerations of material welfare man-

[40] Stigler referred to the aspects of this theory that were later generalized, as a result of the replacement of the additive utility function by the generalized utility function, and of the measurable utility function by the nonmeasurable one.

[41] It should be noted, in this paper we have not dealt with the question of whether Stigler's judgment is appropriate for economists of generations earlier than the material welfare school.

dated concentration on an aspect of the significance of commodities for which the canonical concept of human behavior is the satisfaction of needs or "wants." While intensity of preference among people could not be ranked in any way that would not be considered arbitrary, interpersonal intensity of needs could be ordered in a way that would only be considered arbitrary by a sceptic. However, in the presence of confusion as to the concept of utility being appealed to, it was possible for the scarcity school to characterize material welfare economics as guilty of subscribing to arbitrary conventions or "value judgments," and to explain the persistence of these practices by the neglect of positivist scientific method. Similarly, it was possible for the material welfare school to interpret the strictures of ordinalists on interpersonal comparisons of utility as mere scepticism on the part of economists who were prepared to hamstring the science by giving disproportionate weight to possible but unlikely configurations of utility among people.

The received view is that ordinalism represents scientific progress relative to the material welfare school, but one can talk unequivocally about the progress of a science only when it continues to address the same questions. The period offers two yardsticks with which the achievements of economics are to be measured because the questions asked by economics changed. The evaluation of the schools is thus confounded by the fact that the work of neither encompassed that of the other. It is necessary to balance the gains in understanding markets which the ordinalist framework facilitated against the losses in understanding human welfare, suffered by abandoning the material welfare framework.

An important feature of the received view of the ordinalist revolution is that the explanation of why it occurred is a simple corollary of its evaluation: it happened because all economists, sharing the goal of advancing their science, perceived the merits of the ordinalist approach. In contrast, our account makes it necessary to dissociate the explanation from the evaluation of the change. As far as the explanation is concerned, we have shown that the two schools had different frameworks, the older framework consisting of a material welfare definition of economics, an empiricist conception of method, and an interpersonal conception of utility, whereas the newer framework consisted of a scarcity definition of economics, a positivist conception of method, and an ordinalist conception of utility. The essential unity of each framework explains some features of the change, such as the difficulty each side had in comprehending the other's arguments.[42] In order to provide a more complete explanation of the change in doctrine, an examination of the relationship of the two schools to the wider intellectual and political climate of the time now seems indispensable. For the moment, we can do no better than to echo Lindley Fraser (1937, p. 36) who, having discussed the scarcity and material welfare definitions of economics, despaired of objective criteria for adjudicating among them. He concluded that the choice "would have to rest largely on the individual temperaments of the persons concerned."

References

ARROW, KENNETH J. *Social choice and individual values.* 1st ed. Yale U. Press, 1963.

AYER, ALFRED J., ed. *Logical positivism.* Glencoe, IL: Free Press, 1959.

BAUMOL, WILLIAM J. *Welfare economics and the theory of the state.* 2nd ed. London School of Economics, [1952] 1965.

[42] Our account suggests that the ordinalist revolution was not unanimously accepted by economists. Indeed, Pigou (1951) maintained his belief in the material welfare program into the 1950s, and there do not appear to have been any notable conversions of faith among other members of the material welfare school.

BENHAM, FREDERIC C. "Economic Welfare," *Economica*, June 1930, *10*, pp. 173–87.
BENTHAM, JEREMY. *A fragment of government and the principles of morals and legislation.* Ed.: W. HARRISON. Oxford: Basil Blackwell, [1776] 1948.
BEVERIDGE, WILLIAM H. *The London School of Economics and its problems, 1919–1937.* London: Allen & Unwin, 1960.
BLAUG, MARK. *Economic theory in retrospect.* 3rd ed. Cambridge U. Press, [1962] 1978.
CANNAN, EDWIN. *Wealth.* 3rd ed. London: Staples Press, [1914] 1928.
______. "Review of Robbins' *An Essay on the Nature and Significance of Economic Science,*" *Econ. J.*, Sept. 1932, *42*, pp. 424–27.
CHURCHMAN, C. WEST. "On the Intercomparison of Utilities," in *The structure of economic science: Essays on methodology.* Ed.: SHERMAN ROY KRUPP. NJ: Prentice Hall, 1966.
EDGEWORTH, FRANCIS Y. *Mathematical psychics.* NY: A. M. Kelley, [1881] 1961.
EDWARDS, PAUL, ed. *Encyclopaedia of philosophy.* NY: Macmillan, 1967.
FISHER, IRVING. "A Statistical Method for Measuring 'Marginal Utility' and Testing the Justice of a Progressive Income Tax," in *Economic essays contributed in honor of John Bates Clark.* Ed.: J. H. HOLLANDER. NY: Macmillan, 1927, pp. 157–93.
______. *Mathematical investigations in the theory of value and prices.* NY: A. M. Kelley, [1892] 1965.
FRASER, LINDLEY. "How Do We Want Economists to Behave?" *Econ. J.*, Dec. 1932, *42*, pp. 555–70.
______. *Economic thought and language.* London: Macmillan, 1937.
______. "Review of *Lament for economics* by Barbara Wootton," *Econ. J.*, June 1938, *48*, pp. 196–210.
FRISCH, RAGNAR. *New methods of measuring marginal utility.* Beitrage zur Okonomischen Theorie #3. Tubingen: J.C.B. Mohr, 1932.
GORMAN, WILLIAM M. "The Intransitivity of Certain Criteria Used in Welfare Economics," *Oxford Econ. Pap. N. S.*, Feb. 1955, 7(1), pp. 25–35.
HARROD, ROY F. "Scope and Method of Economics," *Econ. J.*, Sept. 1938, *48*, pp. 383–412.
HICKS, JOHN R. "The Foundations of Welfare Economics," *Econ. J.*, Dec. 1939, *49*, pp. 696–712.
______ AND ALLEN, ROY G. D. "A Reconsideration of the Theory of Value," *Economica N.S.*, Feb./May 1934, *1* (Part I, II), pp. 52–76 and 196–219.
HOBSON, JOHN A. *Work and wealth.* London: Macmillan, 1914.
HUTCHINSON, TERENCE W. *A review of economic doctrines, 1870–1929.* Oxford: Clarendon Press, 1953.
JANES, GEORGE M. "Review of Robbins' *Nature and significance of economic science,*" *Amer. Econ. Rev.*, Dec. 1933, *23*, pp. 698–99.
JEVONS, W. STANLEY. *Political economy.* NY: American Book Co. 1905.
______. *Theory of political economy.* 4th ed. London: Macmillan, [1871] 1911.
KALDOR, NICHOLAS. "Welfare Propositions of Economics and Interpersonal Comparisons of Utility," *Econ. J.*, Sept. 1939, *49*, pp. 549–52.
KAUDER, EMIL. *A history of marginal utility theory.* NJ: Princeton U. Press, 1965.
KEYNES, JOHN NEVILLE. *Scope and method of political economy.* 4th ed. London: Macmillan, [1890] 1917.
LONDON SCHOOL OF ECONOMICS. *Calendar.* London: 1920–1940.
MARSHALL, ALFRED. *The present position of economics.* London: Macmillan, 1885.
______. *Principles of economics.* 8th ed. London: Macmillan, [1890] 1920.
MENGER, CARL. *Principles of economics.* Trans.: JAMES DINGWALL AND BERT HOSELITZ. NY: NYU Press, [1871] 1976.
MILL, JOHN STUART. "On the Definition of Political Economy; and On the Method of Investigation Proper to It," in *Essays on some unsettled questions of political economy.* London: London School of Economics, Reprints of scarce works on political economy, #7. [1844] 1948, pp. 304–39.
MYINT, HLA. *Theories of welfare economics.* Harvard U. Press, 1948.
PARETO, VILFREDO. *Cours d'economie politique.* Two Volumes. Lausanne: 1896–1897.
______. *Manuel d'economie politique.* NY: Augustus M. Kelley, [1906] 1971.
PARSONS, TALCOTT. "Wants and Activities in Marshall," *Quart. J. Econ.*, Nov. 1931, *46*, pp. 101–40.
PIGOU, ARTHUR C. "Some Remarks on Utility," *Econ. J.*, Mar. 1903, *13*, pp. 58–68.
______. *The economics of welfare.* 4th ed. London: Macmillan, [1920] 1932.
______. "Some Aspects of Welfare Economics," *Amer. Econ. Rev.*, June 1951, *41*(3), pp. 287–302.
POPPER, KARL R. *The logic of scientific discovery.* London: Hutchinson, [1934] 1972.
RAWLS, JOHN. *A theory of justice.* Cambridge, MA: Harvard U. Press, 1972.
REDER, MELVIN W. *Studies in the theory of welfare economics.* NY: Wiley, 1947.
ROBBINS, LIONEL. *An essay on the nature and significance of economic science.* London: Macmillan, [1932] 1937.
______. "Live and Dead Issues in the Methodology of Economics," *Economica N.S.*, Aug. 1938a, *5*, pp. 342–52.
______. "Interpersonal Comparisons of Utility: A Comment," *Econ. J.*, Dec. 1938b, *48*, pp. 635–41.
______. *Autobiography of an economist.* London: Macmillan, 1971.
ROBERTSON, DENIS H. *Utility and all that.* London: Allen & Unwin, 1952.
ROBSON, WILLIAM A. *The relation of wealth to welfare.* NY: Macmillan, 1925.
SAMUELSON, PAUL A. "Evaluation of Real National Income," *Oxford Econ. Pap. N.S.*, Jan. 1950, *2*, pp. 1–29.
SCHUMPETER, JOSEPH A. *History of economic analysis.* London: Allen & Unwin, 1954.
SCITOVSKY, TIBOR. "The State of Welfare Economics," *Amer. Econ. Rev.*, June 1951, *41*, pp. 303–15.

SEN, AMARTYA. *On economic inequality.* Oxford: Clarendon Press, 1973.

———. "On Weights and Measures: Informational Constraints in Social Welfare Analysis," *Econometrica*, Oct. 1977, *45*(7) pp. 1539–72.

———. *Poverty and famines.* Oxford U. Press, 1981.

STIGLER, GEORGE J. "The Development of Utility Theory," *J. Polit. Econ.*, Aug./Oct. 1950, *58* (Part I, II), pp. 307–28 and 373–96.

TAUSSIG, FRANK W. *Principles of economics.* Macmillan, [1911] 1946.

WICKSTEED, PHILLIP H. *The commonsense of political economy.* London: Routledge, [1910] 1932.

WOOTTON, BARBARA. *Lament for economics.* London: Unwin, 1938.

YAARI, MENAHEM E. "Rawls, Edgeworth, Shapley, Nash: Theories of Distributive Justice Re-examined," *J. Econ. Theory*, Feb. 1981, *24*(1), pp. 1–39.

[13]

Journal of Economic Literature
Vol. XXVI (March 1988), pp. 80–91

Communications

A New Look at the Ordinalist Revolution: Comments on Cooter and Rappoport*

By Pieter Hennipman
University of Amsterdam

I. *Two Frameworks Contrasted*

A few years ago Robert Cooter and Peter Rappoport (henceforth referred to as CR) published an intriguing article in this journal titled "Were the Ordinalists Wrong About Welfare Economics?" (CR 1984). It describes the "Hicksian" or "ordinalist" revolution as part of a transition, occurring in the 1930s, to an entirely new and commonly accepted conceptual framework of economics (p. 508). This framework differs from the preceding one in three essential respects or "elements." The old conceptual framework, upheld by the "material welfare school," consisted of "a material welfare definition of economics, an empiricist conception of method, and an interpersonal conception of utility." The newer framework, introduced by the "ordinalists," consisted of "a scarcity definition of economics, a positivist conception of method, and an ordinalist conception of utility" (p. 528; somewhat different wordings of the contrast are given on pp. 508 and 512). CR stress that each framework was an "essential unity" (p. 528; similarly p. 520) and see Arthur C. Pigou and Lionel Robbins as the leading representatives of these schools, with Pigou principally allied with Alfred Marshall and Edwin Cannan in the old school, and Robbins with John R. Hicks in the new school.

* A much more extensive commentary recently appeared in *De Economist* (Hennipman 1987) in which more detailed discussions, further textual evidence, and points only touched upon or omitted here may be found.

The victory of the "ordinalist framework" (p. 528) is seen as a "dramatic change" (pp. 508, 525). Robbins offered, according to the authors, a "complete alternative" (p. 520) so that "the work of neither school encompassed that of the other" (p. 528). CR see the change in view concerning interpersonal comparability of utility as the crucial feature of this upheaval. Their main thesis, vindicating the "scientific integrity" of the older school (p. 509), is that "the ordinalist revolution represented a change, not progress in economics" (p. 508). While it brought about "gains in understanding markets" it also resulted in "losses in understanding human welfare" (p. 528).

CR's claim that a metamorphosis of economics occurred half a century ago invites an assessment of its credibility. This article deals with a complex argument concerning three subjects: the definition of economics, several aspects of utility theory, and methodology.

II. *A Material Welfare School?*

Serious doubts arise at once with regard to CR's concept of the first element of the old school, the material welfare definition of economics, which according to CR maintains that "economics was particularly but not exclusively" concerned with "material welfare" in the sense of the necessities of life, the goods that "people need for the sake of physical and mental well-being," as distinct from comforts and luxuries (CR 1984, pp. 513, 521). CR view propositions about material welfare as "the major preoccupation of the old school" (p. 527).

This depiction is correct in the sense that Marshall and Cannan did adopt a kind of "material" criterion for the scope of economics, but their definitions are much broader than CR's concept and are not limited to necessities (Marshall 1920, pp. 1, 54 ff.; Cannan, 1930, p. 4; 1932, p. 426).[1] Arthur Pigou's use of money as the measuring rod of economic welfare, the subject matter of economics (1932, p. 11) and expressly not denoted as "material" (1952, p. 288), likewise lacks this restriction. So it is very strange indeed that when paraphrasing Pigou CR substitute the expression *material welfare* in their narrow sense for *economic welfare* (e.g., p. 513).[2]

Aside from the question of definition, CR incorrectly characterize the substance of the older school. It *is* true that Marshall and Pigou considered the alleviation of poverty and allied ills to be the principal concern of economics. As Pigou declared, "The main motive of economic study is to help social improvement" (1932, p. IX; also p. VII, the passage cited by CR, p. 519, n. 31; a similar statement by Marshall 1920, p. 4).

This conviction did not, however, move them, as CR make it appear, to devote their writings in the main to "material welfare" and closely related matters. As is well known, they studied a much wider range of subjects. Even in Pigou's *The Economics of Welfare*, the first book one thinks of, the parts dealing explicitly with "material welfare" occupy a modest space. The discussion concerns mainly economic welfare or the "national dividend" in general. In Pigou's vast oeuvre the proportion dealing with what CR consider a "major preoccupation" is still smaller.

Pigou's observation that "economics is *relevant* to social improvement. In an indirect way it may help that improvement on" (1952, p. 82) suggests that this beneficial result was envisaged as an ultimate aim, unlike the rather restricted direct concern that CR believe it to be. Their misapprehension is revealed in their astounding assertion that "price theory was not so central to economics until after the ordinalist revolution" (p. 512).

CR's view reflects a pervasive and disturbing ambiguity about the meaning of the two frameworks. Though CR present the frameworks as pertaining to economics as a whole their elements refer to only a small number of topics and they do not take into account other important parts of the discipline.[3] In effect elements are selected because they are deemed relevant in particular to welfare economics, which the authors say they have concentrated on (p. 510). As a result, their discussion confusingly alternates at critical stages between these points of view. At all events, from both perspectives the material welfare school appears to be an artificial construction.

III. *Objective Utility*

In CR's essay utility theory emerges as the chief bone of contention between the schools. CR view utility as objective and interpersonal in the old school and subjective and ordinal in the new school.

Pursuing the material welfare line CR aver that the old school conceived of utility as "the power of commodities to satisfy material needs" (p. 516) and hence "did not equate utility with preference" (p. 509). Utility in this sense is "an objective, public phenomenon" (p. 520; also p. 509). CR regularly use the term themselves in this idiosyncratic way. Utility in the generally current subjective sense, corresponding with preferences, they mostly call, following Vilfredo Pareto, *ophelimity*.

CR argue further that the objective nature of "utility" makes it "comparable across individuals" (p. 520) and therefore that the adherents of the traditional framework had no difficulty accepting the possibility of interpersonal comparisons of utility based not on subjective desires but on "observable facts" (p. 516).

This interpretation is extremely puzzling and is supported by no textual evidence to speak of. Marshall and Pigou by no means confined the utility concept to material needs and de-

[1] Cannan's membership of the school seems to rest entirely on his misunderstood material welfare definition, for CR hardly mention him otherwise. Therefore Cannan will be only incidentally referred to in this paper.

[2] The same point has been made by Ian M. D. Little (1985, p. 1187, n. 2).

[3] CR's silence on the contemporary Keynesian revolution is symptomatic of this omission.

scribed it in unmistakably subjective terms, "correlative to desire or want" in Marshall's words (1920, p. 93). Pigou's notion of economic welfare, for him synonymous with utility or satisfaction, was, as noted above, equally free from the "material" connotation and typified as a distinctly mental phenomenon (1932, p. 10; 1951, p. 288).[4]

Naturally Pigou and Marshall had the same subjective broad concept in mind in the treatment of interpersonal comparisons of utility. Marshall's discussion of the diminishing marginal utility of income, on which such comparisons were assumed to be based, in the chapter on consumer demand (1920, pp. 95–96), plainly shows the conceptual unity. Pigou's explanations, founded on these ideas, of the effect of income transfers from the rich to the poor were consistently couched in general subjective terms like "economic welfare" or "the aggregate sum of satisfaction" (e.g., 1932, p. 89; 1951, p. 299; 1953, p. 48). It is difficult to understand how CR can detect here "the language of the material welfare school" (p. 517). Obviously, references to "material needs" in illustrations of redistribution (e.g., Pigou 1932, p. 87: "Expensive luxuries give place to more necessary articles, rare wines to meat and bread . . .") do not imply that the theoretical propositions on the subject relate to what CR call utility and not to subjective desires.

IV. *Preferences and Economic Welfare*

The most interesting aspect of CR's assertion that the material welfare school "did not equate utility with preference" is the belief that the school was primarily interested in maximizing objective utility and not ophelimity when the two do not coincide (see, especially, pp. 516–17). Their view is derived from the adverse judgments which Pigou, in particular, occasionally made about certain kinds of preferences and corresponding behavior. It is a pity CR confound this point by the peculiarity of their approach.

The best-known case is Pigou's disapproval of "wholly irrational time preference" (1932, p. 24). Misrepresenting Pigou's vocabulary, CR briefly observe that Pigou condemned time preference because of its "deleterious effect on material welfare" (1984, p. 516, n. 25). There is, of course, none of this in Pigou, who argued at some length that time preference leads to a loss of satisfaction or economic welfare in general because intertemporal allocation would not be optimal.

In another passage Pigou regrets the possible tendency of the poor who profit from an income transfer "to dissipate the extra income in forms of exciting pleasure" which might be harmful (1932, p. 91; there is a similar complaint on p. 756).[5] CR interpret this as reflecting the fear that the money would be spent not to maximize utility (in their specific sense) but to maximize ophelimity (1984, p. 516). It is defensible to view Pigou as being concerned here about "material welfare," but this is not a valid reason to impute to him an objective utility concept. It is clear from his own words that he regarded frivolous expenditure as a failure to maximize satisfaction or economic welfare. Therefore, it is unwarranted to say that he did not equate "utility" with preference; correctly stated, in some instances he did not equate indulging preferences with optimal economic welfare. This distinction is not merely verbal because it bears on a distinctive feature of his reasoning.

Moreover, Pigou's somewhat paternalistic concern about the inclinations of the poor is, though noteworthy, a minor trait in his welfare economics. He looked upon the discrepancies he signaled as exceptions to the prevailing "equivalence of desires and satisfactions" (1932, p. 24). CR themselves acknowledge that, according to Marshall and Pigou, "people typically desire what they need" (p. 517). The fact that they held this sensible opinion undermines CR's claim that they represented a school distinguished by its emphasis on needs irrespective of desires.

V. *The Scarcity Definition*

Like its counterpart in the old framework the scarcity definition of economics is the decisive element in the new one. CR hold it fully

[4] Similarly, Cannan remarked that "ophelimity" and "desiredness" are substitutes for "utility" (1964, p. 197). Dennis H. Robertson, a true Marshallian, called utility, satisfaction, and economic welfare "alternative expressions" (1952, pp. 15, 29).

[5] Marshall also warned that "some indulgences are positively harmful" (1920, p. 531).

responsible for the wholesale revision of economics they aim to describe. This seems surprising because Lionel Robbins disclaimed such an idea. He pointed out that his criticism of Cannan's definition, his main target, did not amount to a rejection of "the body of knowledge it was intended to describe" (1935, p. 22).

Ignoring this judgment, CR regard Robbins' criterion as "instrumental in uprooting the existing body of knowledge" (1984, p. 521). This difference results from the fact that they do not compare it with the real definitions of Marshall, Cannan, and Pigou, but with the spurious material welfare definition. This explains why CR write: "The crucial feature of Robbins' definition is that it expands the list of goods that are equally legitimate concerns of the economist" (1984, p. 521). In line with this it "directed economists to study the production and exchange of all commodities" at the cost of the focus on material welfare (pp. 527–28). The "uprooting" specifically concerns the utility element. According to CR, the abandonment of the old definition entailed the displacement of objective utility by ophelimity (p. 521), notably its ordinal version which was "the most appropriate concept" for the newly favored theory of price (p. 521). On the other hand, the general acceptance of the ophelimity concept had fateful consequences for welfare economics, to be considered in the next section.

Apart from its being improbable that a change in the definition of the subject could have such far-reaching effects, CR's historical record, starting from a fictitious event, is in error. Some of the developments it sketches (such as the promotion of price theory from a subordinate status[6] and the coming into vogue of the subjective utility notion) did not happen at all during the period they study. The move toward ordinalism in utility theory was not furthered by the scarcity definition,[7] nor had it anything to do with a higher esteem for price theory. It follows that the scope and utility elements of the second framework in no way display as "essential unity."

[6] One might think of the rise of the theories of monopolistic of imperfect competition but CR do not allude to them.

[7] It was finally accepted by Pigou (1951, pp. 289ff.) and is, of course, compatible with his measuring rod of money.

VI. *Ordinalism*

As CR's title indicates, ordinalism, "the salient feature of utility" (1984, p. 508), is paramount in the supposed great transformation. Regrettably, the discussion of this key concept is less transparent than one might wish.

The haze is largely due to CR's use of the term *ordinalism* in three different ways without drawing attention to these differences. The first of these is the usual one, namely "the rejection of cardinalist notions of utility" (p. 507). On this they have little to say because they consider it as having small importance for their purpose (p. 508). Next, markedly in the definition of the "ordinalist revolution," the denial that utility is "comparable across individuals" is added to ordinalism proper. Owing to the conjunction of these two attributes CR's "ordinalist revolution," the heart of the matter in their account, is not the same event others denote by this expression (e.g., Paul A. Samuelson 1974; Mark Blaug 1985, p. 368). Thirdly and most frequently, also in contrasting the frameworks, the notion of ordinalism is confined to the exclusion of interpersonal comparisons. Amazingly it appears that the title of CR's paper and the designation "ordinalist framework" refer in particular to noncomparability.

It is this oddly named ordinalism that most conspicuously embodies the "dramatic change" effected by the new framework. The climax in CR's narrative is seen as the direct and inevitable outcome of the shift from objective utility to ophelimity, due to the scarcity definition. They agree unhesitatingly with Robbins that factual or descriptive interpersonal comparisons of subjective utility are impossible (1984, pp. 509, 521). Consequently the momentous questions regarding the effects of the distribution and redistribution of income on economic welfare, which the old school could answer by means of their observable and interpersonal utility concept, vanished from economics (p. 508, n. 2, with a "partial listing" of such questions). Because of the loss of these insights CR deny that the ordinalist revolution represented progress.

Clearly CR are here again led astray by their misconceptions about material welfare and so-called utility. Logically, Robbins' attack on the Pigovian doctrines could not involve a repudiation of an objectivist way of thinking, alien, as shown above, to his opponent. Their dispute was one within utility theory in its ordinary sense.[8] The charge that Robbins confused ophelimity and the utility notion of the old school (1984, pp. 521, 525) is wholly unfounded.

The upshot of all this is that the question posed in the title concerns a nonevent, the disappearance of interpersonal comparisons from welfare economics through the expulsion of objective utility in favor of ophelimity. Hence the answer that, in comparison with the tenets of the old school, ordinalism was not progress is meaningless. In addition CR, once more guilty of the ambiguity noted earlier, exaggerate when they portray the discarding of interpersonal utility comparisons as the final act of a "dramatic change in the conceptual framework of economics" (p. 508). Although Robbins' negation, which involves the elimination of the questions listed by CR, has been important for welfare economics, it did not affect other fields. Furthermore CR overrate the impact of Robbins' intervention. Assuming too easily that his position on this score is incontestable, they overlook the fact that the problem has remained controversial up to the present time.[9] For that matter, neither has the scarcity definition been universally accepted. From this angle too the sweeping triumph of a new coherent school seems imaginary.

VII. *Robbins and Positivism*

CR's contention that Robbins "embraced the positivist conception of method" (1984, pp. 523, 528) is one of CR's most baffling ideas. The nonpositivist tenor of Robbins' methodological classic is evident and regularly attested in the literature (e.g., Blaug 1980, pp. 86ff.; Johannes J. Klant 1984, pp. 56ff.). Yet by failing to go into Robbins' methodological principles, CR do not attempt to substantiate their dissident opinion.

This failure is another instance of CR's tendency to present arguments concerning welfare economics in the guise of more general statements. The alleged "commitment to the positivist line" is, in fact, exemplified only in the assertion that the exclusion of interpersonal comparisons stemmed from "strictures against mental and moral concepts" (p. 522). This more restrictive ascription is, no less than the comprehensive one, at variance with the truth. Far from recommending the banishment of "mental concepts" Robbins forcefully defended the inclusion of "psychological elements" (1935, pp. 88ff.; 1953, p. 102). Somewhat inconsistently, CR recognize subjectivist characteristics in Robbins' views on utility (pp. 522, 523). If one wants to trace the origins of Robbins' view, rather than looking to positivism it is much more plausible to note the repeatedly acknowledged influence of the antipositivist Austrian school as one of the principal sources (e.g., Robbins 1935, p. 56, n. 2; 1953, pp. 103, 104; in this sense also Blaug 1980, p. 87). In this case the opposites converge. Moreover, because there is no connection between positivism and the scarcity definition, nothing is left of the unitary triad.

VIII. *Conclusion*

CR's heretical account of the ordinalist revolution contains numerous historical and analytical errors; hence their views rest on flimsy evidence and dubious reasoning. The two contrasted frameworks did not exist. Accordingly, the dramatic change-over to a "complete alternative" engineered by Robbins is illusory, and it would be futile to balance, as CR recommend, the gains and losses they indicate as its consequences. CR's historiographic enterprise cannot be counted a success.

[8] Paradoxically CR, misinterpreting Pigou, side with Robbins in the controversy.

[9] For an excellent survey see Rudolf Moeller (1983) and for a recent eloquent defense of interpersonal comparability see Subroto Roy (1984, pp. 356ff).

References

BLAUG, MARK. *The methodology of economics.* NY: Cambridge U. Press, 1980.

———. *Economic theory in retrospect.* 4th ed. NY: Cambridge U. Press, 1985.

CANNAN, EDWIN. *Wealth.* 3rd ed. London: King and Son, 1930.

———. "Review of L. Robbins, *An essay on the nature and significance of economic science*," *Econ. J.*, Sept. 1932, *42*(3), pp. 424–27.

———. *A review of economic theory.* 2nd ed. London: Frank Cass, 1964.

COOTER, ROBERT AND RAPPOPORT, PETER. "Were the Ordinalists Wrong About Welfare Economics?" *J. Econ. Lit.*, June 1984, *22*(2), pp. 507–30.

HENNIPMAN, PIETER. "A Tale of Two Schools. Comments on a New View of the Ordinalist Revolution," *De Economist*, June 1987, *135*(2), pp. 141–62.

KLANT, JOHANNES J. *The rules of the game: The logical structure of economic theories*. NY: Cambridge U. Press, 1984.

LITTLE, IAN M. D. "Robert Cooper and Peter Rappoport, 'Were the Ordinalists Wrong About Welfare Economics?': A Comment," *J. Econ. Lit.*, Sept. 1985, *23*(3), pp. 1186–88.

MARSHALL, ALFRED. *Principles of economics*. 8th ed. London: Macmillan, 1920.

MOELLER, RUDOLPH. *Interpersonelle Nutzenvergleiche*. Göttingen: Vandenhoeck & Ruprecht, 1983.

PIGOU, ARTHUR C. *The economics of welfare*. 4th ed. London: Macmillan, 1932.

______. "Some Aspects of Welfare Economics," *Amer. Econ. Rev.*, June 1951, *41*(3), pp. 287–302.

______. *Essays in economics*. London: Macmillan, 1952.

______. *Alfred Marshall and current thought*. London: Macmillan, 1953.

ROBBINS, LIONEL. *An essay on the nature and significance of economic science*. 2nd ed. London: Macmillan, 1935.

______. "Robertson on Utility and Scope," *Economica N.S.*, May 1953, *20*(2), pp. 99–111.

ROBERTSON, DENNIS H. *Utility and all that*. London: Allen & Unwin, 1952.

ROY, SUBROTO. "Considerations on Utility, Benevolence, and Taxation," *Hist. Polit. Econ.*, Fall 1984, *16*(3), pp. 349–62.

SAMUELSON, PAUL A. "Complementarity—An Essay on the 40th Anniversary on the Hicks-Allen Revolution in Demand Theory," *J. Econ. Lit.*, Dec. 1974, *12*(4), pp. 1255–89.

[14]

Reply to Professor Hennipman*

By Peter Rappoport

Federal Reserve Bank of New York

In our paper, we advanced the thesis that different views of utility, rather than of the role of normative statements, lay behind the debate on interpersonal comparisons of utility of the 1930s and 1940s (Robert Cooter and Rappoport 1984). We argued that economists who made such comparisons based them on an objective view of the satisfaction of human wants, and could be usefully grouped together as the "material welfare school." According to Professor Hennipman, we have perpetrated an elaborate hoax: The material welfare school is a product of our imagination, and therefore, the fact that it stands in opposition to the contemporary perspective on utility is irrelevant to understanding the ordinalist revolution.

In this reply, we demonstrate that none of Hennipman's principal criticisms is valid. Usually, his reasoning seems to rest on a rather obtuse reading of our paper or original sources. His contention that it is wrong to talk of a material welfare school is based on the fact that the economists in question dealt with many other subjects. But this indisputable fact is irrelevant to our argument that it is appropriate to regard them as a school of thought because of their particular shared perspective on utility and the satisfaction of human wants. He notes that these economists equated "desires" and "satisfactions," but misses that this was a practical judgment, rather than a matter of definition. The material welfare perspective is distinguished by its consideration of both these concepts rather than desires alone, and by the fact that desires, while the focus of modern economics, were actually of secondary interest.

The body of this reply is devoted to substantiating these statements. The first section sets the stage by recapitulating in a simple form the argument of our paper. This serves to highlight the important contrasts between the material welfare perspective and that which has supplanted it. The next section addresses Hennipman's charge that there was no material welfare school, by providing evidence of material welfare economists' particular perspective, and of the way it figured in their reasoning about redistribution of income. Finally, we clarify the significance of material welfare economists' statements concerning the relationship between desires and satisfactions. Because Professor Hennipman berates us for lack of textual references in general and our interpretation of Pigou in particular, much of the argument will involve detailed reference to passages from Pigou's *The Economics of Welfare*.

I. *Contrasting Material Welfare and Scarcity Approaches*

The gist of our thesis is perhaps obtained most clearly by considering the following passage by Lionel Robbins:

> . . . suppose that A and B fall into conversation about their respective enjoyments and A says to B, "Of course I get more satisfaction than you out of music," and B vigorously asserts the contrary. Needless to say, you and I as outsiders can form our own judgments. But these are essentially subjective, not objectively ascertainable fact. There is no available way in which we can measure and compare the satisfactions which A and B derive from music. Intelligent talk? But that may be misleading. Facial expression? That too may be deceptive. . . . We are left with the ultimate difficulty of interpersonal comparisons that, as Jevons put it, "Every mind is thus inscrutable to every other mind, and no common denominator of feeling seems to

* This reply also reflects Robert Cooter's views on Professor Hennipman's comment.

The opinions expressed in this paper are ours, and do not reflect the opinions of the Federal Reserve Bank of New York or the Federal Reserve System.

be possible." Jevons's emphasis may be a bit extreme; we certainly think we know what other people are feeling, though opinions notoriously differ in different cultural settings and between different people. But it is surely incontestable where scientific proof or measurement is in question. (Robbins 1981, p. 9)

This argument, it would seem, is devastating to reasoning that proceeds from the law of diminishing marginal utility to the conclusion that transfers from rich to poor will increase the aggregate sum of satisfaction (c.f., for example, Pigou [1920]1932, p. 89). One is moved to ask how economists of earlier generations could ever have been so stupid.

But there are several rhetorical elements in this passage that should be examined. First, say A and B are talking about food rather than music. Second, suppose A has below-subsistence means while B is quite wealthy. What does one make now of A's statement "I get more satisfaction than you out of food"? If we are talking about the satisfaction of the gourmand, things are still on rather shaky ground. But if, by "satisfaction," we mean the way food counters the deficiencies caused by malnutrition, then A's statement appears to move out of the realm of value judgments and metaphysical assertions, and into the realm of ascertainable fact. In contrast to Robbins' musical example, the greater benefit in this sense of the marginal meal to A than to B is something that outside observers can meaningfully debate and conceivably verify, not by observing "facial expressions" or "intelligent talk," but physical health, life expectancy, and so on.[1]

Evidently, one can make sense of interpersonal comparisons if utility is understood in terms of the paradigm of the satisfaction of basic needs such as hunger, rather than the consumption of luxuries. In our paper, we attempted to demonstrate that the earlier generation of economists had precisely this perspective on human satisfactions. They were particularly concerned with the extent to which the organization of the economy succeeded in satisfying people's basic material needs, in view of which we called them the "material welfare school."

Material welfare was thus defined principally in terms of goods and satisfactions for which objective verification of other people's conditions happened to be feasible.[2] It was intimately connected with the satisfactions to be derived from the consumption of "necessaries" rather than "luxuries." Of course, even if this objective conception of utility makes interpersonal comparisons feasible, policy directives like "Improve material welfare!" still involve a value judgment, namely that material welfare is a good thing. But for the material welfare school, such imperatives were readily translatable into more conventional policy goals, such as improving the productivity of the working classes, and thus the potential of the economy to produce wealth.[3] Such considerations differ greatly from value judgments asserting the superiority of A's musical sensibilities over those of B.[4]

The focus on particular types of goods stood in sharp contrast to Robbins' proposal for defining economics in terms of scarcity. This places any good under the purview of economics as long as there is someone who desires more of it than he or she can acquire for free. From this viewpoint, music and food are on an equal footing. In particular, it points to preferences or "desires" as the unifying behavioral concept, rather than the physical-based satisfactions that are associated with material welfare.

These differences motivated us to characterize the banishment of interpersonal comparisons of utility (which we saw as the principal event of the ordinalist revolution) as the result of a conflict between two schools of thought

[1] Of course, someone may object that A may be a hopeless case, and no end of nourishment will alleviate his or her sickly condition. But it is a lot harder to support this assertion for entire income groups than for a single individual. (See the discussion of the use of averaging by material welfare economists on p. 518 of our article.)

[2] Subroto Roy (1984) also believes it worthwhile to draw a distinction between Marshallian and "post-Hicksian" accounts of utility. The former, he says, "contrasts very favorably as an empirical description," without which "the natural exercise of sympathy and benevolence does not seem to be possible" (p. 350).

[3] The relation of Pigou's economics to the approach of classical economists is discussed by John Hicks (1975).

[4] To use Amartya Sen's (1970) terminology, the value judgment occurs at a more basic level than in Robbins' view of the problem. The role of value judgments is discussed by Ian Little (1985) and Cooter and Rappoport (1985).

with different research agenda and conceptions of utility. While the bodies of knowledge of these schools were internally consistent, they were mutually incompatible, and substituting one for the other could not be regarded as unambiguous scientific progress.

II. *The Material Welfare School*

Hennipman's first attack concerns the material welfare definition of economics and the concept of a "material welfare school," which he describes as an "artificial construction." He bases this conclusion on the fact that the economists in question studied a broader range of subjects than material welfare, and that, while they "did adopt a kind of 'material' criterion," their definitions are not limited to necessaries. We agree both that the breadth of their interests is "too well-known to require illustration," and that material welfare was not limited to necessities; however, neither of these statements bears on our reasons for claiming that there was a material welfare school. We used this term because we were concerned to differentiate their perspective on questions surrounding interpersonal comparability of utility from the current view. Central features of this perspective were an impersonal and hierarchical view of human wants, and a focus on the material aspects of well-being. These economists did not limit themselves to necessaries; they simply formed the paradigm case: Necessaries were the clearest example of the particular part of welfare in which they were interested, just as luxuries constituted the paradigm from Robbins' point of view.

Robbins himself believed that a focus on material welfare characterized these economists. He stated that

> The definition of Economics which would probably command most adherents, at any rate in Anglo-Saxon countries, is that which relates it to the study of the causes of material welfare. ([1932] 1937, p. 4)[5]

In pointing out the inadequacies of this definition in describing the concerns of economists (for example, the theory of wages), Robbins also offered some passing clues to what it involved. The wages of a sewage collector "are the price of work which may be described as conducive to material welfare" (p. 5), while "the wages of the members of an orchestra . . . are paid for work which has not the slightest bearing on material welfare" (p. 6). In a similar vein, he contrasted bread with a seat at the theater (p. 6). Finally, he described the material welfare definition as "the last vestige of Physiocratic influence" (p. 9). Once again, these statements suggest that adherents of the material welfare definition drew a distinction between different types of goods. Their view was apparently based on necessities, while luxuries were not a primary concern.

One consideration that made this perspective appealing was that it was well adapted to developing practical approaches to the contemporaneous problem of poverty.[6] In their introductory chapters, both Marshall and Pigou cited the possibility of betterment of the conditions of the poor as the primary motivation for studying economics (Pigou 1920, p. 5; Marshall 1920, p. 4). The needs of the poor at the time were evidently at the base of the hierarchy, and so provided the best opportunities for improvements in material welfare. In this sense, the disposition of necessities assumed a particular significance for members of the material welfare school.

Possibly the best example of this hierarchical perspective and its use is given by Pigou in his discussion of how a "transference" from rich to poor would increase economic welfare.

> . . . it is sufficient to reflect on the way in which, in this country, income has in fact been distributed in recent times. . . . . Of households . . . 13.5 percent are living in a condition of primary poverty, i.e. with incomes so low that, even if expended with perfect wisdom, they could not have provided an adequate subsistence . . . not more than 300 millions annually can have been spent by the rich and moder-

[5] He associates this definition with Marshall and Cannan, but not with Pigou, as we erroneously stated in our paper; however, the passage from Pigou's *The Economics of Welfare* discussed below suggest that Pigou shared this approach.

[6] It is interesting to note that Robbins does not consider this as one of the possible reasons for defining economics in terms of the causes of material welfare (1932, pp. 5–11).

ately well-off on any form of luxury . . . when all the qualifications have been made, the figures cited above leave still, a substantial excess income in the hands of the richer classes available "for attack" by way of transference. . . .

We must not hesitate, therefore, to conclude that, so long as the dividend as a whole is not diminished, any increase, within wide limits, in the real income enjoyed by the poorer classes, at the expense of an equal decrease in that enjoyed by the richer classes, is practically certain to involve an addition to economic welfare. ([1920] 1932, pp. 92–96)[7]

Implicit in this analysis is an extremely mechanistic and impersonal view of human wants. Generic groups of people, the "rich" and the "poor," are constitutionally the same, but are in different positions on the same hierarchy of wants. The poor present an opportunity for improving economic welfare because of their below-subsistence incomes, which they are unable to spend so as to escape the necessaries region of the hierarchy. Likewise, the rich are spending their marginal incomes on luxuries, which satisfy "less urgent" wants. Thus economic welfare can be improved by redistributing resources to where more urgent wants can be satisfied.[8]

A hierarchy of wants (and the corresponding goods) that is common to all is vital to Pigou's argument. It enables him to identify the material welfare position (or the "urgency" of the wants) of each group by their income,[9] both relatively and absolutely. Conversely, one cannot make sense of what Pigou says if one does not distinguish among types of welfare and types of goods. Otherwise, how does one know that the lower satisfaction of the dispossessed rich does not outweigh the increased satisfaction of the poor? As we noted in our paper, basing economics on scarcity motivates no such distinctions among goods, and motivates one to regard consumption from the viewpoint of preferences or desires, of which interpersonal comparisons are meaningless. Hence, the concept of material welfare and the mechanistic hierarchical view of goods that accompanied it are vital elements of the view of material welfare economists that distinguished them from their successors. This perspective also informed their view of utility, which brings us to Hennipman's second criticism.

III. *Satisfactions and Desires*

In the next two sections, Hennipman turns his attention to our characterization of Marshall's and Pigou's view of utility as being objective. In Section III, he maintains that neither considered relevant the distinction we drew between ophelimity and utility, and that they consistently used the latter in a subjective sense. As an example, he cites Marshall's statement: "Utility is taken to be correlative to desire or want." This strain of argument is continued in Section IV, where he notes that Pigou regarded departures of desires from satisfactions as the exception rather than the rule. If Marshall's and Pigou's utility had no objective connotation, then it becomes functionally equivalent to the notion used in the Hicks-Samuelson consumer-choice framework, and is subject to Robbins' criticisms whenever one uses it as a basis for interpersonal comparisons.[10]

Both Hennipman and we agree that material welfare economists believed that for their purposes, people's desires for goods would correspond to the satisfactions the good yield; however, we draw very different conclusions from this datum. Hennipman reasons that Pigou and

[7] One reason why Hennipman estimates that the economists in question devoted so little of their energies to the study of *material* welfare is that he insists that Pigou was referring to something else when he talked of *economic* welfare; however, this passage suggests that he used the term in the same way as we have used material welfare.

[8] Marshall expressed a similar opinion: "I contend that it would be possible to provide opportunities of healthy play for all children, and to bring fresh air and light more generously into all urban homes, and in other ways to lesser the *real* evils of the poorer classes, without touching on that expenditure of the rich which is necessary for their *true* well-being" (letter to Mrs. Bosanquet, 1903, reprinted in Pigou 1925). Marshall went on to emphasize (as did Pigou) that it would be a dangerous disincentive to carry out such redistribution quickly.

[9] As we stated in our paper, this is how we understood Pigou's use of the "measuring rod of money" (1984, p. 513).

[10] Hennipman does not appear to agree with this statement. In the longer version of his comment (1987b), he states that the debate concerned "utility theory proper."

Marshall therefore had a *subjective* view of utility; that is, it was the measure of how much someone desired something. For us, however, the important thing is not the correlation between desires and satisfactions. Rather, it is that, in the cosmology of material welfare economists, there are *two* concepts—desires and satisfactions—that relate to people's consumption of goods. This is of critical importance in distinguishing the material welfare view, because the modern concept of utility relates exclusively to only one of these concepts—desires.

It was the inscrutable nature of desires that Robbins used to argue the impossibility of interpersonal comparisons of utility. But for material welfare economists, there was something behind desires, called "satisfactions," which was the object of their comparisons. Desires were, in a sense, the subordinate of the two concepts: They were the bridge by which satisfactions could be connected to the amount of money people were prepared to offer for them, and enabled the measuring rod of money to be used to measure satisfactions. As Pigou put it:

> . . . economic welfare [is] taken broadly to consist in that group of satisfactions and dissatisfactions which can be brought into relation with a money measure. We have now to observe that this relation is not a direct one, but is mediated through desires and aversions. That is to say, the money which a person is prepared to offer for a thing measures directly, not the satisfaction he will get from the thing, but the intensity of his desire for it. . . . The substantial point is that we are entitled to use the comparative amounts of money which a person is prepared to offer for two different things as a test of the comparative satisfactions which these things will yield him, only on condition that the ratio between the intensities of desire that he feels for the two is equal to the ratio between the amounts of satisfaction which their possession will yield him. This condition, however, is not always fulfilled. ([1920] 1932, p. 23)

After saying that there is more to this divergence than just mistaken expectations of satisfaction, Pigou eventually concluded that:

> It is fair to suppose that most commodities, especially those of wide consumption that are required, as articles of food and clothing are, for direct personal use, will be wanted as a means to satisfaction, and will, consequently, be desired with intensities proportional to the satisfactions they are expected to yield. ([1920] 1932, p. 23)[11]

Hence, satisfactions are, *in principle*, distinct from desires, and it is satisfactions that are of primary interest; however, *in practice*, it is permissible to treat people's desires for goods as indicative of the satisfactions they will derive from them.

The nature of the contrast between satisfactions and desires emerges most clearly in the following extract:

> . . . the money which a person is prepared to offer for a thing measures directly, not the satisfaction he will get from the thing, but the intensity of his desire for it. This distinction, obvious when stated, has been somewhat obscured for English-speaking students by the employment of the term utility—which naturally carries an association with satisfaction—to represent desiredness. Thus, when one thing is desired by a person more keenly than another, it is said to possess a greater utility to that person. Several writers have endeavored to get rid of the confusion which this use of words generates by substituting for "utility" in the above sense some other term, such as, for example, Professor Pareto's "ophelimity." It may be suggested that, in English writing, "desiredness" would be equally effective and much more readily intelligible. I shall myself employ that term. (Pigou 1920, p. 23, First Edition)

This passage establishes clearly that Pigou drew the same distinction between desires and satisfactions as Pareto drew between ophelimity and utility. As we said in our paper (1984, p. 515), Pareto regarded utility as the property of goods that made them conducive to survival, and he

[11] To explore the distinction between desires and satisfactions a little further, note that Pigou implicitly distinguishes among the *purposes* to which goods might be put. That is, in order to say what he says here, he must believe there to be other purposes for which one could want something, besides as a "means to satisfaction." We can only speculate here, but it seems that ostentation would be high on Pigou's list and certainly Marshall's. Pigou regarded "the injurious luxury of the rich" as an evil ([1920] 1932, p. vii), and Marshall's discussion of the "desire for costly dress" (1920, p. 87) is less than sympathetic.

suggested "material well-being" as the criterion of whether something possessed utility.[12]

It is because of this distinction between desires and satisfactions, with satisfactions being the correlate of utility and the concept of primary interest, that we concluded that material welfare economists had an "objective" view of utility. Utility was related to aspects of a person's welfare that were observable, the paradigm cases being whether they had food, clothing, and shelter. It was not the personal, private, or idiosyncratic affair that desires or ophelimity would be.

The remainder of Professor Hennipman's comment is devoted to a discussion of our contrast of the material welfare school with the scarcity school, which he argues is fatuous in view of the nonexistence of the former. Because we believe that enough has been said to show that the logical and textual basis of our "heretical" account has not been damaged by Professor Hennipman's principal assertions, we shall not discuss these sections of his paper; however, one puzzling issue remains. Among Professor Hennipman's many pronouncements about what did not happen, one searches in vain for his explanation of how a generation of economists could miss the seemingly obvious point that interpersonal comparisons of utility (in the present sense of the term) are meaningless. The most explicit mention of this issue is his statement that the dispute "concerned a problem within utility theory in its ordinary sense" (1978b, p. 16). The only way we can understand this is as a reference to a dispute about the scientific status of commonsense statements regarding perceptions of other people's feelings. One side of this dispute is offered in the passage quoted from Robbins on pp. 86–87 above. The other side is to assert that, while such commonsense judgments are not foolproof, they make sense in the important practical cases.[13] But surely, the form that such a defense would take would be to argue that these practical cases concern comparisons of basic material well-being.

References

Cooter, Robert D. and Rappoport, Peter. "Were the Ordinalists Wrong About Welfare Economics?" *J. Econ. Lit.*, June 1984, 22(2), pp. 507–30.

______. "Reply to I.M.D. Little," *J. Econ. Lit.*, Sept. 1985, 23(3), pp. 1189–90.

Hennipman, Pieter. "A Tale of Two Schools. Comments on a New View of the Ordinalist Revolution," *De Economist*, June 1987, *135*(2), pp. 141–62.

______. "A New Look at the Ordinalist Revolution: Comments on Cooter and Rappoport, *J. Econ. Lit.*, 1988, pp. 80–85.

Hicks, John R. "The Scope and Status of Welfare Economics," *Oxford Econ. Pap.*, 1975, 27(3), pp. 307–26.

Little, Ian M.D. "Robert Cooter and Peter Rappoport, 'Were the Ordinalists Wrong About Welfare Economics?': A Comment," *J. Econ. Lit.*, Sept. 1985, 23(3), pp. 1186–88.

Marshall, Alfred. *Principles of economics*. 8th ed. London: Macmillan, [1890] 1920.

Pareto, Vilfredo. *Cours d'économie politique*. Two volumes. Lausanne, 1896–1897.

Pigou, Arthur C. *The economics of welfare*. London: Macmillan, [1920] 1932.

______, ed. *Memorials of Alfred Marshall*. London: Macmillan, 1925.

Robbins, Lionel. *An essay on the nature and significance of economic science*. London: Macmillan, [1932] 1937.

______. "Economics and Political Economy," *Amer. Econ. Rev.*, May 1981, *71*(2), pp. 1–13.

Roy, Subroto. "Considerations on Utility, Benevolence, and Taxation," *Hist. Polit. Econ.*, Fall 1984, *16*(3), pp. 349–62.

Sen, Amartya. *Collective choice and social welfare*. Amsterdam: North-Holland, 1970.

[12] The second sentence of this passage is consistent with Pareto's observation that Jevons had used *utility* in the sense of the capacity to satisfy the desires of an individual "whether legitimate or not" (1896, p. 3), for which he proposed the term *ophelimity*.

[13] In our paper, we remarked that Robbins' view appears as a species of sceptical argument from this standpoint. A similar point is made by Roy (1984, p. 357), who casts it in terms of the philosophical position of the solipsist.

Pioneers in Economics

Section I: The Forerunners of Classical Economics

1. The Historiography of Economics
2. Aristotle (384–322 B.C.)
3. St Thomas Aquinas (1225–1274)
4. The Early Mercantilists
   Thomas Mun (1571–1641), Edward Misselden (1608–1634), Gerard de Malynes (1586–1623)
5. The Later Mercantilists
   Josiah Child (1603–1699) and John Locke (1632–1704)
6. Pre-Classical Economists Volume I
   Charles Davenant (1656–1714) and William Petty (1623–1687)
7. Pre-Classical Economists Volume II
   Pierre le Pesant Boisguilbert (1645–1714), George Berkeley (1685–1753), Baron de Montesquieu (1689–1755), Ferdinando Galiani (1727–1787), James Anderson (1739–1808), Dugald Stewart (1753–1828)
8. Pre-Classical Economists Volume III
   John Law (1671–1729) and Bernard Mandeville (1660–1733)
9. Richard Cantillon (1680–1734) and Jacques Turgot (1727–1781)
10. François Quesnay (1694–1774) Volumes I and II
11. David Hume (1711–1776) and James Steuart (1712–1780)

Section II: The Golden Age of Classical Economics

12. Adam Smith (1723–1790) Volumes I and II
13. Henry Thornton (1760–1815), Jeremy Bentham (1748–1832), James Lauderdale (1759–1839), Simonde de Sismondi (1773–1842)
14. David Ricardo (1772–1823)
15. Jean-Baptiste Say (1776–1832)
16. Thomas Robert Malthus (1766–1834) and John Stuart Mill (1806–1873)
17. Ramsay McCulloch (1789–1864), Nassau Senior (1790–1864), Robert Torrens (1780–1864)
18. Thomas Tooke (1774–1858), Mountifort Longfield (1802–1884), Richard Jones (1790–1855)

19. William Whewell (1794–1866), Dionysius Lardner (1793–1859), Charles Babbage (1792–1871)

20. George Scrope (1797–1876), Thomas Attwood (1783–1856), Edwin Chadwick (1800–1890), John Cairnes (1823–1875)

21. James Mill (1773–1836), John Rae (1796–1872), Edward West (1782–1828), Thomas Joplin (1790–1847)

22. James Wilson (1805–1860), Issac Butt (1813–1879), T. E. Cliffe Leslie (1827–1882)

23. Karl Marx (1818–1883)

Section III: Neoclassical Economics and its Critics

24. Johann von Thünen (1783–1850), Augustin Cournot (1801–1877), Jules Dupuit (1804–1866)

25. Leon Walras (1834–1910)

26. Carl Menger (1840–1921)

27. Eugen von Böhm-Bawerk (1851–1914) and Friedrich von Wieser (1851–1926)

28. Knut Wicksell (1851–1926)

29. Alfred Marshall (1842–1924) and Francis Edgeworth (1845–1926)

30. Gustav Schmoller (1838–1917) and Werner Sombart (1863–1941)

31. Dissenters
    Charles Fourier (1772–1837), Henri de St Simon (1760–1825), Pierre-Joseph Proudhon (1809–1865), John A. Hobson (1858–1940)

32. Thorstein Veblen (1857–1929)

33. Wesley Mitchell (1874–1948), John Commons (1862–1945), Clarence Ayres (1891–1972)

34. Henry George (1839–1897)

35. Vilfredo Pareto (1848–1923)

Section IV: Twentieth Century Economics

36. Arthur Pigou (1877–1959)

37. Frank Knight (1885–1972), Henry Simons (1899–1946), Joseph Schumpeter (1883–1950)

38. Edward Chamberlin (1899–1967)